catholic
and
feminist

MARY J. HENOLD

catholic

and

feminist

THE SURPRISING HISTORY
OF THE AMERICAN CATHOLIC
FEMINIST MOVEMENT

THE UNIVERSITY OF

NORTH CAROLINA PRESS

CHAPEL HILL

This volume was published with the assistance of Roanoke College and of the Greensboro Women's Fund of the University of North Carolina Press. Founding Contributors of the fund: Linda Arnold Carlisle, Sally Schindel Cone, Anne Faircloth, Bonnie McElveen Hunter, Linda Bullard Jennings, Janice J. Kerley (in honor of Margaret Supplee Smith), Nancy Rouzer May, and Betty Hughes Nichols.

Designed by Courtney Leigh Baker
Set in Scala, Euro Bodoni Italic, and Din
by Keystone Typesetting, Inc.
Manufactured in the United States of America

Ornament on the title page and chapter openings: © iStockphoto/Dave Smith. Image of Mary on p. ii: © iStockphoto/Mark Strozier. Used by permission of iStockphoto.

The paper in this book meets the guidelines for permanence and durability of the Committee on Production Guidelines for Book Longevity of the Council on Library Resources.

The University of North Carolina Press has been a member of the Green Press Initiative since 1993.

Library of Congress Cataloging-in-Publication Data
Henold, Mary J., 1974–
Catholic and feminist : the surprising history of the American Catholic feminist movement / by Mary J. Henold.
p. cm.
Includes bibliographical references (p.   ) and index.
ISBN 978-0-8078-3224-0 (cloth: alk. paper)
1. Feminism—Religious aspects—Catholic Church—History—20th century. 2. Women in the Catholic Church—United States—History—20th century. 3. Catholic women—United States—History—20th century. 4. Feminism—United States—History—20th century. 5. United States—Church history—20th century. I. Title.
BX1406.3.H46   2008
282'.73082—dc22   2008010529

12 11 10 09 08   5 4 3 2 1

for john staudenmaier, sj

contents

illustrations

acknowledgments

This history was a long time in the making, and I am indebted to a great many people. First on that list are the many women who shared with me their memories of activism, faith, and friendship. I have been inspired by their commitment and enriched by their gracious hospitality. I am indebted also to the archivists who preserve these women's stories, particularly those at Marquette University, the University of Notre Dame, the Schlesinger Library at Harvard University, the Women and Leadership Archives at Loyola University Chicago, Union Theological Seminary, and the Sisters of Mercy–Detroit Province.

Thanks go, as well, to numerous mentors, colleagues, and students whose support helped bring this project to its conclusion, including Lynn Gordon, Dan Borus, Curt Cadorette, and the late Brenda Meehan at the University of Rochester; Mel Piehl, Colleen Seguin, Mark Schwenn, and Dorothy Bass at Valparaiso University; Kathy Cummings at the Cushwa Center for the Study of American Catholicism at Notre Dame, and my colleagues in the history department at Roanoke College. Special thanks are due to my two undergraduate research assistants, Katie Burakowski and Amanda "Dru" Carpenter, as well as to the students in my "Faith and Feminism" seminar at Valpo. I am deeply indebted to my fellow postdocs and to friends in the Lilly Fellows Program, especially Heath White and Kari Kloos. Thank you to Elaine Maisner for her encouragement as she guided this manuscript through the acquisition process.

Generous funding aided me in my research. Thank you to the Susan B. Anthony Institute for Gender and Women's Studies at the University of Rochester, the Cushwa Center for the Study of American Catholicism at the

University of Notre Dame, the Louisville Institute for the Study of American Religion, the Lilly Fellows Program, and Roanoke College.

I've moved many times in the past ten years, and I am profoundly grateful to the friends and faith communities that have supported me in Detroit, St. Louis, Rochester, Valparaiso, and Roanoke. The Henold family, and now the Carlin family, offer me the unconditional love that makes my work possible. Thank you especially to my parents, Ken and Nikki Henold, who—besides being wonderful and generous people—provided a model of honest, joyful faith. My husband, Tim, has made me laugh more times than I could ever count in the seven years it has taken to finish this history. He keeps me sane and happy, and I couldn't ask for anything more. My daughter, Ella, arrived a month after the manuscript—my first baby—was safely delivered. May she grow up in the embrace of a just church, and if not, may she be inspired to make it so. Finally, thank you to my mentor John Staudenmaier, sj, to whom I dedicate this book. I offer it in gratitude for an extraordinary education and the gift of history.

introduction

We affirm Jesus and His Gospel as our life focus and that being said, the
[National Coalition of American Nuns] puts society on notice that women
refuse to accept any longer the straw for bricks that we are forced to make.
— National Coalition of American Nuns

The National Coalition of American Nuns (NCAN) was not known for mincing words. In 1972, this organization of 1,800 women religious, probably the most radical collection of Roman Catholic sisters ever put on a mailing list, released its "Declaration of Independence for Women," demanding "full and equal participation of women in churches," establishment of new democratic church structures, abolition of the College of Cardinals, "reformation of the present economic and power systems," and "complete equality for women." They were so dedicated (and optimistic) that they felt sure they could make substantial progress on these goals by the time of the nation's bicentennial four years later.[1]

As is clear from the opening salvo of their declaration, the sisters of NCAN were self-identified Catholic feminists, that is, women with a dual, integrated commitment to their Catholic faith and to the struggle for women's liberation. And they were not alone. They were joined in the movement by Mary B. Lynch, a laywoman so devoted to the cause that over the course of eight years she moved six times to six different states to help the movement grow, each time with no viable source of income. The movement also included Elizabeth Farians, a theologian and activist who founded the National Organization for Women's Task Force on Women and Religion and led it as a Catholic feminist for five years. Ada María Isasi-Díaz, once a

Cuban refugee, found purpose and a call to leadership among Catholic feminists and was inspired to help create mujerista theology, a theology that emerged from the experience of Latinas. The movement embraced Theresa Kane, who in 1979 stood before Pope John Paul II and called for women's ordination. And who could leave out Margaret Ellen Traxler, the determined and outspoken woman religious who once insisted in a letter to first lady Betty Ford that Illinois congressman Henry Hyde was a "fat ass" . . . and then sent him a copy for good measure.

By 1980, American Catholic feminists, both laywomen and women religious, had been openly confronting the oppression of women for nearly two decades. This may come as a surprise to many people who find the concept of Catholic feminism, let alone a movement of Catholic feminists dating to the early sixties, difficult to fathom. Reluctance to believe in the existence of Catholic feminists is understandable. The worldwide institutional Catholic Church is openly hostile toward feminism and feminists. The Roman Catholic Church was and is patriarchal and androcentric; despite refusing to admit women to ordained ministry and to major positions of authority, the church does not acknowledge that it perpetuates sexism against women. Why would any feminist want to associate with it? While nonreligious feminists are more likely than the church to recognize their Catholic feminist sisters, American feminism has tended to be led by secular feminists who have shown considerable skepticism about the feasibility of a joint feminist/religious identification. Moreover, since 1963, the Catholic Church has at times been enemy number one of American feminism (particularly over the issues of abortion rights and the Equal Rights Amendment). Under such circumstances, how could any woman continue to claim loyalty to both institutional Catholicism and the feminist movement? Even I, a historian of American feminism and American Catholicism, a cradle Catholic, and a Catholic feminist, had to approach my first day of research with the most basic question: was there a Catholic feminist movement in America?

Let's get this out of the way first so we need not dwell on it any further. Yes, there was a movement of organizations and individuals who claimed a dual identification with Catholicism and feminism. This statement must be made up front because the persistent questions concerning Catholic feminism since the seventies, coming from a variety of Catholics and non-Catholics and from both inside and outside the academy, have been, "Is Catholic feminism possible?" and "Why did they stay in the church?" Embedded in these questions, too, is another question, "*Should* women be Catholic and feminist?" While these remain important questions, ones that recognize the tension between Catholicism and feminism, their prevalence means that Catholic feminists and those who study them must continually defend Catholic feminism's viability.

I choose to approach the subject of Catholic feminism from a different angle, as a historian. From this perspective, Catholic feminist viability is a very straightforward issue. The historical record of the sixties and seventies —that is, published and archival sources as well as oral histories—provides more than ample evidence that Catholic feminists existed, that they articulated a strong connection between their faith and their feminist principles, that they formed organizations to forward feminist agendas, that such organizations were networked into a larger movement of Catholic feminism, and that this movement had connections with the much larger American feminist movement. In the belief that it is time for us to look beyond these questions, this study asks not just *if* or *why* women were Catholic feminists, but *how* and thus analyzes the nature and significance of Catholic feminism as a distinct branch of American feminism.

The implications of this inquiry shift are many. At one level, the question "how" reveals a new face of American feminism by demonstrating the unique contributions of another group of women engaged in feminist activism. Catholic feminism derived from distinct origins and ideological roots, and it found expression in new forms of feminist activism. It boasted its own body of activists, drawn from communities of women religious (religious sisters) and laywomen, from inside and outside the academy. Exploring the nature of Catholic feminism in the sixties and seventies, then, reveals a complex, creative, enduring, and significant form of activism that expands our understanding of the feminist movement in America.[2]

Such a contribution is significant, but adding Catholics to the feminist historical narrative and stirring is not this project's goal. If we consider the experiences of Catholic women and, indeed, other religious feminists, we must also be open to the possibility that they used their faith to help shape feminist identity and activism. As many scholars are now beginning to argue, religious feminists from a variety of faith traditions contributed to the larger movement's development in ways that historians of feminism have been slow to consider. This study suggests what impact including these religious feminists will have on the existing historical narrative of American feminism beyond simply widening the movement's parameters.

To offer one brief example, the narrative of "second-wave" feminism's origins in the early sixties changes when we consider Catholic feminists. Second-wave Catholic feminism emerged in the United States in 1963, the same year as the publication of Betty Friedan's *The Feminine Mystique* and the March on Washington. In that year, a small number of Catholic women began writing openly feminist articles in the Catholic press. While they were certainly influenced by these important events, these writers were not motivated primarily by the runaway best seller or the growing civil rights and new left movements. Rather, the spark that ignited the distinctively Catholic feminist movement was the Second Vatican Council (1962–65), an inspiring but overtly sexist event that enraged and exhilarated Catholic women in equal measure.

Acknowledging Vatican II as a catalyst for feminism changes the accepted narrative of second-wave feminism's origins. This is the case not because it adds another point of origin to the story, but because it indicates that women could come to feminism from within their own traditions, even if those traditions were considered historically conservative. In other words, it challenges the idea that feminist ideology must have been imported into faith traditions from the outside.[3] The origins of Catholic feminism are complex, and they include exposure to feminist ideas outside of Catholic culture, but evidence suggests that faith and the changing nature of Catholicism at midcentury had an equal if not more significant impact.[4]

More importantly, the experiences of religious feminists invite a reevaluation of the complex process of adopting feminist consciousness. Historians and feminists tend to characterize the development of feminist consciousness as a sudden revelation, a "conversion experience" sometimes referred to as "the click." The moment of consciousness might have come in a consciousness-raising group, or while reading *The Feminine Mystique*, or during an experience of discrimination, but whenever the click occurred, a woman's eyes were suddenly opened, she felt the full weight of her own oppression, her obligation to fight sexism, and a sense that everything was now possible. As one historian described it, "The heart of the matter, say the women, was 'the click'—the light bulb going off, the eye-popping realization, the knockout punch. It was the sudden comprehension, in one powerful instant, of what sexism exactly meant, how it had colored one's own life, the way all women were in this together. It was that awe-inspiring moment of vision and of commonality, when a woman was instantly and irrevocably transformed from naïve to knowing, from innocent to experienced, from apolitical to feminist."[5]

Too many personal narratives describe this phenomenon to dismiss it. However, it begs the question: what came after the click? Did a woman suddenly become a new person when she came to feminist consciousness, as the above quote suggests? Focusing on the moment of revelation implies that feminism is somehow self-evident and that newborn feminists simply turned their faces forward, ready to leave behind everything that did not fit this new consciousness. For religious women—and indeed, any woman with multiple, conflicting loyalties—such an approach is problematic.

The adoption of a feminist identification might also be seen as a complex process involving innumerable negotiated choices needed to reconcile a feminist outlook with preexisting worldviews. Catholic feminism illustrates this process on the grassroots level, revealing that feminist women of faith needed time, energy, and commitment to discern the relationships between their new feminism and their religious faith. One cannot assume that women automatically rejected their faith traditions simply because, as feminists, they now realized such institutions were patriarchal. In reality, Catholic feminists needed to make complicated choices about what to love, believe, challenge, and abandon in their religion, feminism, and daily lives. These choices were emotionally charged and full of risk. Whatever her background, every feminist made choices to negotiate a balance among multiple loyalties in a culture hostile to women's liberation.

The story of Catholic feminists in America helps us better understand this process. Throughout this narrative, this process will be illustrated on two different levels, that of individuals and of the movement as a whole. We will see individual Catholic feminists struggle to define a sustainable feminism that reflected commitments to faith tradition and feminism. As we shall see, individuals did not all reach the same conclusions as to what constituted a sustainable religious feminism, neither did they all follow the same path. Indeed, throughout the twenty-year period under study, many Catholic feminists chose a path that led out of the Catholic Church altogether, having found it impossible to negotiate an integrated Catholic feminist identity. On a second level, this narrative is written chronologically to show that the Catholic feminist movement as a whole also underwent this process of negotiating multiple loyalties. Although the choices of individuals were diverse, over time the movement shifted from conceiving of feminism as an aspect of church renewal to becoming a more determined (if optimistic) loyal opposition to engaging in a more radicalized critique fueled by feminists' growing anger and frustration, and finally to adopting a chosen position of "sustained ambivalence" on the church's margins. Each of these transitions over a twenty-year period helped clarify Catholic women's conceptions of religious feminist identity, and indeed, the process continues to this day.

Finally, Catholic feminism reveals a different ideological approach to feminism. The history of this movement is not simply the story of women applying feminist principles to the reform of their faith tradition and its institutional structure. If we interpret it this way, the Catholic Church was merely the next arena for the spread of feminism, like the *Ladies Home Journal*, or General Motors, or Congress. (Where should we go next, sisters? Let's storm the cathedral!!!) But this approach misses the richer story. For these activists, feminism itself was founded in their faith, not just applied to it. As we shall see, many feminists asserted a causal relationship between their faith and feminism. When the NCAN sisters cited above began their declaration with the phrase, "We affirm Jesus and His Gospel as our life focus, and that being said. . . ," they were not merely making an obligatory nod toward their status as women religious; they also were expressing a vital link between faith and feminism. Evidence from the Catholic feminist movement overwhelmingly indicates that feminism could originate in, be justified through, and be motivated by faith and religious tradition.

Catholic feminists regularly explained their feminism in terms of their commitment to a gospel mandate for social justice, liberation, and radical equality. They considered feminism a Christian principle, and they named the scriptures, rituals, language, sacraments, social teaching, and ministry of Catholicism as their motivation for and preferred means of pursuing their feminism in the world. They knew that Catholicism and feminism were in conflict; if they had seen no conflict they would not have directed their feminist activism toward the church. But they also believed that their Catholic faith could be life-giving as well as oppressive. This belief shows itself in the unique manifestations of Catholic feminist ideology, in particular its emphasis on theology, liturgical practice, the use of liturgy in feminist protest, the commitment to women's ministry, and a conception of feminism as a manifestation of social justice. While Catholic feminists' commitments to the institutional Catholic Church changed over time, as this study will argue, their belief that *faith* and feminism were compatible rarely wavered.

This last claim necessitates a clearer definition of terms, starting with "church," "faith," and "institution." Particular care must be used here because over time Catholic feminists used strikingly similar language to express their commitments to very different concepts. Throughout, I try to distinguish among three of these concepts. The first is the "institutional church," that is, the global or national structure of the Roman Catholic Church, including the governing hierarchy. At various times, many Catholic feminists did express their commitments to the church in this sense. These commitments usually took the form of loyal opposition. My subjects also spoke of a second concept, which they usually called "the church." They meant this in the sense derived from the Second Vatican Council, that the people (not the structures and hierarchy) are the church. So if Catholic feminists claimed commitments to "the church," they often did not mean "the Roman Catholic Church" as institution but, rather, the people and practices that embody the essence of Catholicism. In this way, Catholic feminists tried to reenvision Catholicism as they worked within it. I also use a third term throughout this narrative, that of "faith" or alternatively "faith tradition." I employ this terminology to make clear that women who ceased to identify themselves in any way with the institutional church usually still linked their feminism to their faith. Catholic feminists claimed their own knowledge and understanding of Catholicism, and they rarely believed it was contingent on institutional affiliation.

Another set of terms must be defined more clearly, as otherwise they may cause confusion. According to canon law, the term "nun," customarily used for all Catholic sisters, properly refers only to contemplative, or cloistered, women. The correct term for noncontemplatives, or those with "active" ministries, is either "woman religious" or "sister." In this case, "religious" is a noun, not an adjective. Women religious themselves only began to make the switch in terminology in the late sixties, so the use of the newer term is inconsistent throughout the period of this study. For example, the name "National Coalition of American Nuns" is something of a misnomer because its members were overwhelmingly women religious. Since nearly all the sisters in the Catholic feminist movement were technically women religious, that is the term I will use throughout. To further complicate matters, under canon law, nuns and women religious are considered laywomen, so in this narrative women religious will occasionally refer to themselves as such. However, I will generally use the terms "women religious" or "sisters" to refer to those who were vowed religious and "laywomen" to refer to those who were not.

Yet another pair of terms in need of clarification is "feminism" and "women's liberation." Some scholars distinguish between the two by labeling the more theoretical and academic form as "feminist" and the organizational form as "women's liberation." Others prefer to make distinctions between the quest for "equality" (which would be labeled feminist) and the more radical desire for "liberation," although the media labeled the popular movement "women's liberation," and a variety of feminists adopted the term. Yet most historians agree that these labels should not obscure significant crossover among ideologies, particularly by the midseventies. In truth, the lines between the desire for "equality" and "liberation" in the lives of rank-and-file feminists blurred to such an extent that the labels often become meaningless. I use both "feminism" and "women's liberation" because the women in my study did so; they did not articulate a distinction. A distinction certainly exists between liberal and radical feminists, which I attempt to maintain, and I use the terms "equality" and "liberation" with care.[6]

Finally, I will be avoiding the term "secular feminist movement" in this study. Instead, I typically employ the terms "larger feminist movement" or "American feminist movement" to indicate the national feminist movement. Labeling the larger movement as "secular" falsely suggests that all of the national and local leadership were nonreligious. Second, using the term "secular" as a blanket descriptor for mainstream feminism automatically designates religious feminists as outsiders. As we shall see, Catholic (and other religious) feminists made myriad significant contributions to the growth and development of feminism in America.

To map these contributions, in other words, to craft a historical narrative for the American Catholic feminist movement, I rely on published, archival, and oral history sources. Although published works are vital to my study, I rely most heavily on archival sources for analysis of the period 1970–80, the major portion of the book. Much of the narrative centers around the following feminist organizations, most of which have substantial archival collections: the Saint Joan's International Alliance-United States Section (sjia-us), the National Coalition of American Nuns (ncan), the Deaconess Movement (dm), the National Assembly of Women Religious (nawr),[7] the

Leadership Conference of Women Religious (LCWR), the National Organization for Women (NOW), the NOW Ecumenical Task Force on Women and Religion (usually referred to simply as the NOW Task Force), the Joint Committee on the Status of Women in the Church, Chicago Catholic Women (CCW), the Women's Ordination Conference (WOC), and the Women of the Church Coalition (WCC).

The collections of these organizations, among others, showcase a wealth of sources that bring Catholic feminists' experiences to life. Diverse sources help fill in the details of everyday life in a modern social movement. These include personal and organizational correspondence, memoranda, newsletters, liturgy handouts, music, poetry, visual art, photographs, recruiting material, conference proceedings, academic papers, lectures, membership lists, minutes, financial records, and press releases.

I have also conducted twenty-three oral history interviews for the project, recording the memories and perspectives of some of the most famous and active participants in the movement as well as those of rank-and-file feminists who never claimed leadership. While these interviews are not the foundation of my narrative, my oral history subjects have provided information and passion that cannot be found in any archive. They have offered me amazing stories, invaluable leads, and more importantly, necessary correctives for my analysis. Their memories of this movement are strong, as are their commitments to justice. I have tried my best to capture both in these pages. Throughout this book, narrative and analysis will be interspersed with biography in an attempt to illustrate larger themes through the lives of individual women. In this way, the analysis stays rooted in women's unique, lived experiences.

The narrative in this book traces the first two decades of the Catholic feminist movement in America from the emergence of Catholic feminist writers in 1963, through the development of the major Catholic feminist organizations in the early seventies, to a major strategic and ideological shift that occurred at the close of the seventies. This entailed a move away from the movement's dominant strategy of seeking dialogue with the hierarchy to an increased emphasis on establishing separate women's communities on the church's "margins." A truly comprehensive history of Catholic feminists in this time period would require some fifteen-hundred pages, so I have chosen to highlight specific subjects, events, and ideological trends to map the movement's course.

Generally, I have chosen to focus on what I term "grassroots organizational activists," those individuals who chose to direct their energies through Catholic feminist organizations. These women have been neglected to such a degree that they have nearly disappeared from historical memory. By necessity this decision places less emphasis on academic theologians, individuals who could also be found at the grass roots of the movement. Theologians will of course appear throughout this narrative, as they can be found throughout the movement, and their influence has been crucial. The academic wing of the movement deserves a history in which it is the primary focus, specifically an intellectual history that tracks changes in theological approaches; this, however, is not that study.

The historical narrative begins with chapter 1, "Origins," in which I explore the forces in both twentieth-century Catholicism and American feminism that incubated Catholic feminist thought prior to 1963. These include such acknowledged forerunners as the Grail, the Christian Family Movement, and the Sister Formation Conference. But I introduce two other crucial catalysts for the movement. The first is the Second Vatican Council. More importantly, one cannot grasp the start of Catholic feminism without an analysis of the second, Catholic attitudes toward "Woman" at midcentury, which encapsulated what came to be known as the "Eternal Woman" ideology. Eternal Woman rhetoric dominated the American Catholic popular (and clerical) imagination in the fifties and sixties, and it became a rallying point for, and the first target of, American Catholic feminists.

Chapter 2, "Demythologizing Ourselves," traces the emergence of Catholic feminist thought through the writings of about forty Catholic women who wrote on the topic of feminism in Catholic periodicals and a handful of monographs between the years 1963–70. These writings did not yet constitute a movement, but they did register as a collective response to the "Eternal Woman." Early elements of Catholic feminist theology, as well as the strategies that would shape the later movement, can be found here. The writings of Mary Daly, Rosemary Radford Ruether, and Sidney Callahan will receive particular attention.

By the late sixties, the organizational phase of the movement had begun. Many key Catholic feminist organizations emerged in the period 1965–74, and other preexisting organizations adopted feminist agendas. To begin my exploration of this burgeoning organizational movement, I have emphasized the ideological distinctions already clear among Catholic feminist activists. In chapter 3, "No Cakes in Hands unless Ideas in Heads," I focus first on the women who identified with radical feminism, principally the theologians Mary Daly and Elizabeth Farians. These women provided considerable leadership—both in theology and in concrete organization—as well as created the first Catholic feminist public protests. They largely chose to leave the movement by 1972. Chapter 4, "The Spirit Moving," follows a second ideological wing of the movement. These women, represented by the feminist "new nuns" and the women of the Deaconess Movement, chose a path of loyal opposition and posited a clear causal relationship between Catholicism and feminism. Here we see women articulating their feminism as a ministry of social justice and a means of obtaining ordained ministry.

Chapter 5, "The Love of Christ Leaves Us No Choice," slows down the narrative to view the Catholic feminist movement in the midseventies through the lens of a single event, the first national Women's Ordination Conference in 1975. The first woc conference brought together representatives from all of the major Catholic feminist organizations as well as the emerging leadership; it provides the best opportunity to take the pulse of the movement—its ideological focus, its agenda, its leadership—at a critical moment in the movement's development.

Just as chapters 3 and 4 form a pair to explore different ideological approaches in the early organizational movement, so do chapters 6 and 7 form a pair, to analyze movement strategy in the latter half of the seventies. Chapter 6, "Making Feminism Holy," investigates the extensive use of liturgy by Catholic feminists to reconcile faith and feminism on the individual and communal level as well as the use of Catholic women's spirituality as a form of public protest. Catholic feminists literally sacralized feminism through liturgical practice. The following chapter, "A Matter of Conversion," takes as its subject the movement's primary strategy of the midseventies': dialogue. We can see the limits of that strategy through analysis of the movement's reaction to the Vatican's declaration against women's ordination in 1977.

Finally, chapter 8, "Sustained Ambivalence," argues that as it became increasingly radicalized, the movement found itself divided and uncertain. Some wished to continue as they always had, simultaneously lobbying the hierarchy and organizing at the grass roots. Others questioned how they could ever retain ties with the institutional church. The second Women's Ordination Conference in 1978, the centerpiece of the chapter, illustrates this time of confusion. Ultimately, however, the movement (and many individuals) adopted a position of "sustained ambivalence." This concept, discussed in detail, describes women's choices to distance themselves from the institutional church and to establish new ways of being feminist women of faith, often on the church's "margins." The epilogue explores this shift and how it affected developments in the Catholic feminist movement through the mideighties.

By asking the question "how" in addition to "why," this narrative history expresses the richness of Catholic feminist thought and activism and suggests the movement's contribution to the development of both American Catholicism and American feminism. The history of Catholic feminism in America is a dynamic, and occasionally dramatic, story, full of intriguing characters, life-changing moments, laughter, anger, hope, and hopelessness. It is far too rich and compelling a story to lie in obscurity.

origins

1

When the woman seeks herself the metaphysical mystery is extinguished,
for in uplifting her own image she destroys the one that is eternal.
—Gertrud von Le Fort, *The Eternal Woman*

In a 1965 article for the Catholic magazine *Marriage*, a Redemptorist priest named Henry Sattler asked a question he believed to be of monumental importance for the welfare and salvation of mankind: "*Why Female?*" He asked his readers, primarily young wives, to ponder why God created both man and woman. Sattler acknowledged "procreation" as the obvious answer but sought an additional theological reason for woman's existence. He concluded that "towards the activity of God in grace all of mankind is feminine," that is, humans, like women, are expected to surrender their will freely and face God with an attitude of "receptive surrender." He explained, however, that "[man] is too busy *doing* things to surrender. So God gave him dependence-in-the-flesh—woman" as a daily reminder.[1]

Imagine you are a Catholic woman circa 1965. In the middle of a hectic day, you plop down on the sofa and pick up a Catholic magazine. It could be *Marriage*, or *Ave Maria*, or *Catholic Digest*. Imagine reading that your chief goal in life should be the surrender of your will (not to mention your body and your personality). Now imagine the thousands of ulcers in the thousands of stomachs of American Catholic women told just one too many times that they represent "dependence-in-the-flesh." Long before women's ordination came to dominate the agenda of Catholic feminists, a fundamental desire burned deep in the guts of innumerable Catholic women. As God as their witness, they would never again pick up a Catholic magazine to be assaulted by a know-it-all priest's theological justification for "Woman."

Read enough articles like "Why Female?" and the emergence of a Catholic feminist movement ceases to be such a mystery. But this understanding does not explain why Catholic feminism appeared when it did. After all, American Catholic women had been exposed to arguments such as Sattler's dating back to at least the mid-nineteenth century.[2] Why would this generation become the first to challenge such gender prescriptions publicly and on a large scale? To understand why, one must pinpoint with greater accuracy when Catholic feminism actually came into being in the United States. I date the emergence of Catholic feminism in the "second wave" of American feminism, that is, during the resurgence of feminism in the sixties and seventies, specifically, to 1963. This claim runs contrary to popular perceptions about the movement's history. Those scholars who discuss the movement's origins tend to date the appearance of Catholic feminism to the late sixties and early seventies, not the early sixties.[3]

Such an assumption is not far-fetched. Most of the major Catholic feminist organizations were established in the seventies, the period also of the rise of collective activism. For the most part, these organizations formed after the pioneering liberal and radical feminists of the larger second-wave feminist movement had arrived on the scene but roughly at the same time that popular and media interest in the movement reached its peak, in the first half of the seventies. One might then conclude that Catholic feminism was an offshoot of the larger feminist movement, an effort to take feminist principles and apply them to the religious sector. But what if Catholic feminism was not a by-product of a trendy and highly publicized movement in full flower but instead came into being in the early sixties, without a readily established feminist vocabulary, ideology, or agenda to build upon and with little if any connection to the larger national movement? If this was true, how would we need to reassess the history of Catholic feminism and, indeed, of second-wave feminism itself?

In fact, the first Catholic feminists began to make their presence known in 1963, the same year that Betty Friedan's *The Feminine Mystique* was released and several years before the formation of the National Organization for Women (NOW) or the emergence of the American radical feminists. A search of Catholic periodicals reveals nearly forty Catholic women writing openly feminist articles or letters to the editor between 1963 and 1970. I make this claim not as a misguided attempt to vie for the title of first feminists of the second wave, but to challenge the concept of Catholic feminism as an offshoot of secular feminism. Catholic feminists have unexpected origins that from the beginning mark them as substantially different from nonreligious feminists within the larger feminist movement.

They are different because, in large part, Catholic feminism was not imported into the church; it grew organically within Catholicism. So feminism is not, as many in the church would like to claim, a contagion brought in from outside to corrupt the faith. Nor is it a late-blooming form of feminism solely inspired by the actions of secular feminists. Rather, Catholic feminism was born of women's experiences as Catholics, their wrestling with the injustices, inconsistencies, and inspirations of their own faith tradition, as well as exposure to and participation in feminist and nonfeminist activism outside the church. They were not just feminists who happened to be Catholic. Their feminism itself was Catholic.

These early origins explain so much about Catholic feminism as it developed over its first twenty years, as will be shown throughout this study. It explains, for example, why Catholic feminists so often used Catholic language, symbols, scripture, and social teachings to describe the nature of their feminism. So, too, it explains why liturgy became a central theme of Catholic feminist activism and why Catholic feminists focused on priestly vocation not simply as a goal to be won, but also as the call to serve. Finally, it suggests an explanation for why so many Catholic feminists chose not to leave Catholicism entirely, despite their deep ambivalence toward the church. The following chapter begins this exploration into Catholic feminists themselves, and their distinctive approach to feminist consciousness and activism, but before we can fully analyze the nature of their feminism, we need to know from whence it came.

RELIGIOUS OR SECULAR ORIGINS?

Consider Joan Workmaster, a Catholic laywoman who became a feminist in the sixties. When asked to describe the origins of her feminism, Workmaster named both secular and Catholic influences. She believed her participation in civil rights and peace demonstrations helped lead her toward feminism, and by the early seventies she was an avid reader of *Ms. Magazine*, both traditional explanations for feminist consciousness. But she named as the greatest influence her involvement in campus ministry at her Catholic women's college and, specifically, liturgical changes after the Second Vatican Council that encouraged women's participation.[4] Marsie Sylvestro, another Catholic laywoman, dated her consciousness-raising to experiences in her Catholic high school. She vividly recalls the day her teacher, a woman religious, rounded up the class and marched them out to hear the revolutionary Angela Davis speak on the quad at Yale.[5] Their experiences as Catholic women among other Catholic women at a time of renewal, while not the only influence, played the most significant role in the development of their feminism.

Catholic feminists shared many of the same influences with other feminist women of faith and with secular feminists. In the sociological climate of the late fifties and early sixties, middle-class Catholic women experienced "the feminine mystique" much like other white American women of their class did. Claimed one such woman in a 1961 letter to the left-leaning Catholic weekly *Commonweal*: "Exhortations to find oneself in the bosom of the family can not hide the conflict [between maternity and intellect] nor convince women who are suffering as a result of it that they are not suffering."[6] Catholic women who were tired of trying to be "happy little wives and mothers" (as another Catholic woman memorably phrased it in 1955) read and were influenced by Betty Friedan's book when it appeared in 1963. Participation in the civil rights, student new left, and peace movements, often cited as major factors in the development of feminist consciousness among secular movement leaders, appears to have had an impact on some of the first Catholic feminists as well.

But evidence from the Catholic feminist movement suggests that these influences were limited. First, surprisingly few Catholic feminist writers and activists mentioned *The Feminine Mystique*. If its publication sparked the first generation of Catholic feminist writings, authors would have discussed it more frequently. When a researcher suggested to Elizabeth Farians, one of the first Catholic feminist activists, that her life had been changed by reading Betty Friedan, Farians replied, "Right, well, she didn't change my life. I mean she didn't open my eyes. . . . Oh [I read her book] but what I meant was that was not what made me a feminist."[7] Those who did write about the book found it enlightening, but they also criticized its bias against Catholicism. More significant, the first Catholic feminist writers pursued questions of faith as central to their understanding of feminism. Belief in and commitment to the transcendent as a means of ending oppression was a theme absent in Friedan's work.[8]

As for the impact of protest and reform movements in the sixties, they too were influential. The most prominent Catholic feminist to connect her experiences in the civil rights movement to the development of her feminism is theologian Rosemary Radford Ruether. Margaret Ellen Traxler, cofounder of the National Coalition of American Nuns, also identified the civil rights movement as a major influence, as did Maria Riley, a participant in the civil rights and antiwar movements. But, again, too few writers and activists cited them as major influences to credit them with the development of the Catholic feminist movement.[9]

Perhaps most important, Catholic feminists in the sixties and early seventies were relatively isolated from the larger feminist movement; their writings were self-referential and rarely mentioned the major secular organizations, events, and leadership. This can be explained, in part, by the larger movement's reaction to institutional religion in this period. The liberal and radical feminist strands that emerged in America in the sixties were not particularly welcoming of feminists who claimed their faith as a primary motivator for their activism or who showed strong ties to their faith traditions. Such a reaction probably stemmed from secular feminists' eagerness to condemn the perpetuation of sexism by institutional religions. This wariness, if not outright hostility, seemed to last into the early seventies. NOW could be an exception; among its founders was a Catholic sister, Mary Joel Read, and a year after its founding, NOW organized its task force on women and religion that welcomed religious feminist activists and their concerns.

Yet among NOW's leadership were many nonreligious women who seemed hostile toward the idea of encouraging religious feminism. As the pioneering religious feminist Elizabeth Farians recalled, many members of the NOW board ". . . didn't think religion was important. . . . Some of them were ex-Catholics; they were very turned off by religion." An Episcopalian feminist, Georgia Fuller, who later went on to head NOW's Task Force on Women and Religion, recalled the hostility of nonreligious feminists in the early years: "But there were only one or two feminist sisters with whom I could share my faith. Only one or two could understand that I gave classes in self-defense as a Christian; that I wrote testimony and fact sheets naming rape a political crime as a Christian; that I struggled, sometimes with high visibility, with the internal fighting of a turbulent new movement as a Christian. Yes, I was a closet Christian! For in the early seventies, god was indeed dead for feminists."

Jewish feminists also sensed reluctance on the part of secular feminists to recognize their specificity and their desire to integrate their Jewish and feminist identities. Jewish feminist Letty Cottin Pogrebin asked "why Jewish women *are* validated by the Women's Movement when we trudge through Judaic subcultures ruffling beards with our demands for reform but not when we bring Jewish consciousness back the other way into feminism." In addition, anti-Semitism was perpetuated by both secular and Christian feminists well into the eighties.[10]

For radical feminists, exodus generally emerged as the main theme when discussing religion and especially Catholicism. An extreme example of radical feminists' hostility toward the Catholic Church in the movement's early years was Ti-Grace Atkinson's 1971 speech at Catholic University. Atkinson, a former NOW officer and leader of the radical feminist exodus from NOW in the late sixties, accused the church of "conspiracy to imprison and enslave women," after which she proclaimed, "Motherfuckers! . . . The struggle between the liberation of women and the Catholic Church is a struggle to the death. So be it!"[11] Such a climate would not have attracted many nonradical Catholic feminists who, in this period, were self-consciously committed to integrating Catholicism and feminism.

If Catholic feminists had only loose connections to the larger movement in the early years, and their participation in civil rights and new-left activism also was limited, then what else explains their emergence? The history of American Catholicism in the twentieth century does suggest some possibilities. While some Catholic women did participate in the first wave of Catholic feminism (i.e., the woman suffrage movement), that participation was very limited and does not seem to have a direct link to the origins of a Catholic feminist movement in the second wave.[12] As numerous scholars have argued, however, Catholic feminism has roots in a variety of Catholic women's initiatives and groups founded in the United States as early as the thirties. For example, a variety of lay groups in the Catholic counterculture from the thirties onward, such as the Catholic Worker and Friendship House, laid the groundwork for a critique of church power and control from a position of loyalty. They also provided an American precedent for claiming Catholicism as a rationale for social change. In particular, three movements in the antitriumphalist wing of the Catholic community during this period can be labeled as direct antecedents of American Catholic feminism: the Grail, the Christian Family Movement (CFM), and the emergence of the "new nuns." While not explicitly feminist prior to the seventies, these movements provided opportunities for women to lead, theorize, and devote themselves to reform inspired by the Gospels.

Founded in 1940, the Grail was an exclusively female movement designed to train women as "lay apostles" who would bring Christ's work and message into the modern world. The Grail welcomed young women eager to be trained in the lay apostolate, a means of dedicating one's life to Christ without becoming a woman religious.[13] Women came to Grailville, the movement's headquarters in Loveland, Ohio, for a week, month, or span of years to live an ascetic, monastic lifestyle centered around liturgical celebration; some eventually formed small communities of Grail women around the country.

The Christian Family Movement (CFM), a movement for married couples and families, emerged in the late forties. Couples in CFM, largely middle-class and suburban, committed to transforming their lives by trying to bring Christ into their families and communities. CFM couples looked for ways to combat racism, alleviate poverty, promote community, and tackle systemic injustice. Steeped in the Catholic revival and familiar with the Catholic counterculture, members of CFM were "disturbers of the peace, not content with the status quo."[14] At its peak in the early sixties, CFM boasted 40,000 couples worldwide, with the majority of those couples in the United States.[15]

The Grail and the Christian Family Movement were both associated with "Catholic Action," an umbrella term for a multitude of international programs designed to facilitate lay participation in the mission of the church. While these two movements possessed the spirit of Catholic Action, they were far more sophisticated and in some ways more radical than typical Catholic Action groups directed at youth. They shared two other characteristics that set them apart: they were founded and led predominantly by women, and they were intentionally not official Catholic Action groups. Because of this, they retained lay—and female—autonomy in a church dominated by men.

Achieving and sustaining lay autonomy on a large scale was a bold proposition for a woman in the Catholic Church in the mid-twentieth century, yet most of these women should not be considered feminists. Women of the Grail promoted female essentialism and complementarity, the belief that God ordained different and complementary roles for men and women. As historian James Fisher noted, "the Grail offered an undiluted vision of womanly self-surrender." Grail proponents believed that woman had a special capacity for surrender, contemplation, and spirituality necessary to the work of the apostolate. CFM also provided unprecedented leadership opportunities for Catholic women, modeled by its cofounder Patty Crowley who became a prominent challenger to the Vatican's prohibition of artificial birth control and, by the seventies, a Catholic feminist activist. But CFM women also espoused complementarity; they acknowledged their husbands as heads of their households and leaders within CFM meetings.[16]

The Grail and CFM may have been seedbeds for Catholic feminism by providing precedents for laywomen's authority and action, but judging from the writing of feminists in the sixties—who rarely mentioned them—they did not have a direct influence for most.[17] However, changes in the Catholic sisterhoods had a measurable, palpable influence on Catholic feminism. In the fifties, women religious faced a crisis; their traditional apostolates—teaching, nursing, social service work—demanded a higher degree of education and professionalism. Yet the majority of women religious entered religious life out of high school, and many became teachers in parochial schools without sufficient training. The discipline of being a sister included a rigorous schedule encompassing work, prayer, and responsibilities to the life of the community, leaving little time for education. To gain bachelors degrees, many attended classes in the summers; it was not uncommon for women religious to spend upward of fifteen summers to earn their degrees. In addition, to gain a foothold in their professions, sisters needed a high level of personal ambition and a willingness to enter the secular world, both traits that normally were discouraged among women religious.[18]

In 1954, a group of sisters established the Sister Formation Conference (SFC) to promote education and professionalization for women religious. Through newsletters, annual conferences, and summer programs, a community of women religious began to develop across congregations. The Vatican supported their goal of training, but the hierarchy did not foresee the consequences of encouraging women religious to seek higher education or of gathering so many sisters in one place. Women religious began to be influenced by the works of the Catholic revival, bringing the spirit of change in the American church of the fifties to the sisterhoods. Discussions of teaching credentials and training gradually led to talk about anachronistic dress, the desire for new apostolates, and how to modernize the sisterhoods, all happening well before the Second Vatican Council. Sister formation also led women religious to assert themselves before the hierarchy and the leadership of their communities, insisting that new sisters receive adequate education before beginning to teach.

In the early fifties, the superiors of women religious also organized, forming the Conference of Major Superiors of Women (CMSW) in 1956. In the fifties and sixties, CMSW quietly began a dialogue with the Vatican and American hierarchies, seeking the necessary autonomy to begin reforming orders that seemed out of step with the times. Major changes did not occur until after Vatican II, but they originated in the work of women religious in the fifties, who were asking if sisters could do more to make themselves relevant in the world.

Thus by the time the Second Vatican Council began in the fall of 1962, progressive women religious were more than ready for reform. A buzz surrounded women religious in the early sixties; the Catholic media was full of stories about the "new nuns." Sisters marched in Selma, wore shorter habits without veils, worked in inner cities, wrote theology, earned graduate degrees, and expressed opinions on controversial topics. Debate over the "new nuns" raged in the media, some of it outraged, some faintly amused, but most of it supportive. Between 1963 and 1970, the "new nuns" were on the cutting edge of church renewal. More than any other group they seemed taken with the spirit of Vatican II and ultimately provided much of the leadership for the new Catholic feminist movement of the seventies.

But although the Grail, CFM, and the "new nuns" were important precedents for and influences on Catholic feminism, none of them was the immediate catalyst for the emerging movement. That honor belongs to the institutional Catholic Church, which itself must take the credit for both provoking and inspiring Catholic feminism in the early sixties through the Second Vatican Council (1962–65). Shortly into his papacy John XXIII called for a worldwide council, the first since 1870, with the goal of "aggiornamento." In his own words, he hoped to open a window and let fresh air into Catholicism; the Second Vatican Council invited the church to open itself to the modern world. After a two-year planning process, bishops from both the Roman and Eastern rites descended on the Vatican in 1962, along with hundreds of experts in church doctrine, canon law, liturgy, history, and theology. Of all these thousands of official observers and participants gathered from around the world, none were Catholic women, although twenty-three Catholic women observers were eventually invited for the third session.[19]

Women's rights in the church and society were not on the council's agenda, but other vital reforms were, changes long under discussion by reformers yet still unfamiliar to the vast majority of Catholics. By the time the council ended in 1965, it had changed how the church prayed, defined itself, related to other faiths, and how it understood itself in the modern world, for the first time openly struggling with the challenges of modernity. As a whole, the sixteen Council documents asked Catholics to rethink the church radically. Instead of an institutional church with all the power and importance residing in the hierarchy, Vatican II promulgated the image of the church as the People of God. In this definition, laypersons were called to be full participants in the mission of the church. The council rejected the image of church as judge and monarch in favor of a servant church, "placed in the service of the human family."

The spirit of the council was openness—to people of other faiths, new ideas, dialogue, and most especially, dissent. Through the media, Catholics around the world heard bishops debating central ideas and disagreeing. The church did not speak with one voice, a shocking concept for Catholics. Many Catholics commented that the council was above all an invitation for Catholics to grow up. The church was open to change, it was fallible, and Catholics needed to start taking responsibility for their own faith.[20]

Feminists' relationships to Vatican II were complex. Many American Catholic women were outraged by Vatican II, viewing the council as a blatant large-scale display of the church's entrenched sexism. As women, they found little to commend beyond a few speeches supportive of women. In fact, Vatican II gave already frustrated Catholic women a focal point for outrage and a subject that sent them running to their typewriters. Catholic periodicals burgeoned with commentary about the council, and emerging feminists took advantage by exploring women's issues in the context of that analysis. Vatican II was one of the topics most often discussed by the first Catholic feminist writers.

Ironically, Vatican II also deeply inspired these first feminist writers. Like other liberal American Catholics, feminists found in the documents of Vatican II hope for a modern church awakened to the apostolate of its people and to its responsibilities in the world. These women were eager to apply what they interpreted as the vision of Vatican II to their own lives, to their parishes and religious communities, and to American society. Moreover, they interpreted council documents, particularly the Constitution on the Church in the Modern World, as supportive of feminism, an interpretation surely unintended by the majority of the council fathers. As Margaret Mealey, the moderate executive director of the National Council of Catholic Women, remarked in 1966, "By the action and pronouncements of Vatican II, women have been given their wings. But too many pastors and bishops are reluctant to let them fly. . . . Catholic women are growing tired of being ignored . . . but they are still ready to step forward and assume an adult role in the Church with intelligence and grace when it is offered. It is not yet too late—but it is surely high time."[21] Although it revealed the church's entrenched sexism to the world, Catholic feminists found in Vatican II a catalyst for feminist consciousness. It gave Catholic women the opportunity simultaneously to name the source of their oppression and imagine a new world without it. According to Mary Daly, the council served a larger purpose than renewal; the response to it among women proved to be "a timid beginning of the assertion of their existence."[22]

These peripheral and direct influences, from Vatican II to Betty Friedan to the "new nuns," have been well documented, but a vital piece of the story has been overlooked. We commonly date Catholic feminism to the seventies because this is when Catholic feminists became organized, with well-defined objectives. The battle over women's ordination, the focal point of much feminist activity in the seventies, is well-documented with clear protagonists on each side.

Not being organized, Catholic feminists in the sixties are harder to locate, but when their work is compiled and compared it is clear that they too shared objectives and, indeed, a common opponent. Their target was an idea, a construction of Catholic womanhood known at the time as the "Eternal Woman." When Catholic feminists began to challenge the idea of the Eternal Woman they created a debate that helped fundamentally shift how American Catholics conceptualized women in the Catholic media. The articles and books of a small but growing number of educated laywomen and women religious writing in the sixties provided the first counterpoint to the postwar American Catholic rhetoric of "woman." These early feminists wrote bold polemics exposing the history of Catholic sexism and patriarchy, hopeful essays using the language of the Second Vatican Council to insist on women's individual freedom of vocation, angry articles decrying and denying that pious, suffering, *imaginary* being, "Catholic woman." As they challenged the eternal woman construct, Catholic feminists explored the relationship between their faith and their feminism.

These early rhetorical skirmishes, scattered and unorganized as they were, have fallen through the cracks of collective memory. In fact, this lack of awareness is the measure of feminists' victory. Consider, for example, the word "woman." When did you last hear the term used to encompass all members of the female sex, as in the following sentence: "Woman represents the very power of surrender that is in the cosmos"? This usage, jarring to those who live in a world reshaped by religious as well as nonreligious feminism, has been rendered nearly archaic. Generally, we no longer use the singular form in this manner because most people no longer believe that all women share a common destiny. When students in my women's history courses read Sattler's "Why Female?" they respond with confusion or laughter, not anger. Henry Sattler might as well be from fifteenth-century Mars. American—and American Catholic—culture has changed so drastically that I have to work to help my students take such writing seriously. And we do need to take it seriously.

An assessment of these feminist writers' early work on questions of female essentialism is significant beyond a persnickety academic's need to establish the origins of a social movement. In 2004 the Congregation for the Doctrine of the Faith (CDF), the Vatican body responsible for Catholic doctrine, released a document called "On the Collaboration of Men and Women in the Church and in the World." The document praised women and "feminine values," outlining the appropriate theological justifications for distinct gender roles in the church and beyond. In the United States, the document was most noted for its denunciation of feminism, which the CDF blamed for antagonism between the sexes and the heightened debate over gay marriage.

While the authors claimed not to be returning to an "outdated" concept of woman, the document is chock-full of eternal woman imagery, language, and logic. The most obvious clue is that the document purports to be about men and women, though the authors spend two-thirds of the document defining woman's role but never once define man's. The document's preoccupation with women indicates that the Vatican still conceives of its gender study in terms of defining and limiting women's roles. Vatican officials are not the only group returning to these themes. So-called New Feminism, a growing movement of socially conservative Catholic women who decry the repercussions of second-wave feminism, also seems to argue for a new interpretation of essentialism.[23]

Feminists rushed to analyze and dismiss the Vatican document, but few recognized the rhetoric for what it was, a worrying return to mid-twentieth-century Catholic rationalizations of gender difference centered around eternal woman ideology. Having taken it for granted that such questions were long settled, Catholic feminists have ceased to discuss them with any urgency, leaving room for more conservative voices to reclaim the debate.

Catholic feminists may well find themselves having to reargue the ideas so carefully and forcefully put forward in the sixties. The work of these early feminists is too valuable, then, to be forgotten.

THE AMERICAN "ETERNAL WOMAN"

Although this generation of Catholic feminists was the first to openly confront the Henry Sattlers of the Catholic world, these women were certainly not the first to encounter them. Efforts to promote a church-sanctioned gender ideology through American Catholic periodicals date back to as early as the mid-nineteenth century. Catholic magazines offered prescriptive advice designed to reinforce the "True Catholic Woman" ideology—an image of woman as pious, pure, submissive, domestic, and confined to the private sphere—for the emerging Catholic middle class.[24] The institutional church, from popes to the local parish priest to the Catholic media, upheld strict gender demarcations and behavioral guidelines to protect both the institution of the family and the integrity of Catholic faith and culture. The burden of maintaining such boundaries, and the consequences of failing to maintain them, usually fell on women, to whom exhortations on the proper roles of the sexes were most often directed. Gender boundaries and guidelines gradually shifted, however, as both American Catholic culture and its relationship to the larger American culture changed over time. Therefore, the image of woman required periodic readjustment; the mid-twentieth century was one of those times.

After World War II, the Catholic community seemed particularly concerned about women's sexual morality and "place," as Catholic urban ghettos gave way to suburbanization and upward mobility. The extended family networks and tight communities of the old ethnic neighborhoods could no longer regulate women's behavior; thus Catholic priests, sisters, and pundits showed their anxiety by attempting to define Catholic womanhood for a new age. At the same time, America witnessed a general preoccupation with women's domesticity. On one level, then, Catholic redefinitions of woman reveal the desire of an assimilating group to emulate dominant cultural norms. The new Catholic woman of the fifties touted by the Catholic press was often indistinguishable from the happy housewife ideal then ubiquitous in American popular culture. But the Catholic woman ideal was also distinctively Catholic, reflecting the fears and expectations of the powerful in the Catholic community.

Catholic writers combined the popular urge for feminine domesticity with the ideology and trappings of devotionalism. Robert Orsi has vividly analyzed how in the twenties through the fifties purveyors of devotional literature narrowly defined "woman" and her call to sacrifice herself for others. Orsi found that through the rituals of devotionalism, Catholic women in the mid-twentieth century "incarnated the story that the culture told about them."[25] At midcentury, devotionalism, with its emphasis on feminine piety and the centrality of the Virgin Mary, lent sanctity to the church's attempts to regulate women's lives, providing a ready cosmic rationale for strict gender roles in changing times.[26]

Articles and books that defined gender through the lens of devotionalism peaked in the late fifties, a few years behind the trend of declining devotionalism. Yet Henry Sattler's article, a near perfect example of the form, appeared in 1965 at the dawn of the postconciliar era. "Why Female?" might be considered a relic of the past, a throwback to the heyday of American devotional culture, but for the existence of similar nonfiction articles appearing in a wide variety of Catholic periodicals through the late sixties. Even as the church struggled in Vatican II to bring itself into the modern world, explanations of every woman's duty to sacrifice her body, her will, her work, even her personality, for the sake of her family and the kingdom of God persisted in American Catholic culture.

The term typically applied to such gender constructions as the eternal woman or eternal feminine ideal, a set of beliefs describing woman as an archetypal personality with special characteristics and responsibilities for maintaining balance in God's kingdom. The most comprehensive portrait of this archetype appeared in the United States in 1954 with the publication of *The Eternal Woman*, written in 1934 by a German historian, philosopher, poet, and Catholic convert named Gertrud von Le Fort. Traces of Le Fort's thought can be followed through Catholic magazine articles and books from the midfifties through the late sixties. When Catholic feminists addressed the eternal woman myth, often it was Le Fort's ideas they were attacking, whether ascribed to her or not.

The eternal woman myth rested on the idea that woman had a vital symbolic importance in redemption, distinct from the reality of existence. This made her timeless and eternal, her characteristics fixed. As Le Fort noted in the first sentence of her introduction, "this book is an attempt to interpret the significance of woman, not according to her psychological or biological, her historical or social position, but under her symbolic aspect."[27] According to theologian Maria Clara Luchetti Bingemer, the eternal woman myth purposely separated "the historical and temporal from the eternal and eschatological, setting up revelation and the history of salvation as a dimension above and beyond real, chronological, factual history, leaving no possibility of dialogue between the one and the other."[28] "Woman" could only exist as an archetype in a cosmic realm, yet Le Fort wrote her book for the express purpose of bridging the gap between the eternal and the temporal. In her view, real women could be taught to model the eternal woman.

Le Fort's ultimate concern was saving the world from what she perceived to be a crisis of epic proportions: humans' refusal to surrender to the will of God, in her view, their one contribution in the mystery of redemption. Le Fort argued that both men and women must enact their parts by surrendering to God's will, yet she insisted that God gave woman a special capacity for surrender that she must demonstrate for men, thus exercising the power of surrender for the good of humanity. As she asserted, "the passive acceptance inherent in woman, which ancient philosophy regarded as purely negative, appears in the Christian order of grace as the positively decisive factor."[29] But in assigning the duty of sacrifice and surrender to one sex, in delineating only one way to be "woman," eternal woman advocates like Le Fort "imposed on women a single prototype and a single way of living their identities."[30]

These advocates gave their construct a theological justification by pointing to the Virgin Mary's example of surrender. At the Annunciation, Mary announced her "fiat," her "yes," to God when the angel Gabriel appeared to her and asked her to be Christ's mother. Mary surrendered herself completely to the will of God, and became a crucial factor in the incarnation and thus the redemption of humanity. Because she said yes, Christ was born, and could then die to redeem the world. Mary "represents at the same time both man and woman" as Le Fort explains in the introduction, yet woman alone, as inheritor of Mary's role by virtue of her gender, symbolizes surrender and must demonstrate that surrender at every stage of her life.[31] Mary's power is monumental but ironic; she exercises power only by surrendering it. So, too, for Mary's spiritual daughters. Le Fort argued, "as woman primarily denotes not personality but its surrender, so also the endurance that she is able to give to her descendants is not self-assertion, but something purchased at the expense of submerging herself into the universal stream of succeeding generations."[32]

But what if woman failed to "submerge" herself for the good of the world? Le Fort sketched the consequences in apocalyptic terms, claiming that "when the woman seeks herself the metaphysical mystery is extinguished; for in uplifting her own image she destroys the one that is eternal."[33] Women who refused their "eternal" role were little more than demons. Because woman represented "the very power of surrender that is in the cosmos, that woman's refusal denotes something demoniacal and is felt as such. . . . Even the belief in witches during Christian centuries, however tragically it may have erred in individual cases, signifies in its deeper implications the utter rightness of the aversion against the woman who has become unfaithful to her metaphysical destiny."[34] To Le Fort, then, "woman" was a mystical creature but not a mythical one. All women, no matter how rooted in the realities of time and space, must conform to the eternal woman's destiny.

Like Le Fort, American Catholic authors tended to discuss "woman" in the language of symbols, divorced from earthly reality. Woman is "the vessel on which God has principally relied to unfold the mystery of human freedom and redemption. . . ," one author wrote. Like Le Fort, these authors predicted cosmic consequences if women failed to accept their symbolic role. In an enthusiastic review of *The Eternal Woman* in the journal *Worship*, Therese Mueller wrote, "It makes one tremble, this book, with awe and with fear . . . fear lest we, our own generation as well as each individual woman, fail in our metaphysical and religious vocation."[35] Andre Aubuchon predicted a more specific apocalyptic result in a 1963 issue of *Priestly Studies*: "If she shuns her role as woman, she turns her back on the world and her God-given nature . . . without which the very life of the world will wither up and die."[36] "Catholic woman" carried a very heavy burden, indeed.

But according to these articles, woman was given the very traits she needed to fulfill her metaphysical destiny. Echoing centuries of female stereotypes, writers characterized woman as gentle, tender, humble, and loving. She was person-oriented, more attuned to the individual, whereas man was immersed in larger societal and intellectual interests. "Men are probably attracted to the less personal wonder of scientific and philosophical mystery, women to the more person-oriented depths of intersubjective mystery," a priest asserted.[37] Another author went so far as to say, "when we hear women using intellectual arguments excessively we grow dismayed—and she grows sharp because she is displeased with herself."[38] She expresses her love of people through humility, prayer, "abhorrence of the vicious, heroism in suffering and tenderness in sympathy."[39] Occasionally, authors revealed the other side of the coin, those negative traits that debased women. This was often the case, for example, when authors wanted to prove the impracticality of ordaining women. Women were characterized as emotionally possessive, gossipy, interfering, moody, tending toward emotional imbalance, and most important, unlikely to keep the confidence of the confessional.[40]

Of woman's God-given characteristics, the favorite trait by far was woman's special capacity to surrender herself totally and suffer for the good of humanity. This surrendering of self was both symbolic, as we have seen, and practical. It is worth noting here that self-sacrifice is a central tenet of Christianity. Christ told his disciples, "If any want to become my followers, let them deny themselves and take up their cross and follow me . . . those who lose their life for my sake will find it."[41] The metaphor of the grain of wheat falling to earth and dying before it can bear fruit is another passage explaining this deeply held belief.[42] Self-abnegation was promoted by more than just the eternal woman advocates; it was a concept particularly popular with the American Catholic counterculture at midcentury. For these Catholics, self-abnegation meant antimaterialism, direct service to the poor, and living a radical Christianity, virtues they believed all Christians should practice.[43] But the difference here is that eternal woman advocates believed that woman carried the burden of self-abnegation for all. Man might be called to sacrifice, but as it is not in his nature, woman must model it for him.

Exhortations to women to sacrifice their lives to the point of self-effacement were ubiquitous in American Catholic periodicals. Hers was to be a "total self-surrender," her greatest gift a "hunger . . . for a total dedication."[44] As Mother M. Gregory Lacey phrased it in *America* in 1959, "Of her very nature, woman is made for sacrifice. Hers is the more self-effacing lot in life, and she is happy to have it that way. She wants to give, and she is not happy until she has given her whole self."[45] Another author found the phrase "live her own life" to be "tragic."[46] Woman was described as empty space, the "chasm . . . that exists between God and man," or more succinctly, "to be a woman is to be a cradle."[47] Literally, woman was to forgo her own personality as part of her sacrifice for others. She was told to strive for "silence of mouth, mind, and will" and that "losing herself in other people" was her vocation; woman was "desirous of diffusing herself into others."[48] Her only self-expression was to be her sacrifice and suffering. It should be noted that the eternal woman ideal applied to all Catholic women, including single women and women religious, who often were encouraged to be "spiritual mothers."

Authors made frequent references to Mary to help women relate to the ideology of suffering and submission. Ironically, many authors stressed Mary's awesome power in the cosmos even while highlighting her meekness and eagerness to surrender herself. Mary could be portrayed as a powerful woman who "dared to be the Mother of God."[49] Some authors translated this to women by encouraging what they called "active surrender," by which the Eternal Woman energetically exercised her power of suffering. This way, authors gave woman a sense of agency coexistent with her passivity.

Although Mary possessed enormous power as Co-Redemptrix, many authors chose to highlight that she was simply a happy housewife. On one level, this attempt to humanize Mary and root her in the temporal worked as a necessary counterpoint to the majestic Mary of the Assumption. Such a flesh-and-blood Mary could provide a powerful, supportive image for Catholic women. But the eternal woman authors, following the customs of Marian devotional literature, often sentimentalized this housewife Mary into a saccharine, pious nonentity, no more real than the triumphant Queen of Heaven.

Emphasis on the cosmic and eternal aspects of woman did not preclude the physical. The rhetoric of surrender, receptivity, and suffering often took on sexual overtones, revealing that women were to sacrifice their bodies as well as their personalities. The connection emerged in the occasionally erotic language of devotional literature, as in this passage by a woman religious in a 1966 issue of *Cord*: "While the attitude of the bride is one of ever deepening receptivity to the Spouse, the response of the mother drives this submission to a depth of surrender which she never could have assessed or surmised in that first Nazarene moment of her 'fiat mihi.' Yet, as the shafts of faith, trust, and love are plunged to the very bottom of her will, a resurging peace of completeness is released."[50]

More concretely, authors linked the concept of sacrifice to the debate over artificial birth control. In 1964, Nicholas Lohkamp called woman's refusal to bear children "selfish," claiming birth control was "diametrically opposed to the essential surrender and other-centeredness of the mother."[51] Four years earlier, a Catholic husband and father of six wrote to *The Liguorian*'s advice column about his wife, who refused to have sex with him anymore for fear of pregnancy. She told him that if he did not like it, she would take a separation or divorce. Donald F. Miller replied that she must be "mentally abnormal" and "so neurotic" that "she needs to consult a good Catholic psychiatrist." He wondered "whether a wife who would go that far is not in some way possessed by the devil himself."[52]

At their most extreme, the American eternal woman articles took on sadomasochistic overtones. "Women's nature" according to one author, "responds intuitively to the vocation of victim."[53] Another referred to Mary's fiat saying, " 'Be it done to me' echoes in the life of every woman."[54] Yet another approvingly called housewives a "living sacrifice."[55] Women religious often were the subject of this type of rhetoric. A nun was "a host to be consumed"; religious life was a "crucified" life.[56]

But the most frequent of these references were to self-immolation. One of the greatest sins was that of a "woman who feels the call of self-immolation within her but refuses to answer that call," according to P. Parrain writing in *Family Digest*, the Catholic equivalent of *Reader's Digest*.[57] Woman was to be like a candle that achieves its perfection by "burning itself out bit by bit," formed by God "in the fire of submission."[58] The Dominican priest Athanasius Van Noenen told sisters that to help priests attain the qualities they needed, "we have the silent immolation of a multitude of lives; the purest, the most crucified, who dwell in cloisters."[59] Another referred in passing to "the mature, self-immolating woman."[60]

In 1963, priest and sociologist Andrew Greeley wrote an article on women for young people in *Ave Maria*. He tried to break away from the eternal woman model yet continued to write within an ideology of female essentialism, stressing the importance of sacrifice. Greeley referred to women who looked "for the wrong things in the wrong places and [took] their frustrations and disappointments out on their husbands" as "witches," a term he felt was perhaps "too charitable." In depicting the alternative, a woman who sacrificed when necessary and fought for justice, he remarked, "there ought to be a touch of Joan of Arc . . . within every woman."[61] Whether a witch or a St. Joan, either way she was likely to get burned.

Other Catholic authors revealed their unease about changing gender roles by making frequent, often vituperative statements about feminism throughout the period in question. Curiously, a majority of these comments appeared before the feminist resurgence in the early sixties.[62] Many of these attacks on feminism came from priests and were intimately tied to the eternal woman ideal. In 1955, a homily published in *Homiletic and Pastoral*

Review warned Catholics "to be wary of all those brawling, screaming, hot-eyed social movements that go by the general name of feminism. . . . Christian women must glorify God by being feminine, not feminist."[63] A second cleric claimed that because of feminism, "motherhood is decried as an enemy whenever it interferes with personal aspirations. . . . And what is the result of this abnormal development? It is eating like a canker into the heart of woman. It is eating deep into her happiness, her dignity, her every virtue and prerogative which Christianity has assured her." Calling on another aspect of the eternal woman model, he urged readers to pray to Mary as the best way to stop feminism.[64] Antifeminism continued to appear after 1963, taking a particularly hostile form in conservative publications.

By the early to midsixties, some authors writing on "woman" abandoned the cosmic rhetoric, attempting to update the Catholic woman image for a new generation. These authors stressed woman's intelligence, independence, and right to self-fulfillment. The result, however, while more positive, was often contradictory. An example of this awkward synthesis is F. X. Arnold's *Woman and Man: Their Nature and Mission* (1963). Arnold went to great pains to reject Catholic stereotypes of woman, asserting that "she is a human individual, whose value and rights must be recognized and whose most important counterpart is not the man but God."[65] Yet he perpetuated the stereotype he seemed determined to discard by claiming that man's desire was for "strength and personal courage," while woman's greatest desire was for "self-surrender."[66] Because it was the most prominent incarnation of the eternal woman thesis in the midsixties, Catholic feminist authors targeted Arnold's book as yet another thinly disguised attempt, in a long line of such exhortations, to make mortal women eternal.

Perhaps the best example is the Jesuit magazine *America*, which between 1959 and 1963 printed a series of editorials on women, each demonstrating a desire to break stereotypes about "woman" and advocate equality yet at the same time reflecting essentialist rhetoric. A 1959 editorial decried female stereotypes, for instance, but went on to argue that woman's primary function was motherhood and that " 'woman's place is in the home'. . . reflects the ideal pattern of a perfect human society." Two years later, *America* used the occasion of Theresa of Avila being named a Doctor of the Church to argue for women's equality. However, the editorial quoted Pope John XXIII: "Whatever is the work of love, of giving, of receptivity, of dedication to others, of unselfish service—all this finds a natural place in the feminine vocation," to which the editors replied, "No narrow vision here." A third editorial, published in 1963, applauded the decision to invite female auditors to the council but ended by saying that "no one in his right mind would advocate a religious feminist movement."[67] These authors argued for women's equality but could not yet abandon the Eternal Woman.

In contrast, a few Catholic women began to speak out against the Eternal Woman in the fifties and sixties. One of these was Katharine M. Byrne, a lonely voice in the Catholic media in 1956. Her article, "Happy Little Wives and Mothers," criticized the portrayal of women in Catholic magazines. It is striking not simply for its content, but also for its tone. Unlike other Catholic articles on women in this period, Byrne's writing is sarcastic and frustrated:

> The happy little wife and mother is really busy these days, and she is making my life no easier. . . . Her two year old's hands are folded in prayer. Yours has just bitten his little brother's arm. . . . It would be a real comfort to me to hear the H.L.W. and M. admit that once, after three bleak winter weeks of unalleviated pressures, she walked out on her whole family and took a bus ride to the end of the line alone. . . . We would welcome from the Happy Little Wife and Mother the admission that while the way of life which she chose, and the one which, with God's grace she is trying to live well, is the one she wants, it is nevertheless a somewhat monotonous life. And often very lonely.

Twice Byrne tried to make the Happy Little Wife and Mother speak like a flesh-and-blood woman and admit she was not perfect, but characteristically the Eternal Woman had nothing to say.[68]

Byrne's article represents the first crack in the eternal woman façade, a hint that perhaps real Catholic women could not and did not aspire to this ideal. By the early sixties, at the height of America's preoccupation with women's domesticity, a handful of Catholic women again took up the theme. Their position is best summed up in the words of one author, long disgusted with "the constant insistence of the world in general that we be happy, happy, happy."[69] These writers questioned the eternal woman without putting forth a feminist agenda or calling for equality. The editors of *America* in the same period called for equality without challenging the Eternal Woman. For a Catholic feminist movement to come into being, someone had to link the two in an analysis of Catholic women's identity and a critique of the Catholic Church. Whether *America* was ready for it or not, the "religious feminist movement" was about to make its appearance.

2

demythologizing
ourselves

It is precisely this—the emergence of a significant number of creative women who will *raise up their own image*—that can significantly weaken the hold of the paralyzing stereotypes upon human consciousness.
—Mary Daly, *The Church and the Second Sex*

The person who finally linked a call for equality with an attack on the Eternal Woman was Rosemary Lauer, a Catholic philosophy professor who in 1963 published the first American Catholic feminist article of the second wave in the progressive Catholic weekly *Commonweal*. Titled "Women and the Church," Lauer's article went beyond questioning the eternal woman stereotype to challenge both the church's conception of women and women's roles in the church. While optimistic about the possibilities for change, her message was blunt: "the roots of our tradition require that women be given a 'separate' treatment because they are *not* equal, because they are *inferior*."[1] In attacking Catholic sexism, Lauer did not hold myopic clerics responsible, but the tradition itself, a wildly new approach for Catholic women suggesting the need for radical solutions.

Lauer's article employed a set of techniques that came to characterize Catholic feminist writings to follow, many written by other Catholic women academics. She cited current discrimination and its roots in church practice and theology; detailed the church's patriarchal history, peppered with outrageously misogynistic quotations from the church fathers; engaged in biblical exegesis of both the Hebrew scriptures and the New Testament to offer feminist interpretations of scripture; noted the difference between the rhetoric of Vatican II and the reality of women's experiences; and reported mounting pressure from women demanding change. Lauer's goals were broad in scope as well as daring. She called for a complete reconsideration of women's roles in the church, including a recommendation that women be ordained.

The best way to demonstrate the significance of Lauer's article is to view it through the eyes of a young doctoral candidate studying theology in Switzerland, a woman who shortly became the most prominent feminist theologian in America. In a letter to the editor Mary Daly wrote, "I was ashamed when I read the excellent article by Rosemary Lauer on 'Women and the Church,' ashamed that I had not written it, ashamed for all of us who should be articulate about this subject and have been silent. . . . What is most astonishing of all about Professor Lauer's article is not even the facts that it relates, but the fact that—in view of the facts—this article is so unique." Inspired by Lauer, Daly prophesied the movement to come: "This much I know: the beginnings of these articles and these books (how badly we need these books, especially!) are already in the minds and on the lips of many of us. And—this is both a prophesy and a promise—they will come."[2]

Mary Daly was right; over the next decade Catholic feminism would develop into a full-fledged organizational movement, built upon the foundations of those articles and books she helped call into being. In these writings, the early Catholic feminists needed to reconcile a multitude of new ideas about the church and feminism, as each was in flux in the early to midsixties. They did so through a process of redefining each for themselves. Although these women reevaluated both Catholicism and feminism, their emphasis was clearly more on the Catholic Church in this period.

Like others in the renewal movement, they entered a debate about Catholicism, actively reshaping the church for a new generation. Their critique of sexism was very much about renewal, the process of determining the church's future. How could the church fulfill the intentions of the Second Vatican Council, they asked, if it did not address the archaic myth of woman? Optimism and commitment to renewal mingled with the anger and insight attending feminist consciousness, producing a reevaluation of Catholic women's identity and a searing criticism of Catholic tradition, theology, clerical culture, and hierarchy.

Such an approach resulted in a distinct faith-based feminism coupled with a complex, often ambivalent relationship to the church. Ironically, the

Catholic Church was from the beginning both a rationale for and a target of their activism. Throughout the period under study in this book, Catholic feminists were aware of contradictions between Catholicism and feminism and experienced uncertainty about their position vis-à-vis the church. However, in this first phase, Catholic feminists were generally optimistic about the church's future and their relationship to it.

Indeed, the feminist visions the writers created in this earliest period were overwhelmingly Catholic visions. They countered Catholic sexism with uniquely Catholic responses, steeped in the language of faith. As they experimented with new feminist voices, they retained a Catholic worldview in which faith, justice, and vocation were viewed as catalysts for personal and social transformation, revealing their calls for equality and renewal as two parts of one integrated cause. Far from rejecting Catholicism when they came to feminist consciousness, they seemed to engage their tradition more deeply as a means of understanding and structuring their feminism. Ultimately in this first phase, they chose an integrated Catholic feminist worldview.

DEMYTHOLOGIZING OURSELVES

To identify the extent of feminist activity in the preorganizational period I compiled a bibliography of 480 articles about women printed in American Catholic periodicals between 1954 and 1970. These articles, representing viewpoints from conservative Catholic to Catholic feminist, appeared in sixty-one different Catholic periodicals and journals. Within these I was able to identify over forty articles and letters to the editor written by thirty-seven female Catholic feminists for sixteen different Catholic periodicals.[3] I also studied the three major Catholic feminist monographs from the period: Sidney Callahan's *The Illusion of Eve: Modern Woman's Quest for Identity* (1965), Sally Cunneen's *Sex: Female, Religion: Catholic* (1968), and Mary Daly's *The Church and the Second Sex* (1968).

The thirty-seven feminist writers in this study came from a variety of backgrounds and perspectives. Roughly two-thirds were laywomen, ranging in age from the early twenties to late sixties; they include mothers and housewives, like Anne Tansey and Lucille Harper, who worked part-time as freelance writers; women religious, such as Mary Luke Tobin, Margaret Ellen Traxler, and Maria Del Rey Danforth, with experience in leadership, teaching, sister formation, civil rights, and missionary work; Arlene Swidler and Sally Cunneen, two founders of ecumenical journals; a regular colum- nist for *Sign* named Katherine Burton; and a variety of scholars, such as Rosemary Lauer, Rosemary Radford Ruether, and Mary Daly, in philosophy, theology, and psychology. The thirty-seven also included several prominent non-American feminists who wrote in the American Catholic media, such as Rosemary Goldie from Australia, a council auditor; Gertrud Heinzel- mann, a Swiss lawyer who filed one of the first petitions for women's rights at the council; and Hilda Graef, a German theologian with expertise in Catholic mysticism.

A handful of the writers went on to notable careers in feminist theology and/or leadership in the women's liberation movement. The majority, how- ever, did not rise to prominence either in the sixties or in later phases of the movement. For the most part, each wrote only one magazine or journal article on the subject of women's liberation. A small portion of the articles from scholars such as Mary Daly and Rosemary Radford Ruether displayed a thorough command of theology and an academic depth of analysis. The majority of articles and letters show a lesser degree of scholarly insight but a notable willingness to make new forays into church history and theology, to draw connections between abstract theories and personal experience, and to speak out on new and controversial topics.

The three authors making the most significant contributions in this period were a trio of laywomen: Mary Daly, Rosemary Radford Ruether, and Sidney Callahan, each with a unique approach to Catholic feminism. Mary Daly was born in 1928 to working-class Irish-Catholic parents in upstate New York, raised Catholic, and received a Catholic education. As Daly grew up she valued independence and freedom, dreaming of traveling and be- coming a scholar. Although never particularly pious, her threat to join a convent was a useful "flyswatter" against those wanting her to marry and settle down. While she "was not exactly insincere" about joining religious life, "it just seemed indefinitely postponable."[4]

Daly's real passion was scholarship, particularly philosophy. Beginning a remarkable academic career, she majored in English at the all-female Col- lege of Saint Rose only because the school did not offer a philosophy major, a subject her priest philosophy professors thought unfit for women. She earned a masters in English at Catholic University ("the only respectable university available to me as an inhabitant of the spiritual, intellectual, and economic catholic ghetto") and a doctorate in religion at St. Mary's College, the first American program of its kind for women.[5] She then sought the highest degree in Catholic theology, a doctorate from a pontifical faculty of sacred theology, but the only such program in America, at Catholic University, refused to accept women. In 1959, Daly moved to Fribourg, Switzerland, in pursuit of a Ph.D. in sacred theology. By the time she left Fribourg in 1966, she held doctorates in both sacred theology and philosophy, bringing her doctorate total to three.

After a month-long stint as an unofficial observer at the Second Vatican Council (she borrowed press passes so that she could attend the sessions), Daly took a position at Boston College and worked on her first book, *The Church and the Second Sex* (1968), the first major scholarly critique of Catholic sexism, its origins, and its impact on women. Together with her previous feminist articles in *Commonweal* and other liberal Catholic periodicals, *The Church and the Second Sex* made Daly a national figure as the country's most prominent Catholic feminist. The book also provoked a battle with conservative Jesuit theologians at Boston College who attempted to fire her in 1969 but were dissuaded by massive student protests on Daly's behalf.

Daly's scholarship in the sixties was thorough, well-reasoned, and innovative. A pioneer in feminist theology, she explored the church's accountability in the history of patriarchy and did not hesitate to target Catholic misogyny. As of 1968, Daly believed the church was redeemable—it could be the impetus for change—but she soon rejected this idea as untenable. At that time, Daly was a respected Catholic pundit on a variety of subjects, but by the end of the sixties she had become more a part of the emerging radical feminist community than of the liberal Catholic community, and her work began to reflect this shift. She emerged as one of the first "revolutionary" feminist theologians, that is, a theologian who rejected Christianity as irredeemably oppressive. By the early seventies, Daly no longer considered herself Catholic and was well on her way to repudiating Christianity.

Rosemary Radford Ruether, another pioneer feminist theologian, had a very different background and took a different stance than Daly. Born in 1936 in Georgetown to a Catholic mother and an Episcopalian father, Ruether grew up in a religious but ecumenical and humanistic environment far removed from Catholic triumphalism. She earned a bachelors in classics from Scripps College, then a masters in classics and Roman history and a doctorate in classics and patristics, both from the School of Theology at Claremont. While still in college she married Herman Ruether, a political scientist, and by the early sixties had three young children.

In the sixties, Ruether became deeply involved in the civil rights and peace movements as well as the Catholic left. In the summer of 1965 she worked for the Delta Ministry in Mississippi, witnessing firsthand the struggle for racial justice. In 1966, she took a position at Howard University, a historically black college in Washington D.C., a post she held for ten years. While pursuing her academic career as a theologian, and raising her children in a racially integrated Washington neighborhood, she could frequently be found at demonstrations, on picket lines, and occasionally in jail. She also sustained a significant correspondence with the Catholic monk and social activist Thomas Merton and emerged as a pundit in the American Catholic media.[6]

Ruether insists that, like other feminist theologians, she came to feminism by way of the civil rights movement. "Well, when Stokely Carmichael made his famous remark that the only role for women in the revolution was prone," Ruether remembered, "we were already doing a race and class critique and we began doing a gender critique from within these movements. I was taking my ideas from these movements into the classroom."[7] Here was a praxis model that influenced much of Ruether's later scholarship. In the late sixties, Ruether began to publish articles in the Catholic and secular press on the issue of Catholic sexism and women in the church as well as make initial forays into feminist theology. Ruether's major feminist works did not appear until the midseventies, but in the sixties she offered a foretaste of what was to come.

As the first major Catholic feminist theologians, Rosemary Radford Ruether and Mary Daly are often compared. In the sixties, they produced complementary exploratory work, challenging the eternal woman construct, patriarchal tradition, and searching for liberating Christian symbols and themes. Both began as "reformist" feminist theologians in the optimistic postconciliar mood of the midsixties, that is, they recognized the problems inherent to Christianity but believed, with reform, that Christianity could lead people to justice and liberation. In other words, they espoused renewal. By the late sixties, both Daly and Ruether had written complex critiques of the church, displaying considerable ambivalence about the possibilities of reform. But while Ruether deepened her ties to the Catholic renewal and ecumenical theological communities as she came into the feminist movement, remaining a reformist even as she became more radical, Daly was drawn to revolutionary feminist theology.[8]

The third major figure was Sidney Callahan, author of the first American Catholic feminist monograph. She achieved brief prominence as the Catholic feminist spokesperson of choice in the midsixties, but while the scholarship of Ruether and Daly led to new fields and movements, Callahan's early feminist writings marked the transition between eras and have since faded into obscurity. Sidney Callahan was born in 1933 in Washington, D.C., to nonreligious parents with deep roots in southern culture. Callahan was raised to be a southern lady which, in her experience, meant downplaying her intelligence and ambition. A natural scholar, Callahan eagerly attended Bryn Mawr, a college her family feared would corrupt her with northern liberal values. Their fears were justified.

At Bryn Mawr, Callahan undertook studies in literature but spent considerable time as a spiritual seeker. She drifted from the Quakers to low-church Protestants, and after a brief stop with high-church Episcopalians she converted to Catholicism. Callahan was an "enthusiastic Catholic," a product of the midcentury Catholic revival. She embraced the energetic, dedicated Catholic spirit that emerged through the work of Dorothy Day, the Grail, and the new reformist liturgists and theologians. With her husband, Daniel Callahan, a philosopher (and by the midsixties associate editor of the magazine *Commonweal*), she joined a vibrant community of like-minded liberal Catholics who were eager to make the church alive for the modern world. Catholics like the Callahans wanted to make the church the center of their lives and embrace its teachings, among them the ban on artificial contraception. Such enthusiasm prompted Sidney Callahan to claim that she would have six children by thirty (and a Ph.D. by thirty-five).[9] She gave birth to seven children in ten years, losing one child in infancy. She was, as she recalls, "very naïve."[10]

The Callahans struggled to make ends meet, and Sidney faced increasing isolation as an overwhelmed young mother who longed for the intellectual life. Sheed and Ward, the publishing house at the center of the Catholic revival, offered her entry into that life when it asked her to consider writing a book on Catholic women in the early sixties. She had never thought of herself as a writer but jumped at the chance. Her competitive nature said that if practically every other liberal Catholic she knew could write a book, including her husband, she could too.

She began the project as a firm believer in the eternal woman ideology so prevalent at the time, but as she researched she reversed her position. The work conceived as an affirmation of the Eternal Woman transformed into the first American book-length indictment of the ideology. *The Illusion of Eve: Modern Woman's Quest for Identity*, published in 1965, can be viewed as the Catholic woman's *The Feminine Mystique,* albeit without the runaway success of Betty Friedan's book. Callahan wrote for an audience of young married Catholic women, searching for a middle ground between the intolerable eternal woman ideal and Catholic sexism, on the one hand, and what she viewed as a modern feminism fixated on equality at all costs, on the other hand. Callahan confronted sexism and church backwardness as she put forth practical solutions for women trying to juggle motherhood, marriage, career ambitions, and social concerns. She hoped to help women lead meaningful Christian lives, in whatever way they chose, while accepting their responsibilities for their families and communities.

Like Ruether and Daly, Sidney Callahan wrestled with themes of Catholic women's identity and the relationship between feminism and renewal, but her work had a different focus and tone. Her writing lacked the theoretical underpinnings of the two theologians, focusing instead on practical solutions in the everyday lives of Catholic women and their families, but her thought, while moderate and transitional, is significant. Her feminist voice provides a window into how liberal Catholic women initially approached the process of integrating Catholic faith and feminism. She also represents those women writers in the sixties who did not become active participants in the feminist movement. By the late sixties Sidney Callahan had moved on to other projects as she continued to juggle scholarly and family commitments. Although she remained a feminist, she had difficulty reconciling the growing national feminist movement—which she perceived to be too prone to anger and bitterness as well as hyperfocused on abortion rights—with her own understanding of a nonviolent Catholic spirituality. She also believed women "should take on other questions beyond the feminist one and not let themselves be confined."[11]

Finally, a third Catholic feminist monograph appeared in the midsixties, *Sex: Female, Religion: Catholic* (1968) by Sally Cunneen, cofounder of the liberal ecumenical journal *Cross Currents.* Cunneen and Callahan shared a similar feminist outlook in this period. In the midsixties, Cunneen conducted a study of *Cross Currents* readers on the subject of women and the church; their responses, many of them feminist, constitute the bulk of *Sex: Female, Religion: Catholic* and generally provide a perspective akin to *The Illusion of Eve.*[12]

As was evident in Callahan's writing, one of the primary subjects for analysis in these articles and books was the Catholic Eternal Woman. Catholic feminist authors in the sixties spoke of the eternal woman construct not as a vestige of the past, but as an ongoing problem needing to be addressed. The monographs by Callahan, Cunneen, and Daly noted a steady stream of eternal woman articles, although Daly considered them to be on the wane by 1968. She likened these authors to antique dealers "who manage to do a thriving business with a narrow range of customers, but hardly can be said to be altering the course of history."[13] Time and again these feminist writers demanded reality in place of the cosmic eternal woman myth. In describing Rosemary Lauer's pioneering 1963 article, Daly said Lauer had "broken through the myth." Daly argued how difficult it was to "shake off the inhibiting effects of myth" because promoters of the myths claimed them to be a result of divine revelation. She found these ideas "amazingly incoherent" and "flagrantly unjust."[14] Summing up the thoughts of many early Catholic feminists, a respondent in *Sex: Female, Religion: Catholic* remarked simply, "It's impossible to live in an archetypal pattern every minute."[15]

Writing in the usually conservative American clerical journal *Priest*, German theologian Hilda Graef urged women to begin the process of "demythologizing ourselves."[16] In effect, she called on women to jettison their own internalized myths of Catholic woman as part of their transition to feminist consciousness. Over the course of the sixties, writers systematically exposed every stereotype, myth, falsehood, and glorification perpetuated by the eternal woman advocates and the hierarchy while exhorting Catholics to speak of women as they actually were.

Like Katherine Byrne's tongue-in-cheek response to the "Happy Little Wives and Mothers," authors tried to break through the mask of cosmic unreality with reason, humor, anger, and sarcasm—anything to portray women with a sense of humanity. Displays of anger and sarcasm represented a revolutionary development for women in the public life of the American church. The Eternal Woman not only never expressed anger, she never felt it. In a world of placid submission, sarcasm and irony were unknown. So when feminists adopted a tone that revealed how infuriated they were—and what's more, turned their anger on the church itself—they signaled the beginning of a new era.

As a first step, feminists insisted on plurality. Gone was the singular "woman" meant to encompass all of Eve's daughters, what one woman referred to as "that big gray blob womankind."[17] Writers consistently spoke of "women," emphasizing differences of personality, gifts, and vocations. The Eternal Woman was "self-less," as Mary Daly playfully phrased it. Daly directly confronted Le Fort's *Eternal Woman*: "the characteristics of the

Eternal Woman are opposed to those of a developing, authentic *person*, who will be unique, self-critical, self-creating, active and searching."[18]

By rejecting the personality-free Eternal Woman, writers disdained gender essentialism. In a historical overview of patriarchy for *Cross Currents* in 1967, Rosemary Radford Ruether offered a sophisticated critique of that concept, arguing that women had heads as well as hearts and had "the right to exercise both of them." Furthermore, "if this is to be a true maturation and not just an antagonism of competing egos, then the male ego too must recover its lost psychic self from those groups which have become its shadow side. . . . He must discover that the emotive, affective nature he projected on the woman is none other than his own emotive nature which he needs to integrate with the rational logos in order to arrive at integrated personhood."[19] Other writers picked up the theme, arguing that women's nature was human nature; integrated, balanced personalities were far more valuable than archetypal symbolism and faceless perfection. A less sophisticated, but astute writer insisted that "women are neither that idolatrously good, nor that poisonously bad. They are just people—of the female sex, pretty much like men, bumbling fools of more or less good will."[20]

Feminists recognized those personality traits that the Eternal Woman did display—passivity, receptivity, sacrifice, and suffering—as especially damaging and rejected them as exclusively female traits. "When the difference between men and women is overemphasized," Sidney Callahan argued, "the corollary is always discrimination in the guise of an irrational mysticism of sacrifice."[21] One of the earliest writers to address this theme in the American Catholic media was Gertrud Heinzelman, a Swiss feminist often cited by American Catholic feminists. After describing church sexism as "a forcible strangulation," she argued with eloquence against the idea that woman must demonstrate receptivity for humanity. "It is incomprehensible that the rhythm of receiving and giving should not be analogous for the two sexes," she explained, "as the rhythm of inhaling and exhaling is the same for both sexes."[22]

Catholic feminists began at rock bottom, then, constructing new identities for Catholic women, establishing their existence as individuals, with unique personalities, human imperfections, and the right to self-determination. But if Catholic women rejected the essentialist role of women's receptivity in the cosmology of redemption, what was to be their purpose in God's kingdom? Far from rejecting the need for such a purpose, the writers specifically offered an alternative vision of liberated women actively engaged in the responsibilities and opportunities of the Christian community. Liberated Catholic women had the same task as men, "to grow-up in the fullness of Christ," as Sidney Callahan phrased it.[23] Or as one of the female council auditors argued in 1966, if the church limited women to the "cozily maternal," it was "likely to exclude them from such 'masculine' tasks as formulating the Gospel message for today's world."[24]

Arguments like these explain some women's extreme frustration with Vatican II and why it was such a strong catalyst for the movement. Women felt called to contribute, swept up as they were in the excitement of *aggiornamento*. Yet accounts brought back to the United States by the media and other observers clearly proved women's forced exclusion starting from the council's opening days. These women were angry, and it showed in their writing. Anyone looking for deep theological analysis of the council documents from these feminist writers in the Catholic media will be disappointed. They did not analyze so much as vent. They did this by telling—and retelling—stories. Stories of insults, of slights and rejections experienced by women at the hands of bishops and Vatican officials, appeared over and over again in feminist writing for at least five years.

Why dwell on the insults? Vatican II gave these women concrete evidence, on an international scale, that they were second-class citizens in their own church. The discrimination they might have experienced at the hands of their pastors or bishop or the local parochial school board may have seemed isolated and personal, so much so that they might not mention it at all. But Vatican II was a dramatic, symbolic event, and the slights took on a heightened significance when they took place amid such rich symbolism.

The Eternal Woman was given corporeal form against the backdrop of the council. Vatican efforts to keep women silent and segregated reinforced the Catholic ethos of the eternal feminine. "There was no sign of a woman anywhere in the Council Hall, not even a cleaning woman," one unofficial woman observer wrote about the first session. "Only the stone images of some saints and queens looked down from the walls of St. Peter's, silent and unwanted witnesses."[25] Mary Daly remembered "the tremendous impression of seeing those old men in red sitting up there in their higher seats and then the few [women] auditors . . . sitting in very humble positions. They were not allowed to speak, having no active role at all."[26] Two widely reported incidents involving female journalists in the first sessions made the symbolic silencing of women concrete. One reporter was asked to remove herself from the main floor during a session and to sit in the balcony instead. Another was inexplicably denied Communion at a council liturgy, presumably because she was simply a woman among men. The most retold incident was probably the experience of Barbara Ward, a highly educated and capable woman with expertise in the field of global poverty. She asked to address the assembled council fathers during debate on the schema that would become the Constitution on the Church in the Modern World (*Gaudium et Spes*). She was refused, and a layman took her place.

Some Catholic women were heartened by speeches and interventions on the part of a few bishops who called for the end to sexism. Moreover, world-wide agitation by men and women finally resulted in the inclusion of twenty-three female auditors in the third session, so the Vatican was attempting to respond. But the addition of auditors did little to assuage women's anger; instead it highlighted the lack of women in the proceedings prior to the third session and their lack of power once they arrived.

Mary Luke Tobin, a Sister of Loretto head of the Conference of Major Superiors of Women, was the only American woman auditor. When told that the auditors could only observe sessions of interest to women, Tobin replied that meant she should observe everything. The women auditors made their presence known and followed the debates closely, asserting some influence by contributing to the discussion of key council documents on the commission level, most notably *Gaudium et Spes*. Six women, including Mary Luke Tobin, were named as full voting members of the commission preparing the Constitution on the Church in the Modern World, a move considered something of a coup.[27] The auditors' role was extremely limited, however, as they were unable to speak before the council fathers.

For Sidney Callahan the final insult was the construction of a separate café for the women auditors, in effect separating them from the two official cafés that had become the de facto centers of behind-the-scenes political maneuvering. "What was the final count?" she asked, "a spectacular six or seven feminine 'observers' duly segregated from the sacred precincts of the coffee bar? What a ridiculous situation for an institution numbering millions of women members. . . ."[28] No doubt many echoed the sentiments of Katherine Burton, who demanded "Just whose council is this anyway?"[29]

Feminists' perpetual recounting of the insults of the council did not stop them from joining in the process of renewing the church. After all, many of these feminists were also captivated by the promise of change implicit in the council. Insults to women notwithstanding, Sidney Callahan was so affected by watching "the good guys" unexpectedly triumph, she claims it made her "an optimist for life."[30] Elizabeth Carroll, a Sister of Mercy who became a major leader among women religious and Catholic feminists, recalled that when the council's preparatory commission solicited ideas from American women religious in the early sixties, she "had nothing to say." She was too indoctrinated with the eternal feminine. But by the midseventies she could claim that "the Council helped immeasurably, if accidentally, by force of the very logic of its central themes: the Church as people of God and the dignity of personhood." She also knew that she would have to challenge the institutional church to see the promise fulfilled.[31]

Many saw the challenge to Catholic misogyny as the first and most vital step in that process. One author asked simply, "Our Lord likes us. The Gospels—written by men—show that. Why then don't these men who are supposedly carrying out His teaching like us?"[32] The writers quickly set about identifying and denouncing Catholic misogyny and the barriers it raised to women's participation, just as they tore down the myths restricting women's humanity. Well-informed and connected, Catholic feminists offered a broad critique of the church, from its use of Mary and the concept of "woman" to its treatment of flesh-and-blood women; from exposure of misogyny in the teachings of church fathers to analysis of sexism in contemporary theology and liturgical practice; from criticism of clerical behavior to universal denunciation of the church's teaching on birth control.

A focus on three of these areas, clericalism, sexuality, and Mariology, highlights major aspects of their critique. Writers aimed to expose the true relationship between clergy and women beginning with the church's long history of misogyny. One such writer was Katherine Burton, an outspoken lay columnist for *Sign*, who often pointed out contemporary church sexism and its roots. These columns marked a transition for Burton, a convert, from religious conservatism in the postwar years to a vocal if moderate feminism in the midsixties.[33]

Burton insisted that clergymen rarely bothered to think of women at all, but when they did, she claimed they were unduly influenced by the desert fathers: "During the first century A.D. things went all right, but a little later a lot of very religious men went out to live in the desert. In the desert they communed with the Infinite. My theory is that they stayed too long and came back firmly convinced that women were evil—a necessary evil of course, for where else would future theologians come from?"[34] Feminists seemed to relish particularly outrageous statements by the church fathers and medieval teachers. Tertullian, Chrysostom, Aquinas, Augustine, and

Bellarmine were popular targets. Bellarmine received recognition for his claim that three classes of people (idiots, country dwellers, and women) were incapable of learning theology, while Aquinas was cited for his belief that women were "misbegotten males." Tertullian was remembered for asserting that women were "the devil's gateway."

Writers called these statements dangerous, but also ridiculous, undermining the aura of veneration Catholics were expected to adopt when speaking of the church fathers. Feminists argued that these early writings constituted the foundation of the hierarchy's understanding of women, not the nineteenth-century adoption of "different but equal" or "complementarity" rhetoric. They described complementarity, the belief that men and women were equal but had different roles ordained by God, as "a bow to social pressure," used so as not to appear blatantly misogynistic. In practice, writers claimed, the church still taught that women were inferior.[35] For proof, one need only look to the Catholic Mass, they argued. The priest, lectors, and altar servers were male; God was even male—at least that was what women were taught. If women were equal, where were they in the chief expression of the Catholic faith?

Feminist writers held priests chiefly responsible for excluding women and perpetuating sexism, blaming celibacy and male clerical culture (what Sister Maria del Rey Danforth called the "stag party supreme") for the church's entrenched sexism.[36] In their view, clerical culture promoted sexism by isolating seminarians from women and encouraging intense devotion to Mary, reinforcing the eternal woman myth. Indeed, many saw the perpetuation of the Eternal Woman as evidence of a clerical culture so immature that it stubbornly insisted on the comforting illusion of archetype instead of recognizing reality.

Feminists daily witnessed practical ramifications of this deeply rooted culture, ranging from priests' inability to offer meaningful guidance in the confessional to their extreme awkwardness with and avoidance of female parishioners to the ban on artificial birth control and prohibitions against women in the sanctuary, holy orders, and the hierarchy. Sally Cunneen concluded that most respondents to her survey "are convinced that pre-existing assumptions by priests about the nature of woman greatly determine the character of relationships that develop."[37] Frustration with the clerical system that excluded women was clear. One woman asked in a letter to the editor, "How much longer will women accept with docility a prohibition against serving as God's ministers, or even as acolytes at His altar? How much longer can they or any committed Christian accept as authority for abuse an obscure passage from St. Paul written for a tent-dwelling culture, 2,000 years ago? . . . How much longer will women accept rules made by men only for women only? Is not Catholicism wearying of rules made by celibates only for non-celibates only?"[38]

Feminist demands for participation in decision making and liturgical practice grew in response to the council's teachings that the people of God, not the institution, were the church and should therefore assume greater responsibility for Catholic worship and social mission. The council quixotically directed the hierarchy to decentralize and share power ("collegiality" in Vatican II terminology), the curia sharing power with bishops, the bishops with priests, and priests with the people. Lay groups appeared around the country, hoping for influence in diocesan decision making, liturgical reform, and the expansion of laymen's participation as liturgical ministers. However, women reformers quickly realized that the general use of the term "layman" meant just that.

Establishing women as liturgical ministers and eventually priests required substantial reimagining of clerical culture literally to bring women into the same space as men, let alone share equal standing and leadership. Rosemary Radford Ruether suggested that priesthood itself would have to be radically changed because, "in its exclusive maleness and in its clericalness, it exhibits what has now become an archaic form of social relationships."[39] Few suggested radical change in the sixties, but the debate over feminist alternatives to clerical culture introduced in these years snowballed into the seventies, becoming one of the movement's fundamental issues. Ruether herself played a major role in this debate.

Celibate clerical culture fostered men who feared, were uncomfortable with, and even hated flesh-and-blood women, according to emerging feminists. Such ancient aversion to women, women's power, and women's sexuality in Catholicism resulted in an asexual eternal woman construct; seemingly, eternal woman advocates would have all women be virgin mothers if they could. Recognizing church teachings on women's sexuality as intolerably divorced from reality, Catholic feminists confronted both clerical control of women's bodies and its underlying roots in Mariology.

To illustrate the hierarchy's profound misunderstanding of women's sexuality, feminists turned their attention to canon law. Take for example the canon law governing the classification of female saints. At the time, the Catholic Church only recognized three types of women saints: virgins, martyrs, or "neither-virgins-nor-martyrs." The church canonized so few married women that they did not merit a category of their own. Arlene Swidler, a scholar and feminist who in the seventies became a major leader of the Catholic feminist movement, argued this classification system perpetuated the illusion that the vast majority of Catholic women—because they were sexually experienced—rendered themselves incapable of achieving sanctity.[40] Neither-virgins-nor-martyrs could be tolerated and controlled, but the church did not consider them holy. While symbolic, these classifications proved what Catholic feminists already believed: Catholicism had no healthy concept of women's sexuality and could offer no assistance in navigating the challenges faced by modern women wanting to lead full Christian lives.[41]

In the sixties these challenges included difficult decisions about artificial contraception, readily available for married women but condemned by the church.[42] Traditionally, the church taught that artificial birth control violated natural law by separating the sexual act from its primary procreative function. But many Catholic couples viewed birth control as an answer to the burden of large families, abstinence, and the tyranny of the rhythm method of birth control, which required couples to calculate when conception was least likely to occur and restrict sex to that window. Rhythm was notoriously unreliable, and eventually proven to rest on shaky scientific foundations.

In 1964, Rosemary Radford Ruether, then a graduate student with three young children, published in the *Saturday Evening Post* what was arguably the most well-reasoned and frank treatment of the question in the sixties. Ruether argued that Catholic interpretation of natural law was untenable because in real life, more often than not, husbands and wives had sex for reasons other than procreation. The Catholic position was logically flawed; by using the rhythm method, couples were in fact attempting to divorce sex from procreation, yet such intervention was deemed acceptable. She criticized clerics who consistently told overburdened couples for whom rhythm had not worked that their only option was abstinence, a response Ruether herself received when she sought a priest's advice.

But her main argument was about the reality of marriage and women's desire to control their own lives. Ruether spoke in a very personal way of the damage rhythm and endless pregnancies caused marriages and families. Under such conditions, she argued, "sex comes to mean fear, not love." "The more happily two people are married," she wrote, "the more deeply they know that sexual intercourse has a validity and meaning of its own . . .

this union of man and woman is an end in itself, and its fruits are just as real in the sterile marriage as in the fruitful one." But this was also about the rights and desires of women. Ruether argued that one of the worst aspects of the church's teaching was that it required women to abstain from sex at the time of their cycle when they most desired it. Such a sacrifice was both unnatural and counterproductive. She did not call it evidence of church sexism; this article appeared before Ruether identified herself as a feminist, but the ideas were present.

The young Ruether wanted to make her own decisions and shape her own future: "I see very clearly that I cannot entrust my destiny just to biological chance. . . . A woman who cannot control her own fertility, who must remain vulnerable to chance conception, is a woman who cannot hope to be much more than a baby-machine." Many feminists agreed, calling, as the decade wore on, for a reversal of church teaching. In 1968, the year Pope Paul VI released his encyclical *Humanae Vitae* upholding the teaching against the recommendation of his own commission, feminists, like the majority of liberal Catholics, simply refused to accept the teaching and largely ceased to discuss the birth control issue. Their understanding of their own needs ultimately took precedence over their loyalty to the pope.[43]

In 1967, Ruether remarked that "the idealization of Mary goes very well with the contempt for the question of women."[44] If women were to de-mythologize and embrace feminism, they needed to start with the Virgin Mary, who posed a problem for Catholic feminists. Conservatives based the Eternal Woman on Mary. In popular usage Mary was synonymous with passive receptivity and patient suffering, making her a burdensome symbol for those seeking liberation. Yet Mary could also be interpreted as a powerful figure and a courageous woman, a positive role model, if feminists chose to reclaim her.

Feminists exposed what they viewed as the poor logic and cruelty of Catholic theology that created the false dichotomy of Eve and Mary, a construct they considered the root of women's oppression. Catholic theology stressed two female archetypes, one a sexualized, defiant, active woman who brought sin into the world, the other an asexual, submissive, passive woman who willingly relinquished her body to God to help redeem the world from sin. Mary was the "New Eve"; through her fiat she negated Eve's (woman's) fatal error. The connection of real women with Eve dominated Catholic theology for centuries. The mid-twentieth-century eternal woman advocates, however, rarely spoke of Eve, consistent with the effort not to appear misogynistic. But feminists observed that if you retained only an archetype of perfection, the opposite pole of sin and degradation remained.

Ultimately, writers concluded that Mary should not be a model for all women. In *The Church and the Second Sex*, Mary Daly argued that because of a "catastrophic" misunderstanding of the Christ/Mary relationship as analogous to the man/woman relationship, teaching women to emulate Mary and not Christ relegated "the woman to a hopelessly inferior situation."[45] Despite her glorification, Mary would always be viewed as less than Christ, so women would always be seen as less than men. Also speaking of the Christ/Mary construct, Callahan concluded it "implies that Christ saves men while Mary saves women. . . . No, women must choose Christ and live in Christ as men do."[46] But Callahan raised another reason why modeling Mary was inappropriate: as she was then understood, she was not human, whether in her incarnations as Virgin Mother or the pure, humble housewife who "weeps . . . when young Catholic ladies whistle."[47]

Callahan did attempt to reclaim Mary as a role model for modern Catholic women. She was one of the few writers to do so in this period, although Ruether and Daly both acknowledged that Marian devotion could be positive. Callahan began with a traditional argument, valuing Mary for initiating salvation by her fiat. But she visualized Mary's fiat as "the beginning of a great battle," citing as evidence the emphasis on justice in the Magnificat, Mary's prayer to God upon her visit to Elizabeth, mother of John the Baptist. Callahan suggested, "Submissiveness to God does not imply retiring timidity. Mary may well have been a spirited and demanding woman, capable of the righteous anger and irony Christ so often displayed." Echoing this theme was Martha Durkin, a laywoman who in 1966 wrote a letter to the *National Catholic Reporter* urging women, as a symbolic act against oppression, to stop covering their heads in church, a rare call to activism in the sixties. Significantly, she chose the feast of the Assumption, the celebration of Mary being taken up into heaven, as the date for this action, saying that "with a prayer to Mary for courage and assistance in obtaining justice, Catholic women might commence to assume their dignity as full-fledged People of God."[48] But these interpretations of Mary were rare; she was still too neatly tied to the Eternal Woman for the majority of Catholic feminists to redeem her, at least for the present. Only in the midseventies, after the eternal woman construct had sufficiently faded from Catholic culture, could Catholic feminists claim Mary as a feminist symbol.

If feminists had concentrated solely on casting off the bonds of their Catholic pasts, one would be tempted to conclude that they sought a feminist ideology free of the burdens of institutional religion. But these earliest writings prove that such was not the case. The new feminist visions that Catholic women created were nonetheless Catholic visions. Catholic feminists approached the institutional church with ambivalent feelings, raising new questions about the church's capacity to model its own message of liberation. They also approached secular feminism with skepticism, ready to approve of justice for women but sensing hostility toward Catholicism. They had to create a new path that validated their faith yet challenged the church. Some feminists proved more cautious and traditional than others, but overall Catholic feminists' conclusions in this period were consistent. Even as writers identified the sources of their oppression in the church, they turned to the language, traditions, Vatican II vision, and renewal of Catholicism to begin defining an integrated Catholic feminist ideology.

Catholic feminists seemed to spend much more energy working out their relationship to the Catholic Church than their position vis-à-vis the larger women's movement. It is striking how infrequently these feminists mentioned the women's movement. Their early writings seemed fairly self-contained and self-referential. Though presumably aware of developments outside the Catholic sphere, they rarely spoke of secular organizations, leaders, or activities.[49] An exception to this was Betty Friedan, and the limited reaction to *The Feminine Mystique* offers a rare glimpse into how Catholic feminists perceived the larger movement in this period and how well it fit with their own goals.

In October 1963, one month prior to Rosemary Lauer's article, Jean Holzhauer reviewed *The Feminine Mystique* for *Commonweal*. She found Friedan's thesis particularly applicable to Catholic women because "when intelligent American Catholic women are discontented with being the 'heart' of the home to a point just this side of suicide, they blame themselves and their sinful natures."[50] Holzhauer suggested that they should blame the church instead. Mary Daly also spoke approvingly of the book. Other authors agreed with Friedan's theories but objected to her negative comments about large families and her assumption that Catholicism disapproved of careers for women.[51]

Sidney Callahan recognized the book's importance but also took issue with Friedan's portrayal of Catholic women. Callahan cited Friedan's story of a Catholic mother who gave up her political work because her child was not performing well in school, a story Friedan used to demonstrate the difficulties Catholic women faced in working outside the home. Claiming bias, Callahan wondered why Friedan did not consider if the child was, in fact, harmed by the mother's absence. Instead Friedan's "only concern was that this woman (as typical of many backward orthodox types) was being frustrated."[52] In regard to another story she argued, "One can not agree with a Betty Friedan who can tolerantly comment that a wife's going to work to find her identity 'perhaps precipitated the divorce, but it also made her more able to survive it.' "[53]

Despite these challenges to Friedan, writers only occasionally spoke negatively about feminists or the women's movement, indicating what parts of the movement, as they perceived it, they were unwilling to accept. These most often centered around issues of sexuality and the family. Sidney Callahan was openly feminist but found some aspects of feminist ideology distasteful, harmful, or incompatible with her beliefs as a Catholic. As a contented mother of a large family, she objected to talk about women's enslavement to their own bodies. She asked, "at what point does projected control of nature shade into a rejection of the body and physical processes? . . . as a general rule this school assumes artificial contraceptives, does not balk at abortion, and repudiates Christian ideas of marriage and parenthood as outmoded."[54]

She criticized feminist tendencies to value paid work over nonpaid work and to ignore the difficult question of child care. Callahan also argued that feminists too often "pictured men as oppressive brutes" and ignored husbands in their new visions of the family.[55] Another writer believed that the larger movement limited women's choices by valuing work over family: "Let's not fall into a sterile view of human possibilities. I don't see the ability to have children as a handicap or a burden. What a dreary attitude we find in some of the women's liberation material—a postpartum depression in prose and poetry!"[56]

A young Catholic feminist graduate student at Columbia wrote an enthusiastic article in praise of women's liberation, opening her piece with a remarkable pairing of quotations on women's liberation from Pope John XXIII's encyclical *Pacem in Terris* and the New York Radical Feminists' Manifesto. "To me, liberation means a loosening-up of attitudes, a determination to be open-minded, a refusal to indulge in labels and categories," she wrote. But she found herself rejecting a radical feminist view of sexuality: "At a Fem Lib teach-in I attended one speaker categorized sexual intercourse (in all instances, not only in the case of rape) as an act of male aggression and as the prototype of all later male domination. . . . I find myself disagreeing strongly with this characterization. . . . For it seems to me that intercourse is a sign (a sacramental sign in Catholic theology) of the mutuality that should obtain in a man-woman relationship."[57] When Catholic feminists chose to retain a Catholic worldview, for some, this also meant retaining a Catholic moral perspective on sexuality, reproduction, and the family. But this Catholic worldview did not preclude feminist consciousness; on the contrary, between 1963 and 1970 Catholic feminists became increasingly willing to identify themselves as feminists.

When feminists spoke of how Catholicism and the quest for equality could be integrated, they steeped their prose in the language and teachings of the Catholic faith. They revealed deep connections to the church and often a profound love of their religion. "It is because I so truly believe in the joy and beauty of the doctrine of Christ—both for myself and others," a *Sex: Female, Religion: Catholic* respondent remarked, "that I wince at the minor flaws that seem to betray the very things we all wish to serve."[58]

If Catholic feminists were to pursue feminism from within their religious tradition, they needed to reclaim Catholicism as a liberating tradition, seeking redeemable Catholic beliefs and symbols that could be meaningful for themselves. Accordingly, these writers searched scripture and history for female models not limited to roles of passive suffering. While these early feminist writers rejected Mary as a role model, they chose other powerful but long-ignored or misinterpreted female figures and referred to them often. From scripture, they praised Elizabeth, Pilate's wife, Mary Magdalene, and the women who stayed with Christ at the Crucifixion.[59] They found inspiration also from Ruth, Esther, Deborah, and Judith from the Hebrew Bible as well as women of the early church, whom they characterized as active, strong women of faith who were present at Pentecost and served as ordained deaconesses. These writers called on female saints for support and empowerment, suggesting a continuing Catholic worldview, but in place of Mary they emphasized the new trinity of Catholic feminist saints: Catherine of Siena, Theresa of Avila, and Joan of Arc. All of these figures served the church through "unfeminine behavior," according to

Sidney Callahan. She especially praised St. Joan, "a martyr to masculine arrogance," and encouraged women to invoke Joan as "both portent and patroness of this new age."[60]

Early feminist writers used Catholic women's history both to denounce what was harmful and to reclaim the past for women's benefit. As Ruether phrased it, "breaking down the bondage to the past can give you a very authentic carrying on of your own real past. You get the past back."[61] But feminists also refused to be limited by the past, particularly in light of the Catholic tendency to make all new actions contingent on past actions. As Rosemary Lauer argued, "the fact that 'we have always done things this way' can be regarded only by the uncritical as sufficient reason for our continuing to do things this way."[62] Mary Daly concurred, asserting there was no evidence that "the social facts of the past should be prolonged and erected into an immutable destiny."[63]

Many of these writers challenged the church's supposed "immutable destiny" by reinterpreting scripture from a feminist perspective. Ultimately they took from these reinterpretations the belief that Christianity, as grounded in the Gospels, was not fundamentally sexist, although traditional theology was. Catholic feminist theology, in its infancy in the sixties, reflected writers' inclinations to integrate Catholicism and feminism. Writers accomplished this by creating new understandings of scripture that stressed messages of liberation. A full exploration of feminist theology is outside the scope of this project, but a brief discussion of scriptural exegesis will illustrate how early Catholic feminists, theologians and nontheologians alike, utilized it as a tool for defining their new vision.

Katherine Burton regularly used her column in *Sign* to propagate one of her favorite ideas: Christ liked women. Sidney Callahan agreed, arguing that "Christ treated women with a revolutionary equality—and thereby constantly shocked the masculine prejudices of His disciples. . . . He taught women, healed women, forgave them, and cherished them as friends." She concluded that "Christianity is a revolutionary religion; its view of woman is a part of that revolution."[64] Feminists explained their rationale for this idea by citing Jesus's interaction with the Samaritan woman at the well and Christ's close friendships with Mary Magdalene and Mary and Martha. They noted that Christ was first revealed to Elizabeth before his birth and to Mary Magdalene after his resurrection. It did not escape feminists' notice that only Christ's female followers had the courage to accompany him to his crucifixion and that a woman was first charged with spreading the good news of the resurrection. Through this interpretation, feminists claimed their liberating, nonsexist vision provided the authentic understanding of Christianity and therefore was not incompatible with feminism.

But as Mary Daly noted, "although the seeds of emancipation were present in the Christian message, their full implications were not evident to the first century authors." As one of the few Catholic feminist writers with an advanced degree in theology, Daly offered the most cogent and thorough exegesis of scripture, particularly on the subject of Paul. The Pauline epistles, she claimed, should not be read outside their cultural context. A historical reading of biblical texts was not new, of course, but rarely had it been applied by a Catholic to the powerful passages in the Pauline epistles so long used to justify women's inferiority, texts all too familiar to Catholic women forced to hear them "cited approvingly *ad nauseum.*" Arguing that Paul was preoccupied with order and image in the new sect, Daly asserted that Paul's goal was avoiding a scandal if women took too prominent a role. Not limiting herself to discussions of culture, she also argued that Paul's and the other Pauline authors' understandings of women resulted from a fundamental misinterpretation of the creation stories, themselves a favorite subject of reinterpretation by feminists.[65]

Daly condemned clergy who continued to use the epistles to oppress women, particularly since the message was often contradictory and could be interpreted as transcending gender distinctions. Other writers highlighted these liberating messages in Paul, the most often cited being Galatians 3:28: "There is no longer Jew or Greek, there is no longer slave or free, there is no longer male and female; for all of you are one in Christ Jesus." In reference to this passage, one writer claimed that "while some women are bitter about St. Paul's influence on their fate, it is this writer's opinion that he was one of our greatest champions." She aimed to convince women to emphasize his "theological" statements as opposed to his "sociologically oriented" statements.[66] Feminists clearly sought redeeming, liberating messages in scripture that would allow them to remain in the Catholic tradition.

Most Catholic feminists sought the rights of self-determination and equal opportunity, standard feminist goals allowing women to make free choices and determine their own destinies. Yet in harmonizing faith and feminism, Catholic feminists began to recognize spirituality as central to women's understanding of themselves, articulating women's need to follow spiritual callings as well as the desire for a career. Individual consciousness of the need for social justice for women was often accompanied by a spiritual call to priestly ministry, to liturgical ministry, to prayer, to personal and spiritual transformation. The new vision needed to encompass both the right to pursue a vocation and the obligation to Christian service. Catholic feminists did not fully develop this message until the seventies, but it began in the sixties.

Catholic feminism challenged the male stranglehold on priestly vocations in the church, attempting to open Catholicism to explorations of vocation, ministry, and spirituality that included women. Catholic feminists argued for opening all ministries of the church to women, most especially the priesthood. The issue was an umbrella under which writers discussed not only misogyny, clerical culture, and sexist theology, but also the changing nature of ministry and women's God-given right to vocation. Thus the call for holy orders for women dates to the earliest Catholic feminist writings and was a major topic of discussion on which nearly all writers agreed.

Writers also sought to open liturgical ministries, such as lector, musician, commentator, altar server, and sacristan.[67] This emphasis on women's participation in liturgical ministries not only reflects Catholic feminists' struggle against male domination in Catholic leadership and ritual, but also their strong connections to the Mass as the personal and communal center of Catholic spirituality; at this point they did not call on others to reject the Mass or seek alternatives. They argued that the Mass could be a model for justice just as they believed the scriptures could be messages of liberation for women. Catholic feminist writers also advocated for women religious struggling for the self-determination of their orders. While they criticized archaic and limiting aspects of religious life, these writers spoke positively of women's vocations, whatever form they took.[68]

With vocation came obligations and responsibilities, to God, family, community, and the world. This was one of the central messages in *The Illusion of Eve*. To Sidney Callahan, the richness of Christian life entailed sacrifice on the part of both men and women. She extolled sacrifice as a necessary, inevitable, and sacred Christian virtue, challenging secular feminists who believed that women could be "fulfilled" without it:

> The important point missed by so many feminists is that a woman with a mature self-identity can freely choose to sacrifice certain self-fulfillments for the sake of husband and a large family. Admittedly, Christians have overemphasized the tradition of womanly sacrifice . . . but at least they have recognized and conserved a whole spiritual dimension of life totally

absent from current discussions of fulfillment. 'Losing one's life in order to find it' makes no sense to the secular world . . . all such sacrifice has become suspect. . . . However, when all vocations and free choices are encouraged except the traditional feminine role, a new tyranny and a new stereotype have simply replaced the old one.[69]

Callahan spoke specifically of the vocation of wife and mother but applied this idea to any vocation, for men or women.

On the surface, she sounded surprisingly like an eternal woman advocate, advocating sacrifice. But to Callahan, writing from a Catholic worldview, liberation had no meaning without obligation. Her biggest criticism of secular feminism was its unwillingness to speak of women's responsibilities to family and to the world; every woman (like every man) had responsibilities to a calling greater than her own freedom. Her emphasis on sacrifice did not catch on in the movement, but others frequently stressed women's responsibilities to seek social justice, renew the church, care for the poor, support ecumenism, and to liberate other women. As Catholics, their vision of feminism included the right to choose one's call but also the responsibility to serve God's people.

In their efforts to harmonize faith and feminism, Catholic feminists in the sixties were largely optimistic, writing from a position of loyal opposition. Most were also involved in the renewal process, and while they expressed anger at the church and frustration with its slowness, few believed that the church was a lost cause. Rather, feminists assumed a general faith in the idea that a renewed church was their most powerful instrument in the struggle for justice. "I have always been excited about being a part of the Church," one writer claimed, "even when I was *mad, depressed, disgusted, or disillusioned* . . . for I am convinced that *even I* can do something about what is happening."[70] One key question remained unspoken, however: would the church embrace its own messages of liberation, and until that day, could feminists continue to worship in and affiliate themselves with a sexist church? Because this question was not openly considered, the sixties were perhaps the most unambivalent phase in Catholic feminism's history.[71]

Such confidence in the church's ability to serve justice for women on its own did not last. Indeed, it could not last. If Catholic feminists were to mount an effective collective challenge to the church and use their new understanding of Catholic women's identity to embrace liberation, they needed to approach the church with a greater degree of suspicion. Significantly, the most influential and enduring sixties' monograph was not the optimistic, family-oriented *The Illusion of Eve*, but Mary Daly's *The Church and the Second Sex*, a far more complex and ambivalent work.

Daly was one of the few authors to address directly the question of Catholic feminist viability. Like the majority of Catholic feminists at the time, she affirmed a commitment to a renewed church, believing that women's spirituality and the power of Christian community could confront and transcend sexism. This conclusion did not negate her thorough, nearly damning critique of the church, however. Daly gave the movement its most comprehensive overview of Catholic sexism and a new vision of Catholic feminism that pointed to the future in ways that the more conservative *The Illusion of Eve* could not. The book endured precisely because Daly combined a commitment to a renewed church with an openness to leaving it, acknowledging for the first time the love/hate relationship to the church buried at the heart of Catholic feminism.

The Church and the Second Sex focused less on the practical concerns of married women and more on the intricacies of historical analysis and theology. Daly briefly mentioned *The Illusion of Eve*, praising Callahan for providing a balanced solution to the problems of Catholic married women "that recognizes the values of creative outside work as well as the values of domestic life."[72] While both books were hopeful, Daly used much harsher arguments and language to criticize the church. She warned that if renewal failed, there would be no answer to "the mounting suspicion in the minds of many that Christianity—particularly as it is embodied in the Catholic Church—is the inevitable enemy of human progress."[73]

Daly argued that women suffered a "mutilated existence" at the hands of the church.[74] What women needed most was not more talk of sacrifice, but to extinguish the Eternal Woman through empowerment and support of women by women: "It is precisely this—the emergence of a significant number of creative women who will *raise up their own image*—that can significantly weaken the hold of the paralyzing stereotypes upon human consciousness."[75] More than any other writer, Daly focused on the process of and the potential for the liberation of women, foreshadowing her radical/cultural feminist perspective in the seventies.

But in 1968, Daly rooted herself firmly in a Catholic Christian outlook; she believed that faith could support a woman's process of liberation. The centerpiece of her book was an evaluation of Simone de Beauvoir's views of the church in *The Second Sex*. Daly agreed with Beauvoir's condemnation of the church but only to a point. She believed that feminists erred when they assumed they should pursue their goals in secular society because the church was only a hindrance to women. Her main criticism of Beauvoir was that the French feminist acknowledged the possibility of women finding empowerment through transcendent experiences of God but cited only the extraordinary women Theresa of Avila and Catherine of Siena as examples. "We could well argue" Daly asserted, "that there have been others in all ages who have transcended 'the earthly hierarchies,' and, although they have been comparatively few, they have served as beacons, signaling to others the fact of undreamed of possibilities in themselves."[76]

This led Daly to her ultimate message, that the church, because of the gospel mandate for justice and the power of transcendent spirituality, had within it the capacity to lead its members to transform society. Daly spoke for many feminists when, on the final page of her book, she expressed her feminism as a call from God and her belief that the church could act as a prophetic witness in the world to end sexism: "Rather than a philosophy of despair, we choose a theology of hope, not because the former is 'false,' but because we think it represents an incomplete and partial vision. . . . God is present, yet always hidden, and the summons from that Presence gives us a dimension to our activity, by which we are propelled forward."[77]

Daly's assertion echoed in the words of numerous Catholic feminists who saw in both their faith and their church the power to fight sexism. "The very essence of the Church calls her to form a community in which the Christian equality and partnership of all brothers and sisters becomes manifest," wrote René van Eyden.[78] Rosemary Radford Ruether argued that her own vision of a nonsexist, nonhierarchical society was, in fact, the church itself: "The image which I would project for this new communal society of the future is basically the image of the church; not the historical church as it has been, but the reality to which it is directed; that is to say the Kingdom of God, the new society, the community of the New Creation. In this community of the New Creation there will be neither Jew nor Greek, male nor female."[79]

The earliest Catholic feminist writers believed the church contained within it the seeds of liberation, preparing the way for women to pursue feminist activism as women of faith. In doing so, they laid the groundwork for a movement. They reevaluated the old model of Catholic womanhood and concluded that any new vision of women must take as its starting point negation of the Eternal Woman. Feminists located the source of their oppression in the church itself, confronting centuries-old bonds of sexism. They came to believe that reinterpreted Catholic principles, traditions, and ministries could teach, inspire, and sustain, and by linking feminism and renewal into one integrated cause, they remained distinct within the larger women's liberation movement.

Yet *The Church and the Second Sex* signaled the beginning of a new era. Daly's book appeared in the same year as *Humanae Vitae*—Pope Paul VI's encyclical prohibiting birth control—and, most likely, feminists with new doubts about the church's capacity for renewal on that score responded positively to Daly's ambivalence about Catholicism. Daly herself was not ambivalent about the church for long. Shortly after the publication of her first book, Daly began her journey toward radical feminism and away from Christianity. The majority of Catholic feminists did not follow her, choosing instead to apply their Catholic feminist worldview to a new phase of organizational activism.

3

no cakes in hands
unless ideas in heads

You have raped us of our rights
and preached that it was in the name of God.
These are the ashes of your canons,
of your instruction sixty-six.
The color of our caste is pink,
but the color of our mood is ash.
—Elizabeth Farians, "Pink and Ash"

In 1970, the National Conference of Catholic Bishops (NCCB) released a revised version of the Roman Missal, a book that includes prayers and guidelines for Catholic worship. This missal, which included new instructions for liturgical ministers, contained the now infamous "paragraph 66," sanctioning female lectors for the first time but only if they proclaimed the readings standing outside the sanctuary gates. Deeply offended, a Catholic feminist named Elizabeth Farians decided to hold a "liturgical ceremony" at which Catholic feminists burned a copy of the offending section of the missal. They then gathered the ashes, placed them in a package with the above poem titled "Pink and Ash," tied it with a pink ribbon, signed it "Woman," and mailed it to the head of the NCCB.[1]

Elizabeth Farians had had enough. Like several of the early Catholic feminist writers, she was a theologian by training and wrote extensively about women in the church and the ways that religious institutions perpetuated sexism. But in the midsixties she became increasingly involved in founding organizations designed to forward the cause at the grassroots level through lobbying and public protest. By the time of the "Pink and Ash" protest in 1970, Farians had organized every one of the handful of public protests publicized by Catholic feminists to date. Like the demonstration described above they were edgy, confrontational, creative, and liturgical in nature. The protests, as well as the new grassroots organizations, introduced Catholic feminism in a new form across the country and brought feminist protest to the church doors and chanceries for the first time.

By the final years of the sixties, the American Catholic feminist movement was set to explode into action. From the very beginning of Catholic feminist organizational activism, the movement's ideological (if not racial and ethnic) diversity was clear. In this and the following chapter I will try to differentiate among the large numbers of women throwing themselves head first into feminist activism in the first half of the seventies. They range from the midcentury feminists of the Saint Joan's International Alliance-United States Section (SJIA-US), with its focus on bringing women into leadership in existing Catholic institutions (and its faithfulness to parliamentary procedure), to the "new nuns," with their emphasis on feminism as a ministry of social justice, to the Catholic radical feminists known by their insistence that sexism be rooted out of the very foundations of Catholicism before women would consider placing their hope and energy in the church again.

It should be noted that while all of these strands were distinct, they were not isolated from one another, and their interconnections support the conclusion that a true movement was forming. Elizabeth Farians was on the mailing list for the Deaconess Movement (DM); Frances McGillicuddy, founder of the SJIA-US, was friends with Mary Lynch, Margaret Ellen Traxler (founders of the Deaconess Movement and the National Coalition of American Nuns, respectively), and Mary Daly. The National Coalition of American Nuns (NCAN) supported Daly in her battles at Boston College, and Daly supported the founding of NCAN. Daly spoke before the Leadership Conference of Women Religious (LCWR); Lynch spoke before the National Assembly of Women Religious (NAWR). Arlene Swidler, an early lay activist, was a member of the National Organization for Women (NOW), SJIA-US, and the DM, gave talks for the LCWR, and participated in theological seminars organized by Farians and Daly. In 1970, Farians attempted to pull these emerging connections together under an umbrella group, the Joint Committee of Organizations concerned with the Status of Women in the Church (the Joint Committee), with the goal of presenting a united front to the Catholic hierarchy. Yet each strand was unique and made a vital contribution to the development of Catholic feminist activism.

These two chapters explore this diversity by investigating the primary ideological separation to occur in the first half of the seventies. The Catholic radical feminists determined relatively quickly that they could not sustain a Catholic feminist identity if it required commitment to an institutional church that was irredeemably sexist. These women helped launch the organizational movement, provided much of its creativity and energy, and then departed the movement by 1972. The second, much larger, group includes those women who challenged church sexism in a variety of ways yet still believed they could both transform the institutional church and continued to gain spiritual strength within it. In fact, these women claimed that their feminism emerged from their identities as Catholics. The following chapter will explore this outlook by looking in depth at three organizations for feminist "new nuns" as well as the first organization for Catholic women aspiring to ordination: the Deaconess Movement.

THE BURGEONING MOVEMENT

The enthusiasm of American Catholic feminists mirrored the energy found within the larger feminist movement in the late sixties and early seventies. The organizational movement officially began in the United States in 1965 with the founding of the SJIA-US, the American affiliate of the international Catholic feminist organization. Founded by the irrepressible Frances McGillicuddy, SJIA-US served as many women's first experience of Catholic feminist activism. It was small but active in the early seventies, if eclipsed by newer organizations more attuned to developments in feminist theology and the women's liberation movement.[2]

The next major organization to emerge was the NOW Ecumenical Task Force on Women and Religion, which until 1972 was run primarily by Catholic feminists and focused predominantly on Catholic women's concerns. The task force will be discussed in greater depth below. By the turn of the decade the movement had burgeoned with the emergence of the DM, the NCAN, the Women's Rights Committee of the National Association of Laymen, and the Joint Committee of Organizations concerned with the Status of Women in the Church. In addition, in the first half of the seventies several prominent organizations for Catholic women already in existence included feminist members or adopted feminist agendas. These include the NAWR, the LCWR, the National Black Sisters Conference (NBSC), Las Hermanas, and the Grail.[3]

The NBSC and Las Hermanas were both founded (in 1968 and 1971, respectively) as a part of the civil rights movement of the sixties; they sought to increase solidarity among women of color in religious orders and to promote advocacy for underserved and exploited black and Latino populations. By the early seventies, each group included among its members women who could be classified as feminist "new nuns." NBSC was careful to say that racism, not sexism, was its priority and did not pursue a feminist agenda in this period, although its feminist members would, in the latter half of the decade, consistently challenge racism within the Catholic feminist movement. Las Hermanas, an organization for women religious active in the Chicano movement, showed the beginnings of feminist consciousness in its earliest years, although it did not adopt a feminist agenda until 1976.[4] These two organizations will appear later in this narrative.

Although I will not be discussing the Grail in depth, its transition to a feminist outlook and its efforts to facilitate feminist theological education and dialogue were significant factors in the growth of American Catholic feminism. In her memoir *Women Breaking Boundaries: A Grail Journey, 1940–1995*, longtime Grail leader Janet Kalven details her own adoption of feminist consciousness in 1970 (a process she refers to as an "intellectual odyssey") and the organization's gradual transition from a "prefeminist" to a self-identified feminist outlook by 1974. The Grail began consciousness-raising projects for its membership when the group's leadership officially sanctioned a feminist agenda in 1974; however, the Grail's influential outreach to women theologians and seminarians began two years earlier.[5]

In 1972, the Grail, together with the ecumenical group Church Women United, sponsored a weeklong workshop called "Women Exploring Theology." The workshop, also referred to as "Women Doing Theology," invited women theologians and seminarians to explore theology rooted in women's experience. Several prominent Catholic feminist theologians attended, including Rosemary Radford Ruether, Elizabeth Farians, and Elisabeth Schüssler Fiorenza. Schüssler Fiorenza, who had recently immigrated to the United States from Germany, found the experience to be life-changing. "As a newcomer to the United States, I had the privilege to participate in [the workshop]." She remembered. "I had a classical theological training behind me. 'Women Doing Theology' . . . was a decisive experience for me because here I learned to understand myself not as someone who is repeating, transmitting, teaching the theology of the great theological fathers, but as someone who is a theologian, who is *doing* theology."[6] The workshop was so successful it was expanded into Seminary Quarter at Grailville, a six-week summer program that ran from 1974 to 1978 and that helped hundreds of feminist seminarians make connections with one another, explore feminist consciousness, and "do theology." As one feminist seminarian expressed it after completing the course, "I never looked on myself as an authority before, or realized that my questions are valuable and no less real questions because they come from me."[7]

The Grail was attempting to address a new situation in the United States: between 1970 and 1973 women's enrollment in seminaries tripled.[8] Moreover, the rate of women emerging with advanced degrees in theology also had exploded. These theologians and seminarians represent another branch of activity: religious feminists in the academy. Catholic feminists were well represented in the ecumenical groups that characterized feminist activism in this area. Elisabeth Schüssler Fiorenza was especially influential here, helping to found the Women's Caucus and the Women and Religion Group of the American Academy of Religion in 1971.[9] In these groups and others like them, Catholic feminists exchanged ideas and strategies with the most prominent non-Catholic scholars of feminist theology in the country, thus broadening their perspectives and helping to develop foundational concepts in feminist theology and religious feminist activism. Although I will not be studying the academic wing of the Catholic feminist movement in depth, prominent women from this strand of the movement will emerge throughout this narrative; academic theologians rarely confined their feminism to the academy alone, preferring to apply their theology to activism in the larger community and, as we shall see, to help shape the theoretical underpinnings of Catholic feminist activism.

Finally, it should be noted that many Catholic women found their way to feminism outside any of these organizations. For instance, a Catholic feminist I interviewed attributed her feminist consciousness to her experiences in Marriage Encounter, a Catholic retreat program for couples, in the early seventies. While the organizations discussed in this and the following chapters were certainly not the only means of participating in Catholic feminism, they best illustrate major ideological trends emerging in the organizational wing of the movement before 1975.[10]

When I teach the history of feminism to college students who possess only such knowledge as they can glean from the media, the first thing that usually strikes them is feminists' diversity. For some reason, perhaps because they realize feminists are not all humorless man-hating, bra-burning harpies, this diversity makes even reluctant students more willing to explore the subject. Of course, if they delve into feminist studies in any depth they are soon overwhelmed by the myriad feminisms in the United States and beyond as well as the mighty nomenclature developed by feminist scholars to tell them apart. Fortunately feminists, even within the group "Catholic," are quite diverse; unfortunately, this means we must try to fit them into a classification system. While I generally resist shoving my subjects into their little boxes, we must do a bit of that to understand developments within the Catholic feminist movement in the seventies. In particular, we can not proceed until we deal with that most incendiary word: "radical."

Generally, historians of feminism reserve the term "radical feminism" for a specific group of women active at a particular time, that is, those women who developed, espoused, and practiced radical feminist theory in the years 1968–75. These activists, often part of small feminist cell groups, such as New York Radical Women and the Women's International Terrorist Conspiracy from Hell (commonly known as WITCH), sought to abolish or radically transform social mores and systems, not reform them from within. They gave the movement its most creative forms of protest, its emphasis on shared leadership, the consciousness-raising group, the understanding that "the personal is political," and the foundations of second-wave feminist theory.

While respecting the definition of radical feminism, it is helpful to remember that "radical" is a relative term. What might be considered timidly conventional feminist activism from the perspective of radical feminists in New York City or Berkeley might be a truly radical proposition if it took place, say, in rural Ohio. Such is the case in Catholic feminism. Among women religious, for example, the feminist sisters of NCAN discussed in the following chapter could only be viewed as radical. However, they must be officially classified as "liberal," not radical, feminists because they advocated a reformist position.

That being said, there were genuine radical feminists who helped found the Catholic feminist movement in the late sixties and early seventies. The radical Catholic feminists were a loose network of women who were heavily educated in theology, predominantly lay, ecumenical, and had strong connections to both NOW and radical feminism. Therefore we see a mixing of liberal and radical feminism in their activism, a more common phenomenon than historians usually recognize. They valued women's experience and solidarity above all and favored creative public protests and unconventional behavior to demonstrate the need for liberation and the means of achieving it. Their theological writings, organizing efforts, and dramatic protests helped raise the consciousness of countless Catholic women.

But it was their willingness to question the most fundamental aspects of Catholic teaching that sets them apart. The radicals were far less enthusiastic about aligning themselves with the church; theirs was the most radical critique of Catholicism, extending beyond the institution to the faith itself. They were the first to confront the difficulties of combining feminism and Catholicism and to address the ambivalence of being a Catholic feminist. Most left Catholicism behind, convinced this integration was impossible.

As a result, radical feminism nearly disappeared from the Catholic feminist movement for most of the seventies. If we plotted a graph of the Catholic feminist movement's radicalism from 1963 to 1980, it would show two peaks of radicalized activity: the first in 1969–71 and the second a decade later, around 1978, with a valley of about seven years between. Only in the early and late seventies did a significant group of Catholic feminist organizational activists reject institutional reform. When the radical Catholic feminists left the movement and Catholicism, they left it to those who strongly identified with Catholicism and favored a position of loyal opposition.

While their time in the movement was relatively brief, the radical Catholic feminists' contribution was considerable, and we do them a disservice by assuming that their greatest impact was their departure. Their experiences demonstrate early Catholic feminism's passion, creativity, and sense of humor. Through them we can see the limitations of reform and their struggle with ambivalence. The Catholic radical feminists were a loose network of women interested in feminist theology and radical feminism (both in their infancy at the time) rather than a specific organization. The best way to get at their experiences is to explore the lives and work of two theologians and friends, Mary Daly and Elizabeth Farians, the feminists who provided the impetus for this network.

By the end of the sixties, philosopher and theologian Mary Daly was by far the most prominent Catholic feminist in America. As demonstrated in chapter 2, Daly's scholarship helped establish the basic building blocks of Catholic feminism. Her first book, *The Church and the Second Sex* (1968), with its blunt denunciations of Catholic misogyny, its imaginative and rigorous scholarship, and expressed intention of reforming the church from within, was the cornerstone of every Catholic feminist reading list. "I just finished Mary Daly's book, *The Church and the Second Sex*," one budding Catholic feminist wrote to another in 1970, "and now I *know* we have been shortchanged for 2000 years."[11] The student protests demanding her reinstatement to Boston College and the subsequent support from many Catholic activists and pundits further cemented her reputation, as did the almost ceaseless round of lectures and papers she presented around the country. But even as her reputation flourished due to *The Church and the Second Sex*, Daly quickly distanced herself from Catholicism and Christianity. Her autobiography *Outercourse: The Be-Dazzling Voyage* (1992) is particularly revealing on this point.

Daly was invited to write *The Church and the Second Sex* as a result of her highly influential *Commonweal* articles on women and the church in the midsixties. The book was further informed by Daly's experiences as an uninvited observer at the Second Vatican Council's final session in 1965 (as noted earlier, she borrowed a press pass to gain access). But her interest in church reform in the midsixties was short-lived and ended not long after the publication of *The Church and the Second Sex*, as did her belief that Catholicism and feminism could be integrated and, indeed, her identification with Christianity. In fact, her relationship to Catholicism had been tenuous as far back as her student days in Switzerland and probably earlier. Daly viewed her pursuit of theology, like her long-elusive desire for a doctorate in philosophy, as an intellectual challenge. As she recalled, "The more I studied and the more I traveled, ripping away cultural limitations and mindbindings, the less frequently I went to church. I was not afflicted with piety or missionary zeal. I had no desire to be a priest or to minister to anyone. My Lust was for the Life of the Mind. The simple fact is that the more I studied and explored, the more I was in touch with mySelf, and going to church became odious."[12]

At being asked in 1966 to teach Christology at Boston College, her first response was distaste: "The fact was that for years I had found the christian fixation on the 'divinity of Christ' and on the figure of Jesus disturbing and profoundly repulsive."[13] In 1969, after the publication of *The Church and the Second Sex*, Daly continued to write about renewal, but in her own estimation this writing "lacked conviction" and marked "the beginning of the end of my concern over the fate of catholicism."[14] But she did not yet know in what direction she was headed.

A full identification with the feminist movement provided the inspiration for which Daly was searching. For a brief time in the late sixties Daly was involved in SJIA-US and NOW and particularly in the NOW Task Force, but she soon discovered radical feminism, thereby reshaping her life and work. By the early seventies, Daly found support among other radical feminists, and with the help of Daly's theology, they decided that the core tenets of Christianity were misogynist and that further identification with it was therefore untenable.

Daly had a penchant for witty and dramatic acts of public protest, a gift that would unfortunately disappear from the movement for a time after she and the other radical feminists left it. In 1971, she was invited to be the first woman to preach at Harvard's Memorial Church. She used the occasion to call the women's movement "an exodus community" and proclaimed that "we cannot really belong to institutional religion as it exists." At the end of the sermon she called on everyone to stand up and exit the church to symbolize their intention to abandon institutional religion.[15] Daly described the "Harvard Memorial Exodus" as a stampede and a "Metaphoric event [that] *carried* those who participated with deep conviction into Metamorphic Moments/Movements, changing our lives, hurling us beyond the imprisoning cells of patriarchal religion."[16]

After the Exodus came Daly's groundbreaking "post-christian" work *Beyond God the Father: Toward a Philosophy of Women's Liberation* (1973) and the "New Feminist Post-Christian Introduction" to the second edition of *The Church and the Second Sex* (1975). The latter was a revealing and hilarious analysis of her first book, in which Daly referred to the author of the earlier work in the third person, alternately praising her foresight and pitying her enslavement to the church. At the end of the introduction she included a parody of sound bites she imagined would pour forth from her critics when the new work was published: " 'Daly has now gone off the deep end'— Liberal Catholic"; " 'I fear that she will not be taken seriously by the male theological establishment'—Catholic feminist"; and " 'She misunderstands both Daly and St. Paul'—Radical Catholic." She ended with the gleeful, " 'Stunning!'—Myself."[17]

By this point, Mary Daly had no identification with Catholic feminism. She made this clear in the "Introduction" when she peered curiously at the book from the distance of "approximately seven woman-light years" and declared that the "species" Catholic feminist "is by now almost extinct."[18] This claim further illustrated Daly's distance from the movement. The year 1975 was crucial for Catholic feminism and a time of intensive growth. She rejected the idea that women and men could work together for reform, that church renewal was desirable, or that women could be inspired in any meaningful way by Christianity.

After 1969, Daly was not representative of the majority of American Catholic feminists. This fact makes historians' persistent use of Daly as the sole example of Catholic feminism untenable. However, Daly remained a respected figure among Catholic feminists throughout the seventies. Many Catholic feminists understood her choice, even if they did not agree with her or acknowledge such a choice as inevitable. *The Church and the Second Sex* continued to be a much-used resource, and *Beyond God the Father* was widely read and used even in liturgical settings. But Daly's exodus did not cause most Catholic feminists to leave the church. On the contrary, Catholic feminist organizations, networks, and activism grew steadily at this time and were marked by strong identification with Catholicism.

Finally, *Outercourse* reveals a basic difference between Daly and other Catholic feminists. Never in the book did Daly admit to love, affection, or loyalty to Catholicism at any point in her life. She never felt a call to religious life or ministry; she expressed no connection to Catholic liturgy or social teaching. Even her chosen field of theology she described purely as an intellectual, not a spiritual, exercise. In this she was atypical. Significant numbers of Catholic feminists eventually reached the conclusion that, like Daly, they could not remain Catholic and retain their integrity. But most accounts of this decision described gut-wrenching pain and a deep sense of loss. Daly described only jubilation.

ELIZABETH FARIANS

Mary Daly may have been the most prominent American Catholic feminist in the late sixties, but "she wasn't an activist as such."[19] In the arena of organizational activism her friend and fellow theologian Elizabeth Farians was far more influential. As the first chair of the NOW Task Force, Farians initiated the first national effort to organize feminist women of faith ecumenically as well as the first uses of liturgy for feminist protest. She was the driving force behind organizational religious feminist activism as early as

1966. Both Farians and Daly left the institutional church at the same time—indeed, on the same day—but while Daly left Catholicism with exuberance, Elizabeth Farians was far more ambivalent.

Elizabeth "Betty" Farians was born in 1923 in Cincinnati to a loving working-class family struggling with poverty. Growing up, Farians excelled academically and athletically; she saw no need to place limitations on herself or her future plans because she was a woman. Her athletic ability was so extraordinary that in the forties she was offered a contract to play in the women's professional baseball league, but she declined in order to pursue a bachelor's and then a master's degree in physical education at the University of Cincinnati.

She taught physical education until the midsixties, but at that point she decided she had learned all she could and needed to move on. Farians had known from a young age that she wanted to devote her life to some larger purpose. "I wanted to be dedicated," she remembered. "I wanted . . . this kind of integrity that you live your life for. But I didn't want to become a nun because they were so restricted."[20] She also understood that God was inextricably linked with justice; the Catholic Worker movement and Catholic social teachings were early influences.

So she chose to seek a doctorate in theology, a field just opening to women, at St. Mary's College in Indiana. At the time, St. Mary's College, headed by the pioneering woman religious Madeleva Wolff, was the only American theology program to admit women for doctoral study. Farians often felt isolated there, since most students in the program were women religious, but she found a friend in the irrepressible Mary Daly. Unlike the women religious, who were not personally responsible for their fees, Farians had to support herself. To ease the financial burden, Wolff arranged to hire Farians as her personal driver. Farians relished her theological training and the extensive spiritual direction that accompanied it.

It did not take long for Elizabeth Farians to identify herself as a Catholic feminist, and she was one of the first to move beyond the discursive approach to begin protesting church sexism in public. In 1966, she became the first woman to join the Catholic Theological Society (CTS). When she arrived at her first CTS meeting and attempted to go into the opening dinner, CTS officers were baffled and threatened to call the police if she did not leave. She refused.[21] In the end, fellow theologian Charles Curran heard the commotion and summoned a large group of friends to surround her and escort her into the dining room.[22]

Incidents like this convinced Farians that religious feminists needed to organize so that they might change the culture of the church and educate women as to the roots of sexism in religious tradition. She joined SJIA-US, just founded in 1965, but believed they were looking for surface solutions and that they "wouldn't handle the religious questions."[23] She remained active in SJIA, but in 1966, on her own, Farians formed the Ecumenical Task Force on Women and Religion. Hearing of the recent founding of the National Organization for Women, Farians looked up Betty Friedan in the phone book and was soon talking theology over drinks with the NOW founder.

Friedan convinced Farians to make the ecumenical task force a division of NOW. The NOW board approved the move in 1967 but with some reluctance. As Farians remembered it, many members of the board "didn't think religion was important. They already had six task forces, and they thought that was enough. They were very secularized people. Some of them were ex-Catholics; they were very turned off by religion." Yet Farians got her task force, joined the board, and for the next five years worked to confront church sexism and to keep faith alive in the minds of feminists.[24]

Meanwhile, Farians focused on her career as a theologian. She did not publish extensively, but she held a series of jobs at small Catholic colleges around the country. In the late sixties she accepted a visiting position at Loyola University of Chicago, hoping it would provide some measure of financial stability. Unfortunately, Farians was fired, she believes, for being openly feminist and unabashedly political. Unlike Mary Daly who was in a similar position at Boston College, she was not reinstated. As a result, Farians filed the first complaint of sex discrimination in higher education with the Department of Health, Education, and Welfare. Her case lasted through much of the seventies, resulting in a small settlement but not reinstatement. As her case dragged on it was difficult for Farians to find employment. Her feminism threatened perspective employers, and therefore her work as a leader in the feminist movement was constantly threatened by financial insecurity.[25]

Such worries did not dampen Farians's spirit, however. In her autobiography, Mary Daly described Farians as "a rebel who Lusted for justice and fought for it." She also recalled, with delight, Farians's "inappropriate" behavior and fine wit. In 1970, Farians, Daly, and other theologians, including Jan Raymond, Arlene Swidler, and Marie Augusta Neal, gathered for a conference in Massachusetts. "Not exactly a dull crowd," they were interrupted at dinner one day by a man saying grace for another group, in the course of which he loudly thanked "our heavenly father." Without missing a beat Farians yelled across the room "God is *not* our father!" According to Daly, "the ensuing silence was Stunning."[26]

Farians's connections to Daly would suggest that under her leadership the NOW Task Force had radical tendencies, but was it a radical or a liberal feminist group? During 1969, the task force often met in Mary Daly's apartment, and Daly described the meetings as "rather raucous events attended by a variety of characters who had as our common purpose the unmasking and undoing of patriarchal religion. We were virtually rolling on the floor with laughter a good deal of the time."[27] Daly was by this time a radical feminist, and Farians definitely had an affinity for radical feminism. Daly remembers the task force as a radical group, yet Farians's collected papers indicate otherwise.

From the founding of the task force through 1972, it was primarily a liberal feminist organization in agenda, rhetoric, and membership. Farians's larger goal in the first four years of her tenure as task force chair was not the "undoing" of women's faith traditions. Instead, she hoped to introduce the idea of religion to feminists (whom she believed to be largely secularist and hostile to religion) and the idea of feminism to women in religious institutions (whom she saw as largely unwilling to question their religion). In her view, "it became the job of the NOW Task Force on Women and Religion to point out that one of the root causes of the oppression of women is religion."[28] She pursued this goal through traditional liberal activist means, as evidenced by the list of activities she compiled for the national board in 1970: "The task force has operated in every way it could, advising, giving speeches, infiltrating, distributing literature, dispatching news releases, issuing protests, demonstrating, writing articles, planning, plotting."[29]

However, Farians mixed radical and liberal feminist statements and strategies. "Liberal" and "radical" are to some extent artificial constructs and were very much in flux at the time; Farians exhibits both sensibilities in this period. She ranged from a liberal feminist with radical tendencies in 1967 to a radical feminist with liberal tendencies by 1972. As you might imagine, the shift was subtle, with both liberal and radical feminism apparent in her activism for the entire period. This mixing explains her unique position among Catholics and feminists. She was a living bridge between Mary Daly (who was growing more radical by the day) and the much more conservative women of SJIA-US. She traveled freely in liberal Catholic, liberal feminist, and radical feminist circles, carving out potentially fertile ground for collaboration among them. Her ambivalence about staying in the church allowed for such flexibility, helping her find connections with activists from numerous causes and positions.

Farians's radical nature can be seen most easily in the creative and confrontational protests she designed, the earliest and some of the most inspired actions of the Catholic feminist movement. In 1969, the first protest, "the Easter Bonnet Rebellion" or alternatively "The National Unveiling," called on women to appear in church bareheaded. At that time, official practice still dictated that Catholic women cover their heads in church, although not all women treated the policy with the solemnity many Catholics thought it deserved. Catholic women who came of age at midcentury no doubt recall the hasty search for a tissue or even a handy parish bulletin to pin to their heads once they discovered they had left home without their regular head covering.[30] Still, tissue or not, the head covering was symbolic of women's submission, and Catholic feminists challenged it. The protest was centered at a church in Milwaukee, its pastor having recently castigated women for appearing bareheaded. He threatened to deny Communion to any woman without a hat. Fifteen local women appeared on Easter Sunday wearing the largest hats they could find, and they then laid them on the rail when they knelt for Communion. The pastor did not refuse them the Eucharist.

In an attempt to integrate religious feminism into the secular movement, Farians called on women to "strike" the church during the national women's strike on August 26, 1970. Protests included religious liturgies, some centered around intentions "beseeching God to change the church" or "liturgies of anguish." SJIA held a specially written Mass for the occasion. "Do your thing," Farians urged women. "Take over a church—Pray to God, She will help us! . . . No voice—no donations, no cakes in hands unless ideas in heads."[31] Of course, Farians's most widely publicized protest was 1970's "Pink and Ash," detailed at the beginning of the chapter.

These were the first protest actions of the NOW Task Force, and they were overwhelmingly focused on Catholicism. In fact, in its earliest years the task force tried to be ecumenical, but over half of its membership, and most of its leaders, were Catholic. Of seventeen task force press releases written between 1968 and 1971, ten addressed Catholic issues. Moreover, meeting minutes in this period indicate that the majority of participants were Catholic, as do comments made to the national board by Farians. The task force's most active members were the women most heavily involved in Catholic feminist organizations at this time: Bernice McNeela and Frances McGillicuddy of SJIA-US; Arlene Swidler of the Philadelphia Task Force on Women and Religion; as well as the radical Catholic feminists Mary Daly and Jan Raymond.

Elizabeth Farians tried to resign as task force chair in 1970. She struggled emotionally with the burden of being an activist when such activities seemed to be threatening her career as a theologian and educator. "The personal struggle has been very lonely and depressing," she admitted.[32] She was also increasingly frustrated with the Catholic community, liberal and conservative. "My activities and manner has shocked and offended many persons in the Catholic Church" she wrote. "It is not just the men who have ostracized me. Now there are many church women wheedling their way to prattle like 'experts' on women when only a short time ago one could beg them in vain just for the use of their name for the cause."[33] The NOW board found her so indispensable, however, that they refused her resignation. Farians tried to overcome her frustration and agreed to continue her service to the task force.

Recognizing the growing momentum among Catholic feminists, in 1970 Farians made the first attempt to gather the different strands of the emerging Catholic feminist movement under an umbrella lobbying group with the unwieldy title "The Joint Committee of Organizations Concerned with the Status of Women in the Church." Some evidence seems to indicate that the Joint Committee was considered a NOW initiative, at least by NOW members. The member organizations of the Joint Committee seem to have viewed it as an independent organization. In any case, Farians headed both the task force and the Joint Committee at the time, so it could be hard to differentiate. The Joint Committee included the NOW Task Force, SJIA, NCAN, the DM, Women Theologians United (a small group of theologians represented by Mary Daly and Jan Raymond), and the Women's Rights Committee of the National Association of Laymen (the NAL went defunct shortly thereafter).

The major goal of the Joint Committee was to initiate a dialogue with the NCCB concerning women's rights in the church. By this point, Farians already had a history of reaching out to members of the Catholic hierarchy. As early as 1967 she sought dialogue with prominent NCCB leaders Archbishop John Dearden of Detroit, Cardinal Lawrence Sheehan of Baltimore, and Archbishop Paul J. Hallinan of Atlanta. Her letters were frank, but polite, and occasionally full of praise. Farians wrote to Hallinan to thank him for being the only American bishop to speak for the rights of women on the floor of the Second Vatican Council. When Hallinan died in early 1968, Farians sent a letter of condolence to the people of Atlanta on behalf of the task force. "Women are especially grieved to lose such a dear friend because Archbishop Hallinan extended his strong concept of social justice and action to include the discrimination against women in the church," she wrote. "His memory will long be honored by our organization."[34]

While Farians garnered a few positive responses from such letters, she suspected that the bishops would not deal directly with NOW. So she formed the Joint Committee, whose first order of business was to send a proposal to the NCCB stating that the church was betraying its mission by perpetuating sexism. The group demanded the establishment of a national office to implement a plan for women's equality, a proclamation from the NCCB decrying discrimination, the revision of canon law, leadership positions for women in all policy-making bodies, the opening of all seminaries to women, and women's ordination.[35]

When the NCCB failed to move on the proposal, Farians began a dogged correspondence with NCCB's general secretary, Bishop Joseph Bernardin. His responses to the Joint Committee were slow to arrive and short on concrete commitments. Even Jeanne Barnes, the mild-mannered and moderate head of the Deaconess Movement, was forced to conclude that "it appears . . . a grossly ambiguous run-around is being handed to the Joint Committee."[36] It would seem that by late 1970, Farians's long-standing commitment to dialogue could not outlast institutional stonewalling. In her letters to Bernardin she began politely but soon moved to veiled threats: "No 'establishment' yields any rights unless forced to. We are ready to fight for our rights. . . . Please do not force upon us the means that all oppressed people must use to obtain their rights. . . . Our needs are more important than your rules."

By November she referred to the bishops as "artful dodgers," and when the NCCB's meeting rolled around in April 1971, still without any response to the proposal, Farians called a press conference and took off the gloves: "The Catholic Church is a sexist institution. As a result it is also racist and war mongering. It is unchristian in the worst sense of the word. It has identified with the rich, the wealthy and the powerful. It is not the servant: It is the master. It would be difficult to distinguish between the Church and the pentagon. . . . Assertiveness, arrogance and authoritarianism, pomp, power, and privilege are its characteristics. . . . The result is the monster that the Church is today."[37]

Originally, Farians hoped to stage a demonstration, but some members were hesitant. Bernice McNeela, SJIA-US representative and the organizer Farians originally hoped would lead the Joint Committee, was reluctant to "take over" the NCCB meeting. As she remarked to Farians, "I suppose you know that I am not much for demonstrations."[38] Despite the difference in their approaches, Farians accepted this decision and continued to hold McNeela in great regard.[39] In January 1972, the Joint Committee was invited to send representatives to the NCCB Committee on Women in Society and the Church, but the meeting was not fruitful. Her frustration was palpable in a letter she wrote to McNeela after the event: "To see so much time, energy, talent, and money of women drained into the bishops' bottomless pit causes me so much anguish."[40]

In lobbying the hierarchy, Farians was trying to confront the bishops, but she was also attempting to determine if Catholic feminism was possible, a question that other Catholic feminists (particularly those of the Deaconess Movement and feminist women religious) rarely posed in the first half of the seventies. Her writing reveals great ambivalence; Farians's press statement at the NCCB meeting in April 1971 (made in her own name and with other NOW members, not on behalf of the Joint Committee) was a case in point. Her language was stark and angry. She seemed unconcerned with the strategic consequences of her indictment, as if she had given up trying to change the church. "The overmasculinized males are not able to hear," she insisted. "The barrier is too great. Their skin is like leather, they cannot feel and they are blinded by their own power."

Yet her closing expressed the opposite idea: "This sexism . . . is destroying the Church and the men and women in the Church. We want the bishops to listen to us, to women, and to meet with us so that together we can begin to make the Church whole and holy."[41] Her expressed desire for a dialogue with bishops, and to make the church whole, made her sound much more likely to remain connected to institutional Catholicism. Indeed, the attempt to dialogue with and "convert" bishops became one of the dominant strategies of the movement in the seventies.

Farians's ambivalence emerged again in a paper she wrote for the *Andover Newton Quarterly*'s 1972 special issue on women's liberation. She adopted a scholarly distance on the issue of combining religion and feminism and did not reach a firm conclusion. She argued that religious feminists had much to offer a movement dominated by secularists but concluded that combining religion and feminism was an "inadequate" approach that would simply take too long.[42]

In the end Mary Daly helped Farians past her ambivalence; Farians participated in the "Harvard Memorial Exodus" in 1971, and this seems to be the moment when she broke any formal ties with the Catholic Church. Her meeting with the NCCB in January 1972 would be her last act as a leader in the Catholic feminist movement. Farians left the Joint Committee and recommended that it disband. As of June 1972, the umbrella group was still awaiting a substantive response to the proposal.[43] The Joint Committee remained in existence until 1973, but by this time Farians was no longer an active participant, and the committee had lost its impetus. Catholic feminist organizations did not again come together under a single banner until 1978.

In 1972, Farians resigned from the NOW Task Force as well, and this time the national board accepted her decision. When Farians left, most of the prominent Catholic feminists went with her, and the NOW Task Force ceased to be a center for Catholic feminist activity. It was no coincidence that the new Protestant leadership of the task force chose as its first action a protest on Reformation Sunday that included the tacking up of "115 Feminist Theses."[44]

Farians's ambivalence about the church was relatively short-lived, but she raised significant questions that the rest of the movement, confident in its loyalty, did not address until the end of the decade. Why stay in a church that causes you so much frustration, when there are other alternatives? How do you balance public protest and private lobbying? Will there come a time when feminists should stop banging their heads against the walls of the church? Does love of the church outweigh the pain of oppression? Farians's ambivalence was logical because she functioned as the link among the liberal feminists of NOW, the radical Mary Daly, and the more deliberately Catholic feminists. She is an early example of a woman who chose not to live with sustained ambivalence about the church, a path few Catholic feminist activists of the early seventies considered a serious option.[45]

the spirit moving

4

We are feminists <u>BECAUSE</u> we are Catholic.

—Saint Joan's International Alliance-United States Section

In the first days of my archival research, amid the scattered detritus of myriad Catholic feminist organizations, I happened to find a recruitment flyer for the Saint Joan's International Alliance-United States Section (SJIA-US). The mimeographed sheet outlined the organization's history and its goals for the early seventies, but what immediately caught my attention was the brief sentence set apart at the top of the page: "We are feminists <u>BECAUSE</u> we are Catholic."[1] I could just imagine a beleaguered Catholic feminist jabbing the cap lock on her typewriter, pounding out 'BECAUSE,' then backspacing to add the emphasis of underlining, just in case anyone missed the point. That sentence, with its commingled certainty and frustration, its assertion of a causal relationship between Catholicism and feminism, was the starting point for my historical exploration of the Catholic feminist movement in America.

The brevity of the statement notwithstanding, one could not find a clearer statement of identity. Here was the first proof I found of the existence of actual self-identified Catholic feminists. The activists who wrote the flyer unequivocally labeled themselves feminists, just as they allied themselves with the Catholic Church. But that heavily emphasized <u>BECAUSE</u> in the middle opened up a new world of questions and possibilities. What kind of feminists were these, who credited their consciousness to Catholicism? If they believed they were feminists because they were Catholic, how did Catholicism shape their feminist ideology and activism?

As I considered these questions, I also sought to determine if the SJIA-US causality statement held true for all Catholic feminists. I soon discovered that, while intriguing, the statement was not in fact held as a universal truth by all the Catholic feminists under study here. Indeed, the diversity of mindsets presented in chapter 3 proves this was not the case. Catholic women came to feminism in the sixties and seventies through both secular and religious means. Not all Catholic feminists ranked their faith in God or their Catholicism as the forces that most influenced their identification with feminism; certainly many Catholic feminists would bridle at such a statement and be more inclined to say they came to feminist consciousness *despite* Catholicism, not because of it.

Yet this statement does describe the feminism of a large number of women then active in the Catholic feminist movement, particularly in the years 1969 to 1974. As SJIA-US described the feminism of its own members, it also captured the spirit of these early years of Catholic feminist organizational activism. At the start of the decade, women who chose to direct their energy through Catholic feminist organizations spoke openly and often about the positive connections between feminism and Catholicism, even as they organized to challenge sexism and misogyny within the church.

These organizational activists believed that feminism was a Christian virtue best pursued from within the Catholic worldview, which inspired them, and, where, despite its oppression, they felt they belonged. These activists focused on liberating other Catholic women by initiating consciousness-raising, by seeking autonomy for communities of women religious, and by agitating for women's ordination. The period is distinctive also for its optimism about the ability of feminists to transform the institutional church. More than at any other time in the movement's history, Catholic feminists seemed more hopeful than resigned. Their hope may have been misplaced, as proven over time, but this was a period when Catholic feminists believed, with joy, that they could liberate their church from sexism.

The two strands of feminist activity that best exemplify feminism rooted in and inspired by Catholic identity are the Deaconess Movement (DM) and the "new nuns." The women of the DM defined their feminism as a call from God and a gift of the Holy Spirit. Their Catholic spirituality, as well as their quest for ordination, dominated their feminist worldview. In contrast, social justice—founded on the Gospels, Catholic social teaching, and the charisms of individual sisterhoods—was the predominant theme in the feminism of the "new nuns."

FEMINISM AS SOCIAL JUSTICE MINISTRY

Consider the Catholic radical feminist Mary Daly and her deep skepticism about the viability of a feminism rooted in Catholicism as you read the following statement from 1972: "We affirm Jesus and His Gospel as our life focus and that being said, the National Coalition of American Nuns puts society on notice that women refuse to accept any longer the straw for bricks that we are forced to make."[2] Add to this a second statement from 1974: "Whereas the fundamental principles which underlie the movement for women's liberation are one with the principles of liberation in the Gospel, Be it Resolved that NAWR as an organization and each of us as individuals affirm our identification with the movement for the liberation of women, and, when asked about this identification, use the occasion to clarify both the term and the movement."[3]

Recall, too, SJIA-US's bold "We are feminists BECAUSE we are Catholic" from 1971 and you might sense a trend in a movement quickly diverging from the beliefs of the radical feminists. SJIA-US's provocative statement linked feminism to Catholicism, but the feminist "new nuns" of the National Coalition of American Nuns (NCAN) and the National Assembly of Women Religious (NAWR) took the idea a step further. Each placed Christ and the Gospels first, then claimed feminism as a natural extension of their faith and their apostolates as women religious.

In a 1989 book, the theologian Maria Riley looked back on her earliest days as a feminist woman religious in the seventies and offered this explanation of feminism in her own life. "My search for a perspective that would bring together the strengths of my feminist commitment and my faith commitment had begun." She recalled, "In struggling to bring these two realities together, I came to realize that my commitment to the liberation of women was not only about justice for women, it was also about the integrity of the gospel and the authenticity and effectiveness of the church's mission of justice and peace in our age."[4] Each woman religious dedicated her life to Christ and the Gospels, a commitment that could be interpreted as a radical call to egalitarianism, justice, and peace. For some sisters, like Maria Riley, such an interpretation led to a holistic concept of social justice ministry committed to combating sexism, poverty, racism, classism, and environmental exploitation.

This helps explain the shape feminism took in the lives of the "new nuns." Over and over they defined their feminist beliefs and activism in terms of social justice, a principle to which they dedicated their lives as women religious. According to the Gospels, and also the charisms of their orders, they had a responsibility to serve but also to bring justice to oppressed peoples. In the sixties the "new nuns" were inspired by the times to experiment with new forms of social justice ministry, but with the coming of feminist consciousness some realized they too were oppressed and in need of justice. The feminist "new nuns" incorporated feminism into their understanding of social justice, linking the "new nuns'" call to fight for the victims of injustice with their need to liberate themselves.

The roots of this consciousness can be found in the tumult of liberal Catholicism in the sixties as well as further back, to the Sister Formation Conference (SFC) in the fifties. Changes begun with the SFC snowballed with the advent of Vatican II (1962–65). Most congregations followed the council mandate to reevaluate their constitutions, initiating lengthy processes through which superiors and sisters rethought their history, missions, dress codes, rules of behavior, and, most especially, their apostolates. The widely circulated and highly influential book *The Nun in the World: Religious and the Apostolate* (1962) described the apostolate as "the extension of Christ's mission in and through the Church, a mission which consists of giving God to the world, of acting in such a manner that men come to . . . live the whole of the Gospel in every aspect of their lives."[5] Many women religious rushed to try new apostolates outside the traditional fields of teaching, nursing, and administration. Work with the urban poor, particularly work that forwarded the cause of civil rights, proved very popular.

Throughout the latter half of the sixties both general Catholic periodicals and journals for sisters chronicled the brisk renewal efforts of women religious. As a result, sisters were perceived as the vanguard of renewal, mostly because the very visible "new nuns" (as the media christened them) seemed to embrace *aggiornamento* so eagerly. "If all pastors and all laymen were as open and ready to move as many Sisters are, it would be a sweet world indeed," the editors of *Ave Maria* remarked in 1965. "In many, many ways they are the strongest hope of the Church in this time of renewal."[6]

Some of these "new nuns" flooded into the new apostolates; others sought degrees in theology or experimented with new living arrangements outside the convent. Still others reassessed their vocations and chose to leave religious life; the late sixties and early seventies witnessed a steady decline in vocations and a large increase in women religious (and priests) seeking dispensation from their vows. In 1960, 765 women religious left their orders. That number climbed to 2,000 in 1966 and reached 4,337 by 1970.[7] Many women religious who entered their orders in their teens, believing that their lives would change very little over time, suddenly faced new options.

The desire to explore these options soon led to clashes with male authority. In 1965 and 1967, respectively, the Glenmary Sisters of Appalachia and the Immaculate Heart of Mary (IHM) sisters of Los Angeles tried to adopt changes to their apostolates, only to be refused by their local bishops, who wished them to remain in diocesan-approved assignments. After two lengthy and highly publicized standoffs between male and female authority, large portions of each community broke away into congregations not subject to the hierarchy. Though not explicitly feminist actions, in that few of the women involved would have articulated a feminist consciousness, the Glenmary and IHM cases awakened many women religious to the oppression of sisters. The exploration of congregational histories had a similar effect. According to historian Jo Ann McNamara, "Nuns had long been rigorously trained to ignore their history, personal or communal. The prescribed return to their roots paralleled the tumultuous experience of their present, leading them over several decades to a raised consciousness of their relationship with the male hierarchy."[8]

Yes, they were ready to challenge male authoritarianism in the hierarchy, but were these "new nuns" really feminists? The answer is yes, as overwhelming evidence proves. To begin, the "new nuns" were predisposed to adopt some of the most basic beliefs of second-wave feminism. Sisters knew quite well what it was like to be exploited and oppressed by sexism. Their lives were circumscribed by an ancient patriarchal hierarchy in which they had no representation. Men passed ultimate judgment on their choice of work, their living quarters, their salaries, their political activity, their public statements, and what clothes they put on in the morning. Perhaps no other set of American women more intimately understood the complexities and humiliations of patriarchy.

Rooted in a thousand-year-old tradition devoted to the holiness and joy of sisterhood, women religious also did not need to learn that "sisterhood was powerful"; they were already "sisters." American women religious could look back over a century of independent institution building and professionalism. Women religious built and administered extensive educational and hospital systems on their own. Moreover, of all American women, women religious were probably the least enslaved to standards of female beauty and domesticity. Sisters were living testaments that women did not need to define their identity through marriage and motherhood. They had long rejected both to live and work in communities of women.

Yet the particular worldviews of women religious could make espousal of feminism difficult. They were trained to be obedient, docile, humble, and self-sacrificing and not to question or challenge authority within or outside their communities. These traits had been absorbed so thoroughly that many feminist sisters struggled for years to reassess them. We cannot forget, too, that despite their low status in the hierarchy, women religious historically enjoyed privileges over other Catholic women. Because they worked for such low wages, parishes and dioceses often gave women religious preference in hiring, usually over laywomen (or laywomen were forced to work for sisters' wages). Combined with the traditional deference afforded to women religious, these privileges served to divide the potential sisterhood of Roman Catholic women, a barrier feminist sisters were asked (and asked themselves) to confront time and again in the seventies.

Finally, as women who took vows of celibacy early in life, the feminist "new nuns" did not participate in the larger movement's critique of sexuality and romantic relationships. As far as the public record and the papers of their organizations indicate, feminist women religious did not engage in debates over women's sexuality in the seventies; they neither censured nor endorsed the burgeoning sexual revolution; neither did they comment much on sexual harassment. Sexuality just did not make it onto their agenda. Perhaps they did not feel qualified to speak on the topic, judged that their views would be divisive, or were simply unaware. Maria Riley remembered that "because I was a nun I walked around in a rather protective bubble. I was not subject to the kind of sexual harassment that so many of the women endured."[9] Feminist sisters were also oddly silent on the abortion issue during a period when feminists made abortion rights their chief cause and debate raged over the issue throughout American society. However, the worldview that distanced them from some aspects of feminism also provided them with a ready rationale and opportunity to pursue feminist activism.

The best way to demonstrate this rationale is by examining the feminism that fueled NCAN, the first feminist organization for women religious. The specific genesis for NCAN was a newsletter with the wonderfully punny title *Trans-Sister*, founded in the late sixties by Audrey Kopp and Mary Peter Traxler (who became Margaret Ellen Traxler when she reverted to her birth name), both employees of the National Catholic Conference for Interracial-Justice (NCCIJ). *Trans-Sister* claimed a small but devoted following, featuring stories of "new nuns" and their often radical efforts to renew their communities. *Trans-Sister* also had a decidedly feminist orientation. In May 1969, eighty subscribers met for the "Sisters' Survival Seminar" and NCAN was born. Within a year, NCAN claimed more than one thousand members. In the early seventies, membership hit a plateau of around eighteen hundred, or 2 percent of American women religious, and remained there for the rest of the decade.

NCAN's structure was democratic, with an elected executive director and an executive board. The board prided itself on releasing no statements without approval, by vote, of the entire membership. As a self-described advocacy group "united to study and to speak out on issues related to human rights and social justice," NCAN did not gather for annual meetings, as did the other major organizations for women religious. Rather, NCAN devoted much of its efforts to developing and issuing statements on important justice issues, networking with other organizations, and keeping its constituency informed through mailings and its newsletter, the *NCAN News*. NCAN members also participated in direct action on a number of issues as NCAN members, most notably church renewal and the Equal Rights Amendment (ERA). It should be remembered, however, that NCAN members usually worked in some form of social justice or direct service ministry as their primary apostolate and so were involved in a multitude of different issues, causes, and movements on a daily basis.

The new organization's style and purpose were unique, and the direction they took was due in large part to the leadership of Margaret Ellen Traxler. Born in 1924 in rural Minnesota, "Peggy" Traxler became "Mary Peter" Traxler when she entered the School Sisters of Notre Dame at the age of eighteen. For much of the next twenty years, Traxler worked in the classroom, where she introduced her sheltered students to the events and problems of the larger world. According to a former student, she would often "drop to her knees in front of a large picture of Our Lady of Perpetual

Margaret Ellen Traxler marching in her habit at Selma, Alabama, in 1965 (Courtesy of the Marquette University Archives)

Help, praying aloud for assistance with the dumb, the deviant, the ever-daydreaming adolescents in her homeroom." Such was the earnestness—and wicked humor—of Margaret Ellen Traxler.[10]

In 1965, her desire to combat racism led her to a post as educational director of the NCCIJ in Chicago, and later that same year, wearing the full habit, she marched in Selma, Alabama, with Martin Luther King Jr. In Selma she was approached by a poor black woman who offered her fifty cents to pray over the body of her daughter. Traxler was so moved by the experience of praying with this woman that it made her reconsider her role in the world. "Here is where I belong," she concluded, "preparing people for times of crisis and standing by them when crisis comes." In an article detailing that experience, she called on other women religious to do the same: "Like the faithful women of the Gospel, Sisters must follow Christ into the world ministering to His needs in the person of the poor, the sick, the persecuted. When people are in crisis, they are particularly disposed to look inward to evaluate themselves in relation to God. This is one reason why Sisters have a place at the other Selmas."[11] For Traxler "the other Selmas" came to include taking stands for women's liberation.

Traxler's approach to feminism was like her approach to anything else: she was by turns outspoken, prayerful, demanding, playful, loving, and occasionally rude. Her choices could be rash, but under her leadership NCAN swiftly and strongly spoke out on issues of justice, standing alone if necessary. Traxler encouraged a radical Christian outlook among NCAN sisters, asking them to take chances for justice and walk with the oppressed, including their fellow women religious. In 1972, she described the women of NCAN as "icebreakers which prepare the way for frailer crafts," a phrase illuminating both their sense of mission and their dispositions.[12]

Unlike the radical Catholic feminists, the women of NCAN took for granted that the faith itself, rooted in the Gospels, was a liberating message that could be separated from the church's sexism. They claimed this message as the inspiration for their feminism. In testifying for the ERA before the Illinois legislature, Margaret Ellen Traxler began by saying "Another name for God is Justice," a phrase reminiscent of Susan B. Anthony's famous statement: "Resistance to tyranny is obedience to God." NCAN sisters believed "any action which frees a person from discrimination is a holy action."[13]

These women religious did not follow the path of the radicals in leaving the church because it gave them a structure and a lifestyle through which they could pursue justice not as a cause, but as an apostolate. As NCAN member Jacinta Mann explained, "With me, the movement is an apostolate." Her words exemplified NCAN's approach, whether working for justice in the church or in the "world." Indeed, Mann made no distinctions between the church, the world, or the feminist movement. She asked members of her community to "please ask the Lord to keep His hands on my shoulders as I walk about in that portion of His vineyard which has been labeled 'women's movement.' "[14]

NCAN's feminism, then, had two components: efforts to address their own oppression and then the oppression of others. Because NCAN sisters themselves believed they could "bring no one to the table of freedom unless we ourselves are free," I will begin with the former.[15] NCAN sisters based their feminist consciousness on the firm belief that Christ was feminist. "The women of the Catholic Church are in servitude and will remain so until the National Council of Catholic Bishops returns to the pattern of Jesus regarding women," Margaret Ellen Traxler insisted in a press release. "In Jesus' day," she explained, "He never refused the petition of a woman and even told each why her prayer was answered: faith. Only faith in our day can help women persevere in the Church."[16] When writing to bishops, Traxler was known to sign her letters "Sincerely in the Lord who also dissented" and "Very sincerely in the Lord Jesus who treated women with far more concern than the NCCB."[17] Like Traxler, NCAN sisters were inspired by a reading of Christ as an agitator for social justice.

In this they were no doubt influenced by the new liberation theology, still in its infancy, then emerging from Latin America. Most NCAN sisters would have been familiar with the theology, but it would not emerge as a major in-fluence until the mid- to late seventies. They were more likely influenced by feminist theology of the late sixties and early seventies from such scholars as Rosemary Radford Ruether, Mary Daly, and Elisabeth Schüssler Fiorenza as well as, by this point, the stacks of popular articles readily advancing the thesis that Christ applied his message of liberation to women. Such writers—and indeed, NCAN sisters—most often cited Christ's commission-ing of Mary Magdalene to inform the male apostles of his resurrection and his affirmation of Mary and Martha as evidence of the image of a feminist Christ.

This liberating, feminist Christ emerged again in NCAN's response to the American hierarchy's first document upholding the church's prohibi-tion on women's ordination, "Theological Reflections on the Ordination of Women" (1974). The bishops claimed to be "conscious of the deep love for the Church which underlies the growing interest of many women in the possibility of ordination." But Ann Gillen, then executive director of NCAN, countered, "There is no stirring of any hunger and thirst for justice" in the document, "no holy impatience because there are flocks without shepherds, or shepherdesses." According to Gillen, blind adherence to "the male per-spective called Tradition, which NCAN calls 'the male monologue' " damp-ened the hierarchy's desire for justice and warped its understanding of Christ. Jesus "would be the first to reject the 'great Male' tradition which distorts the meaning of the Incarnation," she argued. "He took on the weakness of humanity, both in the flesh of a woman and the physiological form of a male, thus identifying completely with humanity. NCAN deplores the obsession of Male tradition concerning maleness as tantamount to idolatry." Gillen turned the hierarchy's argument on its head, divorcing Jesus from the ominous Male tradition and allying him with the feminists who shared his Spirit, if not his maleness.[18]

NCAN's specific grievances against the institutional church resembled those of the Catholic feminist writers from the sixties. They found Catholic theology, seminary training, papal encyclicals, and canon law openly sexist and were affronted by restrictions against formal female liturgical participation and ordained ministry. Most often, NCAN's feminist activism centered around the relationship between women religious and the male hierarchy. As NCAN member Helen Kelley remarked in 1969, "women religious in particular have been cherished for their willingness to receive direction and instruction without question and to submit their own decisions for review and approval."[19]

NCAN sisters were no longer willing to surrender their self-determination to an all-male hierarchy. "A male-dominated 'mother church' is a painful paradox which must be questioned by those who love the Church envisioned by Jesus," Ann Gillen wrote. "It is imperative that the women of the church speak out to claim [their] rights." These included the right of subsidiarity: "Who is closer to a sister's apostolic work and better prepared to decide what she should wear to do that work if not the sister herself?"[20] Shortly after its founding, NCAN released a statement calling on "all men of the Church, no matter what their hierarchical status, to refrain from interfering in the internal renewal of communities of religious women," to which Mary Luke Tobin, former head of the leadership body for all American women religious, responded: "You have thrown down the gauntlet, and it's about time."[21]

Throwing down gauntlets was Margaret Ellen Traxler's specialty. When in the early seventies officials in the Sacred Congregation for Religious, the Vatican oversight committee for women's congregations, asserted their authority by interfering in the renewal of specific communities and by insisting that sisters wear the habit, Margaret Ellen Traxler let loose several decades worth of pent-up anger in a letter to Cardinal Ildebrando Antoniutti: "Your illusory power in the past was based upon the illusion of poor religious women who now, more and more are realizing the unchristian system you have made of it. This systemic evil of your efforts to control and dominate we reject outright and categorically."[22] This quote derives from a rough draft preserved in the NCAN collection, so it is unclear if this was the final draft. Whether or not she sent the letter in this form, however, it was more restrained than it could have been. In a letter to Bridget Mary Fitzgerald, Traxler asked, "Will you please give me reasons why NCAN should not publicly in the press, call Antoniutti the male chauvinist goat that he is?"

This letter was not unique. Throughout the seventies, NCAN members, particularly Traxler, wrote to men at all levels of authority in the institutional church, sounding off against everything from the prohibition on women priests to the absence of women speakers at divinity school conferences. More than once, Margaret Ellen Traxler was rebuked for sending indignant letters before she checked her facts. She once wrote a hasty letter to Theodore Hesburgh, president of the University of Notre Dame, because she overheard someone in a hotel lobby say Hesburgh had commented that the "open-season" on bishops should be over. He denied making any such comment.[23] As we shall see in a later chapter, Traxler's pen eventually caused a firestorm involving a bishop, a congressman, and a first lady.

At times NCAN seemed uncertain about this strategy of criticizing/ educating/ lobbying the hierarchy, that is, the strategy of loyal opposition. Some NCAN members argued that this approach only served to acknowledge the hierarchy's power over women. When asked for comments on Traxler's letter to the Sacred Congregation for Religious, several sisters encouraged her to stop communicating with Rome altogether as the best way to escape its control. "By sending this letter," Glenna Raybell argued, "you acknowledge, however you may remonstrate to the contrary, that Antoniutti has power over you. He has no power over those who do not recognize it. . . . We have to do what needs to be done in the world and not get bogged down in fruitless disputes with the hierarchy."[24]

But NCAN's loyalty to the institutional church made members loath to ignore the hierarchy as a means of escaping male authority. In 1972, Traxler rebuked Bishop Raymond Vonesh for a "dictatorial and male chauvinist action" he had taken, saying she would be a traitor and a hypocrite had she stayed silent about it. But she told Vonesh, "I want to affirm the leadership of our bishops. I have not and will not participate in any criticism of our bishops because I feel that my Church needs affirmation and not defamation, especially now in our history."[25] Of course, Traxler's correspondence belies her claim that she did not criticize bishops, but she felt the need to say that she did in order to preserve her position of loyal opposition.

NCAN sisters made this choice in part because Catholicism, as they understood it and despite the hierarchy, offered them an ideology that supported their holistic efforts for social justice. NCAN concerned itself with a broad range of social justice causes, including the antiwar movement, the rights of workers, the legalization of prostitution (they were in favor), the plight of Jews in the Soviet Union, political prisoners (including members of the Black Panthers) and fair-housing legislation. But one of NCAN's deepest concerns was poverty, an issue they specifically intertwined with feminism.

NCAN revealed the interconnectedness of these goals in the "Declaration of Independence for Women" (1972), a statement calling for full equality for women in church and society by the time of the nation's bicentennial in 1976. The declaration's goals were the "full and equal participation of women in churches," establishment of new church structures, abolition of the College of Cardinals, "reformation of the present economic and power systems," and "complete equality for women." But the declaration departed markedly from mainstream liberal feminism in its final demand: The sisters of NCAN decried hedonism and denounced consumerism as "worship of false gods," calling for "austerity and simplicity of life styles." They argued "the more goods we consume, the less there is to sustain life in developing nations."

The call for austerity so as not to take resources from the poor was, for the sisters, a radical Christian ideal, and it found its way into this feminist document for a reason. The sisters who wrote the declaration believed that the fight for justice lay not only in challenging the effects of large-scale male-dominated structures on women, but also in challenging how women themselves exploited others, including other women, in daily life.[26] Therefore they moved away from a concept of "universal sisterhood" that disguised imbalanced power relationships between women and the implications of these relationships for the poor. NCAN regularly called on women religious in particular to scrutinize their lives for ways they exploited or neglected people in poverty, asking them to stop wasting money trying to get their founders canonized and to reallocate resources from prestigious and lucrative suburban schools to poorer students.[27]

NCAN also used its extensive activism in support of the ERA to draw attention to poor women. Take, for example, NCAN's castigation of the anti-ERA National Council of Catholic Women (NCCW) on this point. In true NCAN style, the group claimed first that the NCCW possessed a "neanderthal self-image as women." They then invited the women of NCCW "to leave even briefly the parochial company of the Altar Society and to speak with their sister-women who are on welfare or who live in public housing or who are among the thirty-three million women in the US labor force."[28] For over ten years, NCAN's newsletters, memos, and executive board minutes exhorted sisters to get out and pass the ERA. By 1977, NCAN members had testified twice before the U.S. Congress and twenty state legislatures.

But NCAN went beyond rhetoric when, in 1974, it launched the Institute for Women Today (IWT), a project with the dual focus of consciousness-raising for women of faith and direct service to women in prison. IWT referred to itself—rather naively—as the only organization dedicated to "searching for the religious and historical roots of women's liberation."[29] The NOW Task Force on Women and Religion could and did make this claim six years earlier. In any case, the group, led by Traxler, recruited a faculty of over fifty women lawyers, professors, and activists to conduct a series of consciousness-raising workshops around the country, thirty in all by 1976. These weekend sessions were unique in that they were designed for mixed groupings of Jewish, Protestant, and Catholic women.

IWT's other focus was a ministry to women in Illinois prisons; organizers encouraged IWT faculty and participants to make their beliefs concrete by serving incarcerated women directly. IWT's prison projects included professional training, college courses, psychological counseling, language instruction, poetry writing, and anything else that would foster women's spiritual and emotional well-being. Traxler was especially concerned that women not be exploited by male guards, so IWT successfully lobbied to ensure that women's prisons had female wardens and that jails hired female guards.[30]

NCAN sought to live the social principles of a radical Christianity, and frankly they were about as successful at converting the world to these as was Jesus. The American Catholic Church did not change its priorities by closing its most profitable schools merely because NCAN demanded it; NCAN did not revolutionize society's "power systems," abolish the College of Cardinals, or even convince the Sacred Congregation for Religious to stay out of its business. On the other hand, NCAN's efforts to reach individual women of all classes with the IWT proved to be very successful, and NCAN members mobilized untold numbers of women by their public stands and personal concerns for those oppressed by sexism and poverty. On another level, this social justice approach to feminism proved successful because it helped the sisters of NCAN integrate faith and feminism in a way that inspired them to act while also allowing them to maintain a preexisting worldview that was sacred to them.

Although NCAN was the earliest organized, and the most articulate and outspoken organization on the subject of feminism and social justice, it was not the only organization for women religious to espouse this type of feminism. The NAWR was founded in 1970 at the urging of over thirty diocesan sisters' councils. Under the leadership of Ethne Kennedy, NAWR was created to be a grassroots voice for rank-and-file women religious. NAWR differed from NCAN in that it was roughly three times larger, it created an extensive regional structure to support the activities of a national office, and its membership gathered yearly in national assemblies. The women religious in NAWR were more conservative than those of NCAN but can nonetheless be classified as liberal. NAWR was created not as a counterpart to NCAN, but as an alternative to the Leadership Conference of Women Religious (LCWR), the organization for superiors, and up to 1969 the only cooperative national voice for women religious in America. The NAWR's chief goals were helping American women religious from diverse communities network with each other, promoting social justice causes, and most importantly, providing a voice to communicate the concerns of rank-and-file sisters to their official leadership and Rome.

For the first few years of its existence, NAWR concentrated primarily on issues of renewal and self-determination for women religious. Ethne Kennedy's style was markedly more subdued than those of her counterparts in NCAN or the radical Catholic feminists, but this does not suggest a lack of determination. Kennedy's introductory letter to Cardinal John Dearden, then head of the NCCB, is a case in point. She introduced NAWR but quickly moved on to express sisters' "anxiety" and "acute disappointment" over the NCCB's handling of the Los Angeles IHM case, hardly incendiary vocabulary. But her careful choice of words, couched in respectful, prayerful Catholic language, did not obscure what in the last line is clearly a rebuke of the NCCB:

> Is there any way that the NAWR . . . can make known to the NCCB the suffering caused by the lack of consultation before decisions which radically affect the lives of thousands of women religious are made? . . . Although no concrete proposals were made at the [LCWR] meeting, other than witnessing to [the IHMS] our fraternal concern, one wonders if a moratorium could not be declared to allow time and the grace of Christ to heal the wounds of all those concerned. *Perhaps the Bishops together may think of a corporate gesture to express Christian compassion.*

Adhering to the epistolary etiquette of women religious, Kennedy followed this barb with assurances of continuing prayers.[31]

Margaret Ellen Traxler, however, expressed considerable frustration with NAWR's leadership and agenda, revealing early tensions between NCAN and NAWR. She cut out an article detailing NAWR's 1970 agenda and annotated it for the members of the NCAN executive committee, commenting that each idea could have been taken directly from NCAN's agenda of 1969.[32] Her biggest frustration with NAWR, however, was its lack of involvement with the feminist movement, either as participants or by addressing issues of women's oppression. Traxler repeatedly complained that NAWR would not sign on to the new Joint Committee then just forming under Elizabeth Farians's leadership, thereby further separating themselves from other women. In a letter to a friend she wrote, "Don't you think that nuns should stop being exclusively 'nunnery' and get with other groups? . . . Ethne Kennedy said she had no authority from her organization to further the cause of women and therefore declined." Yet Traxler claimed, "her steering committee is incensed about this and clearly see how if we are going to make progress, we women should get together."[33] Characteristically, Traxler had no trouble dictating how other organizations should conduct their business, but her perceptions were valid. NAWR did not emerge as a partner in the movement until 1973.

NAWR's progress toward a feminist orientation is instructive for understanding how a group of women religious came to feminist consciousness. The organization began with a strong understanding of sisters' oppression, as evidenced by Kennedy's letter to Dearden, but there remained an unwillingness to call this feminism. Several years later, NAWR willingly identified with the women's liberation movement, a sign that consciousness-raising efforts among women religious were working, but continued to be conciliatory and consciously politic in its approach to the church. Finally, by 1974, NAWR took strong public stands on feminist issues without any attempts to placate the hierarchy. As their public voice emerged, however, they retained a Catholic identification; like the sisters of NCAN, NAWR's members defined their feminism as a ministry of social justice and as a means of validating and integrating their faith lives and their feminism. Their collective espousal of feminist consciousness was a gradual process, as it was for many other organizations and individuals.

In 1971, *Probe*, the NAWR newsletter, surveyed NAWR's four thousand members on the question, "What meaning and importance do you give the phrase: 'new roles for women religious in the ministry of the Church?'" Respondents spoke overwhelmingly of ministry as service: "ministry means being a circumstance of God's grace . . . a deep authentic life of the spirit expressed through service of all, especially the poor and oppressed." The study's author, theologian and Dominican sister Fara Impastato, concluded that sisters were saying, "we want to serve . . . but not servilely," expressing "weariness" with "ritual subordination." Yet Impastato commented that the desire for expanded ministry was not about wanting to "take over": *"There is no reference here to anything like mere woman's lib movement."* In Impastato's view, NAWR sisters seemed reluctant to identify as feminists, because they perceived feminists as lacking humility. Also, it appears these sisters wanted to assure themselves that their desires were not "merely" feminist; their central goal was to serve others, not themselves.[34]

By 1973, however, NAWR not only talked openly about sexism, but the group also used feminist language. In this it reflects the far-reaching effects of consciousness-raising within the larger culture. In a brainstorming session on women in the church at the 1973 national assembly, members spoke of consciousness-raising as a solution to address "woman's own sense of powerlessness and a lack of awareness of her potential." They identified a host of problems in the relationship of women religious to the church, from financial dependence to impenetrable clerical structures to lack of freedom to change careers. Their solutions to the problems were all intrachurch and fairly conservative: encouraging leadership training, liturgical ministry, homilies on women in the church occasionally preached by women, joining liturgy committees and parish councils, and encouraging "pastors to have staff meetings with sisters." The working group urged that sisters "be willing to compromise (with integrity intact) on details to obtain final goals. . . . Be willing to 'politic,' to take one step at a time."[35]

It might have been cautious, but overall the approach was innovative. Nearly all of these strategies concerned liturgical ministry in some form or another, thereby recognizing the intersection between feminism and the essential spiritual needs of the majority of Catholic feminists. NCAN represented the big picture, tilting at the windmills of society's unjust "power systems." NAWR saw that grassroots women, women religious and lay, were feminists in large part because they wanted to be in the sanctuary. In this, NAWR stood closer to the Deaconess Movement and to the NOW Task Force than to NCAN.

Therefore, NAWR's strategies centered around consciousness-raising and the parish battles needed to gain the right to participate in the sacramental life of the church. Most significantly, though, the working group urged women to plan their own liturgies around the theme of women as part of an "action plan." NAWR was the first organization of women religious to recognize the power of the liturgy as consciousness-raising, as expression of a Catholic feminist spirituality. The organization did not yet articulate the next step in this process, that is, liturgy as a form of feminist protest, but they paved the way for the movement's future. Indeed, as we shall see, one of the most dramatic feminist liturgical protests took place at the 1976 NAWR national assembly.[36]

As of 1974, NAWR ceased to talk about the need for humility and compromise and began to take public stands on Catholic feminist issues. Its approach was similar to NCAN in expressing feminism as a Catholic ministry of social justice. In their first public statement on women's liberation they resolved, "Whereas the fundamental principles which underlie the movement for women's liberation are one with the principles of liberation in the Gospel, Be it Resolved that NAWR as an organization and each of us as individuals affirm our identification with the movement for the liberation of women, and, when asked about this identification, use the occasion to clarify both the term and the movement." The authors of this resolution did not indicate how they would "clarify" women's liberation, but their writings on the subject suggested that they would define it as social justice ministry.

NAWR proclaimed its support for the ERA, the diaconate for women, and the opening of liturgical ministries. But like NCAN, NAWR also called for simple living and reduced consumption "to witness to the gospel message of love for poor and starving peoples." NAWR committed to using 1975, declared a jubilee year by the church, "to change unjust structures by working for the equalization of relationships in all levels of society." Again, like NCAN, NAWR focused on women's liberation but did not limit their desire for justice to women. They couched their goal in terms of the jubilee, used by the church to foster reconciliation among all peoples, revealing a commitment to a holistic social justice within a Catholic worldview. No doubt, too, they took some pleasure in proclaiming women's liberation to be an obvious goal of the pope's jubilee year.

NAWR put its vision of liberation into practice on the local level, something NCAN's structure did not allow. The Los Angeles chapter designed a "Liberation Study Day" for over eighty sisters based on a Catholic multimedia resource packet called "The Woman Kit." The kit included discussion topics and a mix of audiotapes and filmstrips on feminist theology, sexist imagery, and other issues designed specifically to raise the consciousness of

Catholic women. Its authors hoped facilitators would use the kit to design programs "on the topic of liberation either as personal growth or a ministry of justice": "the interest and involvement of women religious in the area of women's rights and the liberation of all people—men and women—to be fully human is growing rapidly. . . . Sisters, in an attempt to continue their unique and creative role as bearers of the Gospel, are discovering in the issue of liberation, not only a personally rewarding awareness themselves but also an exciting challenge to share this 'good news' with others."

Giving an opportunity for women to reflect on their role as Catholics committed to liberation, the liturgy included a group "dialogue" homily in which participants discussed "our discoveries about the Christian responsibility to liberate and be liberated."[37] Here, NAWR's consciousness-raising technique reflected the influence of liberation theology, but it also showed how far these women had come since NAWR first flirted with feminism in 1971. By 1974 they clearly understood the relationship between faith and feminism as causal and were ready to engage in feminist activism.

Finally, we'll take a brief look at the LCWR, the third major group of women religious to espouse feminism. Like NAWR, LCWR did not officially identify itself as feminist until 1973, and these sisters also spoke in the language of social justice ministry. LCWR's process of adopting feminist consciousness was more gradual than that of the more radical NCAN. However, it was the first organization of women religious to seek justice for women in the church, as early as the midsixties. LCWR trained and raised the consciousness of some of the movement's most important leaders and helped spread feminism to the rank-and-file sisters the superiors represented. As the official representatives of American women religious in Rome, they often adopted a diplomatic role. In the first half of the seventies, they were feminists who, like the members of NCAN and NAWR, believed they could eventually influence the hierarchy and were willing to work through official channels. Therefore they appear to have been the most conservative of the sisters' groups, although this facade was often strategic.

LCWR came into being in 1956 as the Conference of Major Superiors of Women (CMSW), the first organization to represent American women religious. CMSW invited all general and provincial superiors to be members and instituted its annual national assembly in 1965. The conference of superiors gained much positive publicity in 1964 when Mary Luke Tobin, then CMSW president, was chosen as auditor to the Second Vatican Council. In response to the council, CMSW encouraged the renewal of religious orders and the revision of canon law. They also created a formal liaison committee to facilitate regular meetings with the NCCB.

The midsixties were a transitional period for CMSW, however. For while the superiors began to assert their autonomy within the male-dominated hierarchy, they also attempted to maintain authority over the nation's women religious. A crisis erupted in 1964 concerning CMSW's decision to assert jurisdiction over the Sister Formation Conference (SFC), an organization devoted to raising the educational standards of American teaching sisters. According to author Judy Eby, the sister formation crisis "was, at root, an intense struggle over differences in the theological understanding of religious authority and obedience." The SFC founders' vision of authority was one of shared leadership, a style that suited new apostolates and the loosening of restrictions in convent life.[38]

The painful suppression of SFC was CMSW's attempt to stem the tide of such changes, but ultimately time and pressure from the grass roots helped the superiors recognize the value of collaboration. In 1970, the CMSW amended its bylaws, giving the membership more freedom to choose the organization's leadership and thereby leading to a more liberal outlook. This liberalization was reflected in 1972, when the CMSW changed its name to the Leadership Conference of Women Religious, hoping to de-emphasize the hierarchical connotations associated with the term "major superior." Feminist consciousness did play a role in facilitating this transition.[39]

The leadership of CMSW/LCWR did not refer to themselves as feminists in the sixties, but their actions suggested a strong consciousness of women's oppression, and the desire to fight sexism. As early as 1966, the CMSW began its efforts to gain representation in, or the right of consultation with, the Sacred Congregation for Religious in Rome. The LCWR archives contain a stream of letters, papers, and protests directed at a variety of Vatican officials in America and Rome. The tone rarely changed; LCWR presidents always "requested" more representation or consultation in prayerful and respectful language. Anger in these letters was nearly always coded as "frustration" or "disappointment." This can be read as docility but also as the strategic conventions of nun-speak. Theatrics and rhetorical brashness might rupture already tenuous lines of communication.

LCWR functioned as the voice of all American sisters, and the leadership knew it. Like it or not, the organization carried the burden of being diplomatic with those who barely acknowledged its existence. Their means of expression, however, does not obscure the fact that the leadership of American women religious asserted its constituents' rights for nearly a decade before the leadership labeled itself feminist. As in NAWR, the adoption of feminist consciousness could be a very gradual process, both in individuals and organizations. In a 1970 memo to the NCAN board, Margaret Ellen Traxler wrote positively, if a bit skeptically, of LCWR's emerging feminism: "Enclosed are pieces from the CMSW meeting. I thought that it was all plus for their efforts to open themselves. . . . Old Mother Seraphine, CsJ, came up to me and whispered, 'Do you think better of us now?' I do of course, but am not saying so until I see . . . a few more such 'action proofs' of their new spirit."[40]

Not a few Catholic feminists urged the LCWR to join the movement. Mary Daly spoke of Catholic misogyny to the LCWR in 1968, and canon lawyer Clara Maria Henning stressed the urgency of such a move in an address four years later.[41] Henning tried to spur the leadership to action because "the LCWR comprises a potential for the liberation of women which is providential in scope." Henning referred here to the American sisterhoods' extensive infrastructure and networks already in place, half the battle for a growing movement. She also pointed out that women religious still controlled the Catholic schools "from kindergarten to college"—an opportunity to educate the next generation about justice. Finally, Henning bluntly stated, "Let us not kid ourselves: There exists an incredible amount of animosity between nuns and laywomen, especially on the part of laywomen toward nuns."[42] Henning was not alone in this belief; the animosity was apparent in the seventies and will be discussed in chapter 5.[43] Nevertheless, Henning believed that if the LCWR expressed its solidarity and "sisterhood" with laywomen as women, as opposed to as women religious, it could go a long way toward reconciliation with laywomen.[44]

Once the LCWR went feminist, it did so wholeheartedly, using its conventions to speak out against sexism, support the ERA and women's ordination, criticize the institutional church, and promote consciousness-raising among women religious. In the latter half of the decade, former LCWR members became important leaders in the Catholic feminist movement, namely Elizabeth "Betty" Carroll (Thomas Aquinas Carroll), Joan Chittester, and Theresa Kane, who, in 1979, used her role as LCWR president to personally confront Pope John Paul II on the issue of social justice for Catholic women.

ANSWERING THE SPIRIT'S CALL TO ORDAINED MINISTRY: MARY B. LYNCH AND THE DEACONESS MOVEMENT

In December 1971, a young woman named Karen Whitney was preparing to move to California to begin theological studies at Santa Clara University. Before she moved, she wrote a brief but deeply felt letter to a woman she had never met. Karen began with spirit, saying that she planned "to challenge [a] few of the clergymen" at her new university. But she soon poured out her fears: "I don't know if the sense of calling *is* strong enough—I am very secluded. I have faith and I hope I love. I will try and keep my eyes open and see. We must be strong in our knowing that we share Christ's mission regardless of discrimination. Being a woman and a black woman, I cannot help but feel that the persecution of the Church in the last days will come more from within than from without the church."[45]

Karen Whitney's letter reveals the myriad emotions of a young African American woman with a call to ordination in the Catholic Church. She intended to put up a fight, to be strong, and though she felt persecuted on two levels, she knew she was called to follow Christ through ministry. Yet she struggled with doubt, attributing it to her seclusion. She felt terribly alone.

So many women felt the call to ordination, and each had to learn in her turn that she was not the only one. Feminists, religious and secular, went through similar processes across the United States in this period. No matter their particular experience of discrimination, part of becoming a feminist was learning that your problem was shared by other women. The awareness of oppression as a systemic, not personal, problem and the support found in sisterhood often constituted the first step toward feminist consciousness. The process of consciousness-raising, or CR, was designed to facilitate this awareness by gathering small groups of women to tell their stories so that they might experience sisterhood and learn that "the personal is political."

For hundreds of Catholic women who felt called to ordination in the early seventies, scattered across the country and easily isolated, it was the Deaconess Movement that provided the earliest forum for consciousness-raising. As the first organization for Catholic women aspiring to ordination, the DM served as a clearinghouse of information and provided a forum for discussion. But more than that, it also created a supportive network for women called to priesthood who also tended to be novices in the world of feminist activism.

Through prayerful, earnest, and often achingly vulnerable stories, the women of the DM shared the narratives of their callings. They offered each other encouragement and the certainty that whatever voice was calling, it was valid and they were not alone (nor crazy). No argument in *Common-weal*, however well reasoned, could provide this kind of affirmation. In this way, the DM served as a highly successful form of consciousness-raising. These women also learned of an emerging body of scholarship that provided support—intellectual and spiritual—for their cause. Most importantly, they taught each other that feminism did not require wholesale abandonment of Catholic spirituality or the institutional church. Like SJIA-US and the feminist "new nuns," the women of the Deaconess Movement found the source of their feminism in their faith. As we shall see, however, the DM differed from these groups in the nature of its spirituality and its focus on ordained ministry.

Unfortunately, the history of the DM has been overlooked. Even the Women's Ordination Conference, the direct descendent of the Deaconess Movement, today seems unaware of its existence.[46] Historians can be forgiven for overlooking its importance, however. The DM lasted for only five years. It held no protest rallies, conferences, or regular meetings, and while it quietly lobbied the hierarchy, it issued no press releases. It did not develop a comprehensive critique of the institutional church or notable feminist theology. In this it was quite different from feminists in the other strands of activity. The DM basically consisted of a woman, a typewriter, a mimeograph machine, and a mailing list. But one should never underestimate the power of a woman and her mimeograph in the early days of second-wave feminism.

At the dawn of the new decade Jeanne Barnes, a twenty-two-year-old Catholic college student, was struggling to find her place in her faith tradition. After a long period of "religious confusion," Barnes returned to Catholicism with the zeal of a convert after joining her undergraduate Newman community in Illinois. Within a few years she was acting as the defacto "Woman Chaplain" for that community. Her experience counseling other young Catholic women affirmed her call to the diaconate, a call she first experienced at the age of eleven.[47] Barnes knew this was an ordained ministry and that women were not allowed to receive orders. Nevertheless, in early 1970 she wrote to the NCCB committee on the permanent diaconate, hoping to learn that a training program would accept her. She was told this was out of the question; in fact, the NCCB claimed she was the first woman to ask. Undaunted, Barnes felt convinced that "if my desire was, as I had prayed, a summons from the Holy Spirit, there must be other women who are feeling the same calling."

In late 1969, Barnes solicited advice from Mary Daly, who recommended she write to Elizabeth Farians, who was, by this time, several years into her leadership of the NOW Task Force. Farians encouraged Barnes to pursue her calling through activism and twice met with Barnes to teach her the ins and outs of Catholic and feminist organizational politics. On March 4, 1970, Jeanne Barnes placed a twelve-word advertisement in the *National Catholic Reporter* looking for other women who felt the call to holy orders. Barnes was right; the women did exist. By May she had heard from 120 women from around the country, each sharing stories of isolation and the call of the Spirit.[48]

The Deaconess Movement, as Barnes named it, took shape between 1970 and 1972 through the distribution of a mimeographed newsletter called the *Journey*, edited and largely written by Jeanne Barnes. The *Journey* under Barnes's direction was chatty and prayerful. It included updates on developments in Catholic feminism and the ordination question and was full of stories from women around the country. By 1972, the mailing list contained 400 names and was growing steadily. The mood was generally optimistic, resulting in prose full of hope and the belief that God would guide and inspire them. As Barnes insisted in the *Journey*'s first issue, "I am not the leader of the Deaconess Movement; in a sense, I am not even the organizer. It is the Holy Spirit who is both. May the Seven Gifts of the Holy Spirit grow strong within us and guide us."[49]

Despite her faith, Barnes quickly felt overwhelmed by the movement she called into being. Just as Farians was forced to focus on her own survival, Barnes struggled to make ends meet as she juggled work, activism, and her education. As of August 1970, just as she was putting together the first editions of the *Journey*, she was forced to forgo health insurance and sell off her furniture to pay her tuition. By spring 1972, work responsibilities, combined with the demands of the burgeoning movement, led Barnes to hand over her correspondence and editorship of the *Journey* to one of the original respondents to the NCR ad, Mary B. Lynch.

Like Margaret Ellen Traxler with NCAN, Mary Lynch exemplified the spirit of the Deaconess Movement: gentle, deeply grounded in prayer, supportive of women, and full of faith that God would win the day. Perhaps no one was able to personally integrate Catholicism and feminism more harmoniously than Mary Lynch. Born in 1924, as a young girl Lynch "played Mass" at the dining room table, taking the role of priest. From this point on she was aware of her vocation but, being a woman, chose social work as "the best field where I might at least indirectly reach their spiritual lives." What followed was a wide-ranging and distinguished career in education and social service. She once joked that it would be hard for any priest to match her "spiritual formation," which included a large number of social service positions, from head counselor at a girl's camp to counselor of emotionally disturbed children to psychiatric social worker in a state diagnostic center to ten years of organizing and developing group homes for emotionally disturbed children in four dioceses.[50]

For Lynch, these years were preparation for the events of the seventies: "I knew my life had to be concerned with my relationship to God and I wanted it to be concerned also with others as they related to God. . . . I went on risking and trusting in the Lord."[51] "Risking" led her, at the age of forty-seven, to enter a Catholic seminary; she was the first American woman to do so. Lynch ran the DM while earning a master's of divinity, to her a preparation for ordination. Friends described her as "in a hurry," driven to get the women's ordination movement off the ground. She moved six times to six different states in the span of eight years, always to further the movement in some way and always without a viable source of income. With her for every move went her close friend Eileen Murphy, described as Lynch's companion. The two vowed "to live and work together" before their friend Bishop Maurice Dingman, probably around 1973. Their life together centered around prayer and, by the early seventies, the women's movement.[52]

While in the last year of her master's of divinity program, Lynch traveled extensively to give the DM a concrete reality. She visited DM women all over the country and spoke at numerous meetings and conferences, including official meetings of diaconate program directors. With her fellow activist and good friend Josephine Ford, a theologian teaching at Notre Dame, Lynch determined that what the movement needed next was a bishop to support their cause. Barnes and Lynch had tried to foster dialogue with the NCCB since the beginning of the Deaconess Movement, with only limited success, but developments in the early seventies gave them new hope. At the 1971 Synod of Bishops in Rome, the Canadian bishops presented an unexpected resolution in favor of women's rights. Subsequently, both the NCCB and the Vatican established committees on women's changing roles in church and society.

These developments suggest that, at that time, such optimism was not unfounded. In 1972, Lynch met Bishop Maurice Dingman of Des Moines and was so impressed with his acceptance of the movement and his openness to the Spirit that she moved the DM from Indianapolis to Des Moines, where she knew the diocese would be supportive. While in Des Moines, still working to build the DM, and still without financial support, she also helped found the Paraclete Prayer Center to foster women's spirituality.[53]

Mary Lynch's commitment to spirituality and no doubt her single-mindedness drew other aspiring priests to her. While she actively sought institutional change, she made the fostering of individual women called to ordination her chief priority. She visited such women wherever she traveled but also built sisterhood through letter writing. The *Journey* and her personal papers bulge with letters from women around the country. Her correspondence was voluminous; her personal mailing list, so large it "almost frightened her." Her correspondents, both friends and strangers, saw her as a bedrock of support.

Some of these women were active in the movement already, but many were outsiders—and laywomen—with no connection to other aspiring priests besides the knowledge of their own callings. Lynch understood the need to validate and energize these women through sisterhood. As she wrote in a letter to the membership shortly after assuming leadership in 1972, "Our energies need focusing, our strengths must be analyzed, our convictions need support, our hearts need rejoicing, our heads need to be examined (literally) to learn to live with the overwhelming uncertainties before us. . . . We are women now ready to take initiative and responsibility toward participation in the ordained ministry. Spiritual unity through inter-correspondence and involvement discovering each other is a necessity."[54] She gave women opportunities to share personal stories of faith, calling, and feminism, both among themselves and with the hierarchy, providing a unique forum for Catholic women to express and explore their growing feminist consciousness in the context of their relationship to God.

Mary Van Ackere, a self-employed convert and mother of two with no higher education, revealed her call to Lynch in 1974. "I have a strong call to the priesthood since early childhood," she wrote. "I should speak a lie before God, did I say otherwise." She turned to Lynch, asking for "any news, advice, counsel, or just plain friendliness" to help her actively pursue her calling because in the past she had been content to "wait quietly on door sills and not get my nose crushed when the door swings shut." Lorraine Storck, a grandmother, Sunday school teacher, and aspiring deacon, told of how she recently became the first woman lector in her parish, and this led her to recognize her vocation. She was awed both by the experience of proclaiming scripture within the sanctuary and by the fact that she was so relaxed doing it when she normally feared public speaking.[55]

Women often shared stories of their futile efforts to have their calls recognized. Celia Sells, a thirty-six-year-old Chicana mother of four, knew she was called to the diaconate; she just was unsure about how to have her call recognized. She tried to tell others in her parish about her vocation, "but no one seemed interested or simply laughed it off as part of Women's Lib (as if that is all bad). One women [sic] went so far as to say that she never heard of anything so vulgar in all her life." Sells decided to write about her vocation in a letter to someone in authority, but she struggled because she lacked education in theology. She wrote to her local cardinal asking for a meeting, thinking it might help, but he never replied. Feeling desperate, she approached a visiting priest at her parish, and, in tears, the words tumbled out of her: "I told him that by virtue of my baptism I had the right and that it was a gift and I had accepted it." Luckily for Sells the priest was supportive, suggesting she write simply and from the heart. He offered to pray over her, a gesture Sells found comforting.[56]

Celia Sells finally wrote her letter to Monsignor Ernest Fiedler, a member of the NCCB committee on the permanent diaconate. "I need a big favor from you," she said. "I want to be a Permanent Deaconess. I need your help. . . . I hope that you can speak to the Holy Father for me. I was told that I would have to speak to him concerning this vocation." She was only trying to do God's will, she said; she wanted to "imitate Jesus to my fullest capacity." In reply he sent her a copy of "Theological Reflections on the Ordination of Women," the NCCB's recent denunciation of women's ordination.

Sells's faith in churchmen—and their ability to gain an audience with the pope—may seem naive, but it reminds us that not everyone who sought ordination held advanced theological degrees or was well-versed in the latest church politics. Sells was like many women in the DM, a mature Catholic woman lacking training but holding firm to a call she refused to deny. Eventually Sells's letters found their way to Mary Lynch (infinitely more pastoral than Fiedler), who brought her into the company of the Deaconess Movement.[57]

Even in these earliest days of Catholic feminist organizational activism, Catholic feminists were markedly different from each other. For example, while the radicals maintained a clear focus on liberation and the feminist "new nuns" emphasized feminism as a ministry of social justice mandated by the Gospels, the Deaconess Movement did neither. They did not often speak of feminism itself as a ministry; nor did they assert their obligation to seek justice, like the sisters' organizations. Likewise, they did not scrutinize Catholic tradition and scripture for the roots of their oppression and publicly challenge the institution through protest, as did radical Catholic feminists.

The DM had one feminist goal: ordination. Catholic feminists universally supported this goal—although even at these early stages many were asking if it were possible for Catholic feminists to tolerate entering the priesthood as it was then conceived—but in the first half of the seventies, only the women of the DM made ordination their central focus. This may explain why the DM talked so infrequently about social justice. The intense, individualistic focus on ordination precluded the development of an expansive feminist critique linking feminism to other justice issues in a Gospel context, like that of the "new nuns." The Deaconess Movement rarely explicitly explored the nature of feminism and its relationship to Catholicism, as did the "new nuns."

Their lack of interest in theorizing does not mean that the DM saw no connection between Catholicism and feminism. On the contrary, their feminism took recognizably Catholic forms. Their preoccupation with ordination led them to place their feminism in the context of the sacraments, for example. An American woman religious, very likely Marilyn Sieg writing anonymously of her call, revealed a powerful story of feminism linked to eucharistic devotion. She felt a call to priesthood early in life, but because she was a woman she "gave up the idea of ever becoming one, despite the urgent and deep desire." The Mass was so important to her, however, that she created a ritual for herself to link every action to that of the eucharistic sacrament: "I would work out every facet of my life for that day as it was possible to perceive it and relate it to each segment of the Mass. For example— My dressing in the morning would be related to the priest dressing for Mass. Leaving the room would be like leaving the sacristy for celebration, etc."[58] In a talk to her community on ministry and women's liberation two years earlier, Sieg phrased her feminism explicitly in terms of the Eucharist: "We are called to be prophets of Love, sisters, because we prepare the way for the revolution of liberation through the Paschal Celebration of the Lamb.... What a brilliant future lies in our hands."[59]

Receiving and offering the sacraments was central to D M women. In this, they displayed a profoundly Catholic "sacramental imagination," as Andrew Greeley referred to it, a way of imagining the world that included an emphasis on ritual and ceremony, community, institution, and hierarchy.[60] They wanted sacramental sanction from the church; without it, they felt cheated, and on some level, incomplete. But equally important was the restriction making them unable to offer Christ to others through the sacraments. "God has given me talent and ability to make Him known and loved," one aspiring priest wrote, "and ... official recognition by the Church would greatly widen the scope and confirm the service I feel called by Jesus to render my brothers and sisters."[61]

Many of these women were already working in various ministries that once had been the sole purview of ordained clergy, and were performing ministerial functions in those roles, but were prohibited from administering the sacraments. Women in ministry often described their frustration over being able to counsel people but not be able to offer the sacraments of reconciliation, anointing of the sick, and Eucharist as means of resolution and healing. Virginia Finn, a member of both SJIA-US and the DM, challenged a priest on this point: "Among the tasks performed by deacons listed in the brochure [on the permanent diaconate], only officiating at funerals is now outside what women already do. I wonder if God really holds that the works of women are not 'sacramental' as Her/His 'church' does. I don't believe God is that small."[62]

One need not look far to find the Catholic character of deaconess feminism. These women, more than any other Catholic feminists in this period, were openly prayerful, readily sharing their spirituality in most any form of communication. In doing so, they helped develop Catholic feminist spirituality, arguably the most vital and creative aspect of the movement from the midseventies onward. Expressions of spirituality were certainly more common among those in the DM than among the radical Catholic feminists, who rarely wrote of a personal Catholic spirituality, and even more common than among those in the organizations for feminist women religious. Their spirituality also seemed to be of a slightly different nature. The prayerful use of language appears to have been more personal and visceral for women of the DM. Quite often its members were simply unable to explain themselves without reference to God and prayer. Perhaps this can be accounted for by the fact that women religious had a shared tradition of spirituality that could remain unstated, whereas laywomen rarely had opportunities to express their prayer lives to others.

One of the most obvious characteristics of DM spirituality was a devotion not to Christ the liberator, but to the Holy Spirit. It could be explained in part by an upsurge in devotion to the Spirit, due to the emergence of the charismatic movement in the late sixties, yet this movement was largely conservative in nature, and no evidence suggests a strong involvement by feminists.[63] We can speculate, however, that feminists called on the Holy Spirit because, of the three "persons" of the Trinity, the "Holy Spirit" is most often construed as gender neutral, and this allowed them to avoid the use of "God the Father." The Holy Spirit has connotations distinct from the "Father" and the "Son" that suited the early movement. The Spirit is repre-sented by wind and fire, symbolizing movement and urgency, election and call, mystery and promise. "The Spirit is taking me on" or "the Spirit is at work," they wrote. They invoked the Spirit to bless each other and their cause, and they described each other as "Spirit-driven." By invoking the Spirit, particularly in their call narratives, they instantly expressed their faith in change and the belief that their activism was sanctioned, in fact, initiated, by God.

Spiritual language in the narratives also carried traces of devotionalism that did not often arise among the highly educated women in the other strands. When Celia Sells was attempting to compose her letter for the NCCB, she dedicated her Lenten prayer that year to praying about the letter and was calmed by the act of a priest praying over her. When she finally finished her narrative she ended it with this statement: "So I put myself totally in God's hands. I shall trust in Him completely. And hold on to Our Blessed Mother and St. Joseph tightly. With their help I will do my part in asking for this favor."[64]

But DM women could also be experimental and forward thinking about their spirituality. Mary Lynch collected handouts from feminist liturgies she attended, among the first to be celebrated in the United States. These litur-gies used gender-neutral language, nonbiblical texts, feminist symbolism, and they encouraged women's full participation. These handouts and others like them will be discussed in detail in chapter 6.

Most of the women who wrote their call narratives and organized the DM were openly feminist and knew that the church stood in the way of their calling; in their minds, it stood in God's way. Their letters reveal a growing feminist awareness and willingness to name the source of their oppression in the church. "I was so brainwashed as a child that it never even occurred to me that [a] woman might desire to be a priest!" one woman wrote. "As you can see," she admitted, "I'm also a bit of a rabid feminist." Another DM member speculated that "at the present the leadership does not feel threatened by us. We are not being taken serious [sic]. I think we should stop and reevaluate our work and pose a threat."[65] They were, at first, more optimistic in their relationship with the American hierarchy, perhaps more naive, than their counterparts in NCAN, NAWR, LCWR, SJIA, the NOW Task Force or the Joint Committee. Lynch once contended, for example, that "we may not get all of the powers but if we show that we are sincerely led by the Spirit to serve wherever we are needed, those in authority cannot help but recognize us."[66] Eventually, such optimism faded, as attempts to dialogue with bishops went nowhere.

A few DM women reached the point of leaving the church in this period. Rose Horman Arthur, a woman religious who had recently left her order and married, insisted that women should just perform the sacraments on their own without sanction: "If the sacred mysteries 'don't take,' we're not less holy for trying. . . . The sense of 'calling' has been over-estimated into something mysterious. It's part of life, all of which is mystery." With some regret she concluded, "If it takes much longer I shall direct my energies in the ministry of other Christian churches, which I consider far more Christian than the Roman Catholic one."[67] Yet most members of the DM signaled their continued connection to the institutional church by making the institutional church the center of their protest and the sacraments the focus of their spirituality.

Mary Lynch took most of the Deaconess Movement's call to activism on herself. Besides founding the Paraclete Prayer Center in Des Moines, maintaining the *Journey*, and giving talks throughout the country, she built international connections by affiliating the DM with the International Association of Women Aspiring to Presbyteral Ministry (IAWAPM) in 1974. Lynch then decided the time was right for a national meeting on the subject of women's ordination. On December 14, 1974, she gathered thirty-one individuals—women religious, laywomen, and clergy—to strategize, resulting in an ordination conference task force. On stationery headed with a passage from the Gospel of Luke—"Blessed is she who believed that the promise made her by the Lord would be fulfilled"—Lynch invited the nation's bishops to share in the movement by offering their "spiritual, moral, and financial support. . . . Will you pray for us in this Holy Year, so appropriately coinciding with International Women's Year?"[68]

Lynch then moved to Detroit, and as she helped arrange the watershed Detroit conference, she also began work on a plan to found a lay community based on Ignatian spirituality there.[69] Lynch joined the conference task force but declined to chair it. Frances McGillicuddy of SJIA-US later contended, with hostility, that women religious tried to "use" Lynch as a front to conceal their efforts to take control of the movement in 1974–75.[70] But as Lynch's companion Eileen Murphy remembered it, Lynch knew this was not the case: "Mary didn't see herself as a public person. Mary worried about telling Nadine [Foley] that she was not the one to do it. She saw Nadine as the one. . . . She felt she was in the background. It was just between herself and the Lord."[71] The dream of founding a lay community never materialized. After the Detroit conference, Lynch and Murphy moved, this time to Columbus, but Lynch had difficulty finding work. Not long after, she began a long battle with cancer that forced her to give up her work in the movement and led to her death, at age fifty-four, in 1979.

While seeming to appreciate Lynch and the work of the Deaconess Movement, several high-profile leaders of the Catholic feminist movement, including Elizabeth Farians, Mary Daly, Ethne Kennedy, Virginia Finn, and Arlene Swidler (of the five, only Finn and Swidler were active members) wrote to the DM in the early seventies to offer encouragement but also unsolicited advice. The latter most often concerned the DM's focus on the diaconate as opposed to priesthood. In a note to Jeanne Barnes, Daly refused her support if the movement did not set its sights higher than the diaconate, writing, "As you know, I have reservations about this movement because there is a danger that it could be given as a sop to women rather than granting *full* equality, i.e., priesthood."[72] Elizabeth Farians concurred, issuing a NOW Task Force statement specifically written to warn against concentrating on the diaconate.[73] Arlene Swidler spoke for many when she objected to the word "deaconess." She warned that next it would be "deaconettes," insisting, "we can't take such people seriously."[74]

These comments signaled an attempt to guide the DM toward a more sophisticated understanding of feminism. In truth, the DM gradually shifted from a focus on diaconate to priesthood around the time that Lynch assumed leadership. But women continued to write of calls to both priesthood and diaconate, and the DM never challenged the latter choice as detrimental to the movement. The feminism demonstrated within the DM seems less informed and less connected to the secular movement than that of the other two strands of the Catholic feminist movement at this stage. Yet the DM functioned as a hothouse for developing feminists. For the women of the DM, Catholic spirituality and feminism grew simultaneously in the early seventies, just at the point when secular feminism within the larger movement was particularly hostile toward institutional religion. The women of the Deaconess Movement would have found it difficult to develop an integrated, Catholic feminist approach in this climate.

In the first half of the seventies, Catholic feminists ranging from the members of the Deaconess Movement to the Catholic radicals made crucial choices that would have long-reaching effects on the development of Catholic feminism. For some, the first choice was the most difficult: "now that I've become a feminist, do I still want to be Catholic?" A small number of women decided, early on, that being both a Catholic and a feminist was infeasible. But for the majority, women religious as well as laywomen, this question was less troubling during this period because their feminism was growing directly from their experiences of Catholicism. The movement built its organizations on Catholic foundations by choice. These feminists defined themselves in Catholic terms, celebrating the best of Catholic teaching and spirituality. Yet by constantly trying to engage in dialogue with the Catholic hierarchy and by adopting ordained ministry as a major objective, the movement bound itself to the institution. Marked by optimism and a sense of sisterhood, the movement was in its ascendancy.

5

the love of christ
leaves us no choice

We convene this conference as an act of faith, hope and love
in you and in the community of the people of God. We come
because we must. We have heard your good news.
—Rosalie Muschal-Reinhardt, "A Liturgy of Invocation"

It was late November 1975, and Maureen Hickey Reiff found herself standing in a hotel broom closet in suburban Detroit. She had traveled from
Chicago at the urging of her friend Donna Quinn, who "nagged the hell out
of her" until Reiff agreed to come to Detroit. By her own admission, she
was only marginally involved with Catholic feminism, she was not called
to ordination, and she had no real expectations for this "women's ordination conference." In fact, she had no expectation even of getting in; overwhelmed conference organizers had already turned five hundred people
away. So now here she was, rather ridiculously, hanging around in a closet.
Finally, Donna rushed up with a name tag for "sister somebody or other,"
who had failed to appear.[1]

Not only did Maureen Reiff get to attend the first women's ordination
conference—albeit in the guise of a woman religious—she was so inspired
by the event that she eventually became a prominent leader in the arising
movement. She wasn't the only one. Marsie Sylvestro, a local campus minister and musician who would go on to compose the movement's most
enduring anthems, walked around all weekend wearing the name tag of a
sister who had been unable to attend on account of a death in the family. A

group of others who failed to gain entrance (there were only so many absent women religious) and could not bear to leave put together their own mini-conference in one of their hotel rooms, periodically sending communiqués down to the main conference from what they called "the Upper Room."

Such was the excitement surrounding the first large-scale gathering of American Catholic feminists at the first women's ordination conference. Women and men poured in from across the country with a sense of urgency and, for some, gleeful anticipation. Here they would state their purpose, show their strength, and find solidarity. Here they would stand with other feminists and explain their belief that women must be ordained in the Roman Catholic Church.

The Detroit conference is a major touchstone in the history of the American Catholic feminist movement, the pivotal event of the seventies. Catholic feminist scholarship found a forum there as well as a means of reaching and directly inspiring a grassroots audience. Friendships formed on that short weekend that endured for lifetimes. Some women found in themselves the call to ordination; others, to leadership and activism. One participant described the conference as a "greenhouse" for emerging activists.[2] The majority of my interview subjects attended this first conference, and their memories of the event are universally positive. Some went so far as to call it "life changing." Interviewees described the conference as joyful, enlivening, spiritual, and hopeful, a place where the academy and the grass roots, women religious and laywomen, came together to articulate a new vision of the priesthood and a plan to achieve it. It looms large in the memories of those who participated in it.

Historically, it looms large for other reasons. Because the 1975 Detroit ordination conference was attended by activists representing nearly every sector of the movement, it offers us the opportunity to take the pulse of Catholic feminism at mid-decade. Through the meeting we can identify changes in leadership, pressing concerns, ideological convictions, and mood shifts. The conference also shows the paths that were not taken, the ideas that were rejected or ignored by a movement just finding its direction. Innumerable women were undergoing the process of negotiating a religious feminist consciousness as they listened to panel discussions, met in small groups, or just talked it all over in the hotel bar. In effect, they were struggling to identify what a Catholic feminist was and what she wanted.

The Detroit conference reveals a movement equally concerned with transforming the Catholic priesthood and articulating its own feminist consciousness. Participants spoke as feminists—condemning patriarchy, advocating praxis, extolling sisterhood—but they also spoke freely of their love for the church and their determination to renew it. They found much about the church to condemn, but they did so very much as members of the family. Before long, the movement would succumb to frustration in the face of institutional stonewalling and, eventually, crackdowns. But for the moment, Catholic feminists rejoiced in their dual commitment to church and feminism. They were hopeful enough to put forward what they truly desired both for and from the church. From the first ordination conference, we can learn what these women hoped to achieve, if they could last to the end of the struggle and remake the Catholic priesthood.

THE WOMEN'S ORDINATION CONFERENCE EMERGES

By 1974, the Catholic feminist movement was in a hopeful, optimistic mood. Catholic feminist organizations were growing steadily. Increasing numbers of women were entering graduate study in theology and ministry at divinity schools and seminaries across the country. Feminist theology was emerging as a viable and exciting new discipline that in turn helped to educate and inspire grassroots activists. Developments within the hierarchy also encouraged optimism. At the 1971 Synod of Bishops in Rome, the Canadian bishops presented an unexpected resolution in favor of women's rights. Subsequently, both the National Conference of Catholic Bishops and the Vatican established committees on women. Some of the movement's leaders, most notably Mary Lynch of the Deaconess Movement, also had encouraging experiences "dialoguing" with individual bishops at this time. The now-defunct Joint Committee's inability to breech the hierarchy's walls in the early years of the decade did not seem to faze the new feminists coming up by 1974.

Moreover, Catholic feminists were excited and inspired by the bold actions of Episcopalian feminists in 1974. In an attempt to force the issue of women's ordination, eleven women deacons planned an "irregular" ordination in Philadelphia, presided over by two retired bishops and one bishop who had resigned. Amid a firestorm of controversy, they became the first Episcopalian women priests. Within two years, the governing structure of the Episcopal Church approved women's ordination and recognized the pioneering women's ordinations. Although Episcopalian politics were very different from those of Roman Catholicism, feminists saw similarities. Both churches participated in a worldwide communion, and both required apostolic succession for a valid ordination. Many Catholic feminists attended the irregular ordination, and the women priests became regular speakers at Catholic feminist gatherings. The priests' determination—and success—was cause enough for optimism.

The movement's hopeful mood also had much to do with the arrival of large numbers of women religious to the movement by 1973, which had a profound impact on the movement's politics and its tone. Recall the departure of radical feminists like Mary Daly and Elizabeth Farians by 1973; their leaving created a leadership vacuum that women religious were ready to fill. But sisters differed markedly from the radical feminists in that they were far more likely to have strong ties to the institutional church, or at least to their communities, and they rarely discussed the possibility of separatism. Their approach could generally be labeled "determined loyal opposition." Feminist women religious also began to supplant the predominantly lay Saint Joan's International Alliance, once the most visible of the Catholic feminist organizations. So the movement took on a more "nunnery" cast, as Margaret Ellen Traxler might say. This had many implications, as we shall see, but the first was a determination to remain within the church and renew it from the inside. These women had recently experienced and helped implement the transformation of their orders and the upheavals of conciliar reform. They had reason to believe that agitation for progressive reform of the institution could have an impact.

The women who populated this movement at mid-decade were generally hopeful, but I do not mean to imply that they were naive. Catholic feminists were not without skepticism about the church's willingness to implement feminist reforms. Most of the participants were well-educated, particularly in theology and church history, and many had extensive experience trying to work with members of the American hierarchy. All knew firsthand the struggles of being a woman, either lay or religious, in the Catholic Church. But they sincerely believed that the ideas they put forward could be transformative, on both a personal and an institutional level.

So it was in this hopeful spirit that planning for the conference began. In December 1974, Mary Lynch called a meeting of Catholic feminists to discuss the cause closest to her own heart, women's ordination. This meeting led directly to the Detroit conference, which helped make ordination the central issue of the Catholic feminist movement. We should ask at this point why ordination became the rallying point for the movement, because such a decision was not inevitable. Movement leaders could have focused on other issues, for example, women's participation in liturgical ministry at the parish level, an issue that arguably would have had more of an impact on the majority of American Catholic women. But at this point, ordination was the issue of greatest concern to the majority of leaders in the movement, many of whom were being trained for ministry themselves. More and more women were stepping forward to express their call to ministry; something needed to be done to validate their calls and end the prohibitions against women priests.

But ordination was a highly suitable cause for a number of other reasons. Ministry, ordained or not, proved a central theme for both women religious and lay feminists, and leaders probably hoped it would help unite the two groups. Moreover, the issue drew the attention of both grassroots reformers and theologians, promising an intellectually grounded activist movement. Theologians in particular hoped to use the question of women's ministry to explore the possibility of a renewed priesthood. Finally, the topic of women's ordination was controversial. Catholic feminists realized that if they wanted to push the church toward justice, they needed a controversial issue to capture the institution's attention and rally supporters eager for action.

From the first meeting of the ordination conference task force, the planning process was charged with a sense of excitement. At one point, a task force member said rather ominously that this conference would be the first time in history that the Roman Catholic Church convened on the question of women's ordination. Rosalie Muschal-Reinhardt remembers thinking at that moment, "Do all the people who make history feel as confused as we do right now?" They may not have known what they were doing, but they were "willing to engage," and their enthusiasm was clear.[3] This sense only grew with feminists' overwhelming response to the proposed conference titled, "Women in Future Priesthood Now: A Call to Action." Requests for information poured in, as did endorsements. Originally slated to be held at the University of Detroit, at the last minute, after registrations far exceeded expectations, organizers moved the conference to a large hotel in a Detroit suburb.

The task force capped attendance at twelve hundred, turning five hundred people away. Although statistics from the conference are not precise, it is estimated that women religious outnumbered laywomen nearly three to one. Roughly one-third of the laywomen and one-third of the women religious believed they were called to ordination; one-third of the whole had or were in the process of obtaining degrees in theology or related fields. Nearly all participants were white, middle-class women, although women of color and a significant number of men attended.[4] All of the major Catholic feminist groups then in existence had members present at the conference, and the major Catholic feminist theologians also were present.

The task force envisioned the conference as a gathering of scholars, women aspiring to be priests, and feminists who together would act as a new model of church—challenging, dialoguing, worshiping and sharing in the solidarity of Christ. Central to this model was Marge Tuite, a feminist woman religious active at the time in the ecumenical group Church Women United, who would come to have an enormous impact on the movement through her understanding of fruitful "process," her insistence on an integrated sex/race/class analysis, her strategizing, and her mentorship of young activists. An entire generation of activists can recite her oft-repeated refrain: "Do the analysis, make the connections."

Led by Tuite, organizers built the conference on a model that included sixteen scholarly talks (most of which were responses to a handful of longer papers), followed by facilitated small-group discussions. The groups then divided into specialty groups according to each attendee's interests. The small group meetings were the centerpiece of the conference, providing opportunities for grassroots activists to give input and make connections. Between talks and discussions, participants worshipped together in three liturgies: "A Liturgy of Invocation," "The Love of Christ Leaves Us No Choice: A Liturgy of Blessing," and "Certain as the Dawn Is His Coming: A Eucharistic Liturgy, First Sunday of Advent." The theologian Ada María Isasi-Díaz, at the time a young emerging activist, believes it was the best-designed process of any conference she has ever attended. She remembers being consumed by the conference; it was so intense that she never even looked out the window all weekend.[5] Certainly, the Detroit conference was powerful for those who participated; emotions ran high, and more than one individual reported feeling that her life was transformed by the experience. The movement, too, experienced a transformation as it began to articulate its collective purpose.

In an attempt to synthesize the conference experience for the proceedings published the following year, Mary Daniel Turner elucidated three primary themes that emerged not only in the scholarly talks, but also among the small-group discussions. Together, these three themes help us understand what the women of the Catholic feminist movement wanted to achieve in the midseventies. Twelve hundred people are unlikely to hold one universal opinion, yet it is safe to conclude that the three issues named by Turner carried broad support within the assembly. In order of importance, these themes were: (1) "The need for a reinterpretation of the priesthood within today's pastoral needs"; (2) "a concern for bonding among women"; and (3) "an emphasis on fidelity to the tradition of Church."[6] Each theme reveals much about the kind of church these feminists wanted and what kind of feminists they wanted to be.

RENEWED PRIESTLY MINISTRY

At some conferences, the chosen theme is little more than a flimsy device to hold disparate aims and ideas loosely together for the duration of a weekend. Speakers might acknowledge it politely but then quickly move on to their own agenda. This was not the case in Detroit, where the conference theme resonated through each talk, small group, and liturgy, revealing how vital it was to the movement and its future. The phrase "renewed priestly ministry" took hold of the assembly, which asserted conclusively that a renewed ministry was even more important than women's ordination itself. Most of those women with a call to ordained ministry believed they would only accept ordination into a transformed priesthood and church. Those who did not commit to a renewed priestly ministry, preferring instead to enter the old clerical model, "stand waiting to be co-opted," warned longtime activist Arlene Swidler.[7]

Speakers led the way by describing in detail just how corrupted the priesthood had become, resting as it did on two thousand years of patriarchal tradition. The theologians, particularly Rosemary Radford Ruether, Elisabeth Schüssler Fiorenza, and Margaret Farley, a Sister of Mercy, made accessible to the assembly a decade's worth of feminist theology and historical studies to explain why the ministry must be renewed. Ruether's and Schüssler Fiorenza's remarks were brief, as they were panel respondents, but each took the opportunity to outline the church's systematic exclusion of women, justified through scripture and tradition.

Schüssler Fiorenza called the participants' attention to the early church, where women "exercised leadership as apostles, prophets, evangelists, missionaries, offices similar to that of Barnabas, Apollos or Paul." Women shared in "apostleship," a concept not limited to the formal twelve upon which the institutional church rested its claim for an all-male priesthood.

The Jesus movement (the earliest formulation of the Christian church) attracted those marginal to the dominant culture, she explained, and was not limited by cultural expectations of male superiority. But she went on to outline "the gradual cultural compromise" that led the institution to link priesthood to the hierarchical Jewish and Greco-Roman traditions.[8]

Ruether also outlined a history of patriarchy, concentrating on the formidable power and longevity of symbols. "Patriarchy not only pervades specific dictates about women, but also creates an entire symbolic edifice of reality that reflects the social hierarchy of male dominance and female submission," she argued. "The challenging of male dominance, therefore, challenges the entire symbolic language of order, hierarchy, power, lordship and authority in religion, as these have been shaped by patriarchy." Ruether reminded the assembly that patriarchy determined the nature of the magisterium, the so-called teaching authority of the church located primarily in the bishops and the papacy, which believed that the hierarchy had an exclusive right to determine when tradition should be reassessed. Recent experience over the birth control issue had proved that those at the bottom of the institutional pyramid were unlikely to influence the process. Therefore, not only patriarchy and its attendant symbolic scaffolding, but also the concept of Catholic teaching authority must be disassembled to gain recognition of women's ordination from within the institutional church.[9]

Margaret Farley added a third voice to this grim assessment of patriarchy within the Catholic Church. She noted how cultural beliefs embedded in Catholic tradition explained the institution's refusal to allow women's ordination and asserted that ordination would not occur until each of those beliefs was repudiated. The first such belief was that women were by nature unsuited to leadership, particularly leadership over men. Second, the church held tightly to the long-standing belief that women could not "represent God to human persons nor human persons to God." Men were viewed as representing God, whereas women were seen only as lovers of God. "No wonder that public witness of God's self-revelation seemed appropriately given only by men," she wrote. Third was the belief that women contaminated sacred space, associated as they were with "pollution and sin." Such beliefs derived from the ancient taboos against allowing menstruating women into sacred spaces. The church could see only men as "appropriate subjects" for the sacred responsibility of leading all of God's people into the inner sanctuary. After debunking each of these beliefs in turn, she spoke in the voice of a scholar, concluding that, "the Church ought to open its ordained sacramental ministries to women . . . because not to do so is to affirm a policy, a system, a structure, whose presuppositions are false."[10]

Scholars agreed that the patriarchy did not merely cause the exclusion of women from priesthood; it also helped warp the priesthood into a bastion of hierarchical privilege and power. The portrait speakers painted of the priesthood was dire, at best, although it should be noted that speakers couched their remarks in terms of the office of "the priesthood," not individual "priests." Perhaps they did not wish to tar all priests with the same brush, particularly since a good number of priests were present in the assembly. In any case, the priesthood was characterized during the conference as morally timid, ambitious, rigid, defensive, materialistic, uninterested in dialogue or the sharing of ideas, power-hungry, unquestioning, and too self-involved to truly serve the people of God. None of these traits reflected "the priesthood deserved by the Church of Christ."[11]

The state of the priesthood, added to the weight of all patriarchal history, suggested the enormity of feminists' task. But speakers urged those assembled to take on this responsibility to help guide the church to conversion. Schüssler Fiorenza used the language of conversion explicitly, arguing that "the admission of women to the full leadership of the Church requires the official confession that the Church has wronged women and has to undergo, therefore, a radical conversion." By the end of her talk she was offering practical suggestions for how to proceed; whether she believed such a conversion was likely to occur is unclear, but she obviously tried to convince her audience to try. Rosemary Ruether did ask the question: "can structures so deep-rooted be changed?" She concluded that "the answer we must give is that they must be, for the sake of the Gospel itself."

But the call to conversion was made most powerfully by Margaret Farley. She ended her very academic paper with a surprisingly moving call to the women assembled. She acknowledged that what she was asking was difficult, if not impossible, but the attempt had to be made "because some women will have received a unique imperative by the power of the Holy Spirit and from the Christian community in which we find life." She urged women to seek ordination "without bitterness," although they would be bitter; "in spite of weariness," though "they are subject to the cardinal temptation to weaken and not to struggle forward in freedom and responsibility." And finally, she said that women should seek ordination "because now ripens the time when they must say to the Church, for all women, words reminiscent of the words of Jesus Christ to his disciples (under the continued query for a revelation of his true reality), 'Have we been so long with you, and you have not known us?' "

With that last line, many of the women assembled reportedly broke down weeping. According to one witness, the gathering was racked with the sounds of sobbing for several minutes. Margaret Farley's query resonated with resignation, anger, and the hurt of betrayal. But Christ said this to the apostles, whom he loved, and in that spirit Farley asked feminists to say it to the church. Farley hoped women would find the strength to change the church, which they continued to love, despite the church's colossal failure to recognize in its midst women's full humanity and the gifts they offered to the people of God.[12]

So the conference committed itself to renewing the priesthood, and the women knew how to begin. The feminist academics in the movement proved highly influential because they brought to the conference a commitment to praxis, a cornerstone concept in second-wave feminist theory that figured heavily in the work of Catholic feminist theologians. In a praxis model, women validate and explore their own unique experiences as women, the very experiences dismissed by patriarchal tradition, as the basis for personal development and transformative action in the world. As feminist scholar Josephine Donovan notes, "the concept of praxis also implies the development of alternative arrangements that will themselves provide models for change and will in the process change consciousness."[13] So participants were encouraged to believe that the solution to the problem of priesthood would emerge not from tradition, scripture, or theology alone, but from women's experiences of church, theology, and pastoral ministry and the "alternative arrangements" they created by necessity to work in ministry outside the structures of the ordained priesthood.

Speakers frequently mentioned the ministerial work in which women were already engaged. Elizabeth Carroll outlined the full scope of women's work in ministry, from liturgical ministry and catechesis to theologizing and spiritual direction. "As a result of such experience," she remarked, "women gained insight into what a renewed ministry in the Church might be and at the same time . . . sensed danger as they saw their work separated from the often formal conferral of sacrament and the official communication of doctrine in Gospel and homily."[14]

The impulse to honor women's experience and judgment found fullest form in the Saturday evening liturgy, "The Love of Christ Leaves Us No Choice: A Liturgy of Blessing." After songs and scriptural readings, the female presiders invited those present who felt a call to the priesthood to stand. No one knew what the response would be; no liturgy of this kind had ever been celebrated before. Most in the assembly were astonished and deeply moved when several hundred women (and a few men) rose from their seats and presented themselves to the congregation for a blessing. Consider how isolated most of the women of the Deaconess Movement had felt, sending letters to strangers in order to talk about their calls, whereas here, two hundred women were affirmed and blessed by their peers, all of whom believed that each woman's experience of call was to be honored. Surely this was an event that few could have anticipated in their lifetimes. Maureen Hickey Reiff, a woman not called to priesthood who simply watched from the back of the hall, called it a "mind-blowing" experience, the "Aha" moment that caused her to embrace the movement.[15]

Although everyone could agree on the importance of validating women's experience, a range of ideas emerged about what should constitute the new priesthood. Fittingly, Anne Carr asked the church to "think and act in new ways, to choose imagination over the violence of authoritarian structures of power, prestige, and caste." Feminists let their imaginations roam freely, introducing a number of rather utopian concepts, but their creativity was rooted in common themes. Most of all, they wanted a priesthood that eschewed power and privilege, sought justice, focused on service, and questioned tradition and authority.[16]

Of these, the most common theme by far was that the renewed priestly ministry would reject the power that had corrupted the Catholic priesthood. The "Women Called to Ordination," one of the small interest groups formed at the conference, read a statement in which the aspiring priests explicitly stated that they sought ordination "not because we want to exercise power, but because we are motivated by love and a concern for our Church," suggesting that the two ideas were mutually exclusive.[17]

The most compelling voice on this subject was Marie Augusta Neal, who relied heavily on liberation theology in her talk and emphasized the social justice themes so prevalent in the feminism of women religious. Her topic was abuse of power, and it helps demonstrate a distinct religious feminism evident among some (although certainly not all) speakers at the conference. Her piece was a warning to those who would be priests, that they not replicate a priesthood (its "good-will notwithstanding") that celebrates "the life of a social class as if it was the life of the people." She spoke of the world's poverty and Americans' complacency, insisting that a "theology of relinquishment" must be at the center of any renewed priestly ministry. She explained the need for such a theology: "Theology from the point of view of the oppressed suggests a corresponding theology from the point of view of the advantaged, namely, a theology of relinquishment; so that, when the poor reach out to take what is rightfully theirs, there will be some consecrated hands ready and willing to lead the rich assembly in letting go of their hold on the treasures." It should be noted that Neal placed the women gathered in the category of "advantaged," not "oppressed," because she wanted them to recognize that as white women in a prosperous nation they too wield power.

Anne Carr also asked the assembled feminists to put the needs of others first in order to gain a priesthood that would not exert its power as an instrument of oppression. Carr called on all present to be, within the context of the church, "receivers and sharers," without actively seeking power. "In the secular sphere," she explained, "women justly demand equal rights. . . . In the Church it is different. In a certain sense, no one has rights or even powers. The priesthood belongs to the whole church. And all of us, women and men, are receivers and sharers."[18] Here Carr displayed a type of feminism that would have been anathema to most secular feminists, arguing as she did that women in the church should claim no power at all. Carr also asserted that the very act of welcoming women into the priesthood would make it more service-oriented because women "have traditionally only served." Her argument flirts with essentialism, suggesting not only that women are the cultural symbols of service, but also that service is in their nature.

Dorothy Donnelly echoed the theme of relinquishment, asking the assembled to invite "our brother-priests" to give up privilege and power that the church called ministry. "Don't be afraid to die, dear brother—to a role, a function which may no longer need such a form as yours," she said. But she was not finished, because she recommended that "this dying-rising" happen in each of them: "Are we ready to enter into our dying and rising to be people for others on the model of Jesus?"

Not all participants, however, agreed that Catholic feminists should eschew power as a mark of their identity. Margaret Farley recognized excessive humility as an impediment to feminist consciousness and a capitulation to traditional Catholic definitions of womanhood. She insisted that feminist theologians needed to work on a new concept of sin, recognizing women's tendency not to the sin of pride, which the aforementioned speakers seemed to fear, but to the "sin of failure to take responsibility for their lives, for becoming personal selves, for using their freedom to help make a better world."[19] Farley's emphasis was no less on renewed ministry, but her approach placed the objective of women's liberation first, and she reminded the assembly to banish the eternal feminine ideology from the new church they envisioned.

FROM SISTERS TO SISTERHOOD

Attendants at the Detroit conference spent most of their time happily debating how women would transform the priesthood, but the conference's second overall concern, that of establishing sisterhood, should not be overlooked. The Detroit conference provided an opportunity for women to make connections and establish friendships, some of which have abided for more than three decades. But participants raised this theme because sisterhood was viewed as problematic within this group of Catholic women. If the concept of renewed priestly ministry showed the group's unity, the theme of sisterhood showed their deep divisions.

The traditional division between laywomen and women religious had been a concern for the movement since the early seventies. Women religious received hierarchical privilege by virtue of their status. Even though they had little power in the hierarchy to influence their own affairs, they still had more power than laywomen. Many warm relationships existed between laywomen and women religious, and it should be remembered too that many lay Catholic feminists were once themselves women religious. Yet many lay feminists were frustrated by women religious who would not acknowledge their privilege or who could not see their own attachments to the concept of hierarchy. Economic issues also caused bitterness. If laywomen wanted to work in paid parish ministry or in Catholic schools, they usually were paid the same as women religious, who often earned starvation wages. It was also not uncommon for women religious to be given the advantage in hiring. It should be remembered, too, that most of these women had attended Catholic schools, and no matter how they might try to shake it, women religious represented childhood authority figures. "Sometimes you went back to second grade when the nuns looked at you," one feminist remembered.[20]

Tensions between laywomen and women religious were very evident at the Detroit conference. Frances McGillicuddy, cofounder of the sjia-us, was keenly aware of the recent influx of women religious into what had been, until the early seventies, a predominantly lay movement. She wrote a scathing note to her fellow SJIA member (and member of the conference task force) Rosalie Muschal-Reinhardt shortly after the conference: "You're an intelligent woman—I wonder how long before you realize you've been 'had.' You are no threat to nuns but they are your competition, as you will find." Muschal-Reinhardt replied that "In order to be true to me, I will, and I choose to continue to perceive women as my sisters. I strongly believe that it is only in the 'sisterhood' that we can bond together to make church and society an equal place for women and men."[21] When Mary Lynch declined to chair the task force in favor of Dominican sister Nadine Foley, McGillicuddy was furious. She railed against sisters' "take-over" of the movement and their alleged attempt to disguise this fact by trying to make Mary Lynch their front woman. Although McGillicuddy's conspiracy theories were overblown, she did have a point. Of the twenty-one members on the conference task force, only four were laywomen (and one of the four was actually a woman religious in the process of leaving her community). Furthermore, only six of nineteen conference presenters were laywomen.

At issue here was more than a question of salaries or privilege. If women religious dominated the movement's leadership, they would set the movement's agenda. I do not wish to imply that laywomen and women religious had radically different concerns or that both groups were not equally interested in the ordination question. Women religious and laywomen shared the experience of being female in a patriarchal church as well as the desire for justice. I also wish to avoid lumping all laywomen together in one group, suggesting that they all had the same concerns. But it seems clear that the perspectives of the majority of laywomen (i.e., those outside the academy) did not come to the fore.

For many laywomen, concerns about church sexism were local concerns. The vast majority of laywomen did not root their connection to the church in a widespread community of religious or scholars, but in their parishes and families. The tone of the conference papers was often highly theoretical. This was a conference for dreaming dreams and posing the big questions, not for solving such practical local issues as helping women become eucharistic ministers, or get on the finance committee, or confront sexist parish priests, not to mention dealing with a husband threatened by feminism. Laywomen's most immediate experience of church was the parish, yet the Catholic feminist movement rarely addressed parish-specific concerns on a national level in the seventies, and it appeared to give parish-level consciousness-raising a low priority.

Dissatisfaction about how laywomen's concerns were being treated emerged well before the conference began. In January 1975, Bernice Mc-Neela, president of SJIA-US, wrote that "despite claims to the contrary, there has been little progress in the status of women in the church." The majority of laywomen, she argued, were in a worse position since the Second Vatican Council relative to laymen, who now exercised a variety of new ministries, in and outside the liturgy. McNeela stressed that while official rules allowed for women lectors, many parish priests permitted them "on sufferance" or not at all and flatly denied female eucharistic ministers. The situation on the parish level was bleak, yet attendees at this conference on women's ministry did not seem to want to address it.[22]

Only three talks really spoke to laywomen's specific concerns. They were anomalies at the conference and are indicative of two issues that were missing from the movement's agenda: the parish and the family. The first of these talks was by Eleanor Kahle, Toledo's first laywoman pastoral associate and a mother of six. Her talk addressed what she called "earthy" problems. "What will we do with a woman in the rectory?" She asked; "how will the pastor be able to treat a woman as an equal when first he must deal with his own feelings of resentment, animosity, yes, even rage?" Was it vital to talk about the pastor's feelings when justice for women was on the line? Perhaps not, but as someone working in the parish trenches, she knew that pastors must be considered if women priests were to serve there. She urged the assembly to prepare parishes now by getting women into every possible liturgical ministry. Kahle understood the serious local difficulties that ordained women would face and the responsibility of feminists to lay the groundwork in parishes for female priests.[23]

The second talk was by Arlene Swidler, a laywoman involved in nearly every aspect of the movement in the first half of the seventies and an officer in SJIA. She was not violently antireligious like McGillicuddy. In fact, she and McGillicuddy had a very chilly relationship, and she commented in a letter written shortly after the conference that "the nunophobia has bothered me for a while."[24] But in the same letter she easily chronicled the ways in which women religious had been complicit in the oppression of laywomen. In her talk at the conference, Swidler focused on the need for alternative models for ministry that could include laywomen and suggested that perhaps the married couple could be used as such a model. Swidler's talk asked the movement to affirm and promote egalitarian marriage, a major focus of the larger feminist movement but a theme that was practically nonexistent in the Catholic feminist movement. Also absent was nearly any discussion of women's sexuality. So, too, abortion rights, child care, romantic relationships, housework, career and family, homosexuality, or the lay single life. The near exclusion of parish and family concerns from the national movement's agenda may explain Catholic feminists' persistent difficulties in reaching Catholic women in the pews.

Several speakers, including Elisabeth Schüssler Fiorenza and Dorothy Donnelly, mentioned the divisions caused by sisters who did not understand the resentment of laywomen. But the most straightforward statement came from Leonard Swidler, a theologian and a leader of SJIA. He chose not to indict women religious for shutting out laywomen but to invite them to a more just relationship with their lay sisters. He argued that women religious had the responsibility not only to be laywomen's sisters, but also to let them be their own leaders: "It will only be when our sisters, your *lay* sisters, have reached their maturity, have taken their full roles, as leaders as well as followers, in the Church and the world, that your priestly ministry will have begun to be fulfilled. Then it will be true to say, in every sense, "sisterhood is powerful."[25]

It is important to note that most of these voices were associated with SJIA, which fully backed women's ordination but believed its primary constituency—laywomen—was being neglected as the movement reorganized. The relationship between SJIA and WOC, the organization created after the Detroit conference, was cold at best, at least on the national level. As WOC grew in prominence, SJIA receded. It would be up to local chapters and other feminist organizations to raise such questions vital to laywomen. The organization created after the Detroit conference did attempt to diversify, reaching a more balanced level of participation in leadership by laywomen, but other questions about the lack of sisterhood continued to haunt them.

In 1975, Catholic feminists of color publicly challenged the movement for the first time. Latina and African American women religious organized in the early seventies, forming Las Hermanas and the National Black Sisters Conference (NBSC), respectively, to foster solidarity, encourage work for social justice in their own communities, and combat racism in and outside the church. Feminism emerged early in these groups, and was encouraged, but was always secondary to other goals.[26] By 1975, sisters from these groups had become convinced that feminism was a distraction for women religious.

Their challenge began in a dramatic way three months prior to the Detroit conference during the NAWR national assembly, at which five minority sisters (two Latina, one African American, one Native American, and one Filipino American) presented the "Women in Solidarity Panel." These five women offered a resounding critique of women religious in general, and feminist women religious in particular, no doubt stunning not a few of the women assembled. The most evident emotion in the talks was not anger, but resignation. As one remarked, "I believe in your good will, but good will doesn't accomplish everything." In the words of another, "I do not offer any [hope]. I wish that I could because I wish . . . that I could truly again believe in the great power and potential of the American religious woman."[27] Two sisters in particular, Mario Barron and Shawn Copeland, offered comprehensive and powerful criticisms.

Barron's argument confronted women religious with details of their own racism, misguided ministry, and feminism gone awry. Like Leonard Swidler at the Detroit conference, Barron argued that too many women religious wanted to step in as leaders before they understood the people they were supposed to be serving: "You've got to stand under and learn. And then you can serve. If you're looking for a position of leadership then you can't serve us." Barron believed women religious had to accept their role as oppressors and acknowledge their exclusion of women of color, in and outside religious congregations. Finally, Barron warned women religious that feminism could not be their primary agenda. "I'm all for it," she said, but added that the difference between the oppression of women religious and the oppression of Mexican Americans was like the difference between getting hit by a flyswatter and a bulldozer.[28]

Shawn Copeland demanded to know if sisters had faced the consequences of their decisions to leave educational systems for other, more "fulfilling" apostolates, thereby decimating inner-city Catholic schools that served minority populations. Like Barron, she challenged sisters' preoccupation with feminism and wondered at its motivation:

When I see the American religious woman fascinated to exclusion of other matters with an obsession for ordination, then I ask you. "Will you be any kinder to black people? Will you be any kinder to red people, and brown people, and yellow people once the holy oils of Holy Orders have been poured upon you?" I think not. I think not. Once you raise the question in this same area, concern about our interpretations and fascination with Gospel commitment, I want you to think. . . . What kind of people are we encouraging to be poor? To be meek? To be long-suffering? To be patient? And whom are you encouraging to holy anger and sacred impatience?

Copeland echoed the criticisms of laywomen by arguing that women religious needed "a smaller vision for practical action"; for her, this meant looking inward to find the root, the cause of causes—not sexism, but racism. In the end, her tone was one of stony despair, speaking of African American genocide and the inability of the church to do anything about it: "I believed for a long time that the Church was the last possible institution for societal criticism. I believe that no longer."[29]

The result was that the movement (and the ordination conference) did not garner the full support of minority Catholics. Two women religious, Shawn Copeland representing the NBSC and María Iglesias representing Las Hermanas, made brief statements before the assembly at the end of the conference. Las Hermanas expressed its desire to be involved in a coalition seeking women's ordination, but Iglesias spoke with great skepticism. "We talked here about bonding," she said. "We have mentioned justice. If that is what we're about here, this is for us a joyful occasion. I am grateful to be here where such words are spoken." Noting Shawn Copeland standing beside her, Iglesias stated that "the task before me and my sister is not very comfortable." She went on to lament the continued lack of ministry to minorities.[30] Copeland's statement was extremely pointed and brief. Referring to a metaphor that arose in one of the talks, she said simply: "One of the other parts to the story of Joshua is that after the people took the city of Jericho, Yahweh said to them, 'Never build in this place again, a city like this.' So if you go through the walls and you take the city, then don't build the same city again."[31] These short statements were a sobering reminder that not all Catholic feminists believed that this movement would or could serve their interests. In Detroit, sisterhood had its limits.

THAT SPIRIT IS UNDENIABLY LOVE

The final theme, "an emphasis on fidelity to the tradition of Church," was ever-present. The conference shows that Catholic feminists in this period were still deeply committed to being a part of the larger church; they did not yet see themselves as existing outside the institution. From the very beginning members of the conference task force insisted that their hope for the church was "positive and loving" and that they saw the work of the conference as "an expression of the contemporary life of the Church and as a contribution to its future."[32] According to Nadine Foley, task force chair, the one element of consensus throughout the planning process was that "the conference would take place *within* the Church." Indeed, the first mailing about the conference went out to the nation's bishops, then to the major superiors of men and women, and finally to prominent organizations and leaders in the American church.[33]

In fact, at times the conference seemed weighted more toward church renewal than feminism. According to Foley, conference participants gathered to raise the idea of ministry "out of a sense of responsibility for the credibility and effectiveness of the Church today. . . . The issue is not one of 'women's concerns.' It is an issue of *Church*."[34] Elizabeth Carroll's keynote address emphasized the movement's responsibility to challenge the church not with hostility, but with love: "If love is not enhanced in the struggle for ordination of women we may win the battle and lose the war. The war is the renewal of the Church in the Spirit of Jesus. That Spirit is undeniably love."[35] In fact the word "love" was used repeatedly throughout the conference when individuals described their relationship to "the church," although they usually did not mean the institutional church when they made these statements.

The focus on church renewal was natural for feminists who believed that their feminism originated in the Gospels and Catholic social teaching. As Anne Carr asserted, "Some among us maintain that answers to the dilemmas of women are indeed found in the Christian tradition, in its Gospel of reconciliation, its political and liberation thought, its theologies or religious transcendence."[36] Here was a clear statement of commitment to a feminist identity that could not be separated from faith tradition.

That did not mean that Catholic feminists would not take major risks to challenge the church or, in fact, leave it behind. The most prominent theologian at the conference, Rosemary Radford Ruether, asked the group to give serious consideration to whether the church was redeemable and if women really wanted to be a part of it. She also suggested that women had to choose whether they "want or need to be ordained" because "there is good reason to think that the present clerical and institutional structure of a Church so constituted is demonic and itself so opposed to the Gospel that to try to join it is contrary to our very commitments." Rather than doom women to waiting for something that might never come, she encouraged them to believe that "the full life and ministry of the Church of Christ are already ours."[37] Ruether's remarks stood out at this conference, dominated as it was by themes of renewal and love. Her views did not conflict with these themes, per se; she was not a separatist. She simply saw beyond them, predicting a time when Catholic feminists would view themselves less as members of the family and more as "others" on the church's margins.

But this was not yet the case. The Detroit conference was an overwhelming success, bringing the issue into a national media spotlight and inspiring countless women to embrace feminism and the cause of women's ordination. Women left the conference buoyed and ready for action, so it is not surprising that the conference resulted in the creation of a major new organization, the eponymous Women's Ordination Conference. As a group, they were able to articulate what they wanted at the first conference; for the remainder of the decade they would struggle with how to achieve it. Strategy was the next issue on the movement's agenda.

6

making feminism holy

If we experience ourselves as living along an ecclesiastical San Andreas Fault, then, I suggest, we are to pray for its healing.
—Patricia Hughes, "Strategies for Transformation: Healing a Church"

"Women Pray for a Pope Who Will Treat Them as Equals." So read the heading of a 1978 press release from the Catholic Women's Seminary Fund (CWSF), a Maryland-based Catholic feminist organization dedicated to providing financial and moral support for female seminarians. The group announced a eucharistic service on August 27, 1978, during the conclave to choose Pope Paul VI's successor. According to organizers, the goal of this service was "affirming the wholeness of women and calling on the Holy Spirit asking that She guide the Cardinals to select a non-sexist pope." They especially urged all women called to ministry to attend and to pray that the Holy Spirit would produce another pope like John XXIII.

The above statement from CWSF reveals a crucial aspect of Catholic feminism in the mid- to late seventies: as Catholic feminist organizations grew and multiplied, spirituality and political activism intertwined and became increasingly interdependent. CWSF's brief statement is a prime example of this complex relationship. In notifying the media through a press release, CWSF deliberately made their prayer service a political action. Prayer became an act of protest. Moreover, the women of CWSF believed that their prayer—with its acknowledgment of the feminine aspect of God set within the thoroughly Catholic setting of the Mass—could make women whole. But according to their press release, these women claimed their prayer would do more than simply protest their exclusion from leadership or bring them a measure of spiritual fulfillment. They believed their prayer was powerful enough to affect the conclave in Rome. cwsf asserted the power of prayer to advance feminist goals.

This and the following chapter address the strategies Catholic feminist activists employed in the latter half of the seventies to achieve the goals so apparent at the Detroit ordination conference in 1975: gaining women's ordination, renewing Catholic priestly ministry, eliminating sexism in the church and beyond, and building sisterhood. Chapter 7 explores the more overtly political of these strategies, the effort to dialogue with the American Catholic hierarchy. This chapter, however, analyzes a second strategy so clearly exhibited at the cwsf protest outlined above. Catholic feminist liturgy was, on one level, a new means of worshipping God that validated women's spirituality and experience. On a second level it served a number of strategic purposes. First, it acted as a dramatic form of protest directed at the institutional church. Activists also used liturgy as a way to build supportive and creative communities for women. Finally, liturgy was a means of sacralizing feminist activism, a process that aided Catholic feminists as they continued to experience tensions between faith and feminism on the personal and organizational levels.

How are we to interpret the various strategic dimensions of Catholic feminist spirituality found explicitly and implicitly in Catholic feminist liturgies in the latter half of the seventies? No historical studies of Catholic feminist liturgy in the period under consideration have yet been attempted, so we must turn to more recent studies of Catholic feminist liturgy and the larger feminist spirituality movement (with which Catholic feminist liturgy shares some characteristics and participants) to provide a basic framework for analysis. Yet these recent studies, focusing primarily on the eighties and nineties, can take us only so far.

Scholars of feminist prayer and ritual often mark the separatist nature of feminist liturgical communities. Catholic feminist liturgies in later decades were usually designed for the purpose of creating sacred space for communities of women outside the structures of patriarchal institutional religion or as means of strengthening individual feminist spirituality through worship that valued women's experiences. The separatist approach to liturgy reflects the influence of late-seventies' cultural feminism, which encouraged women to form their own networks and institutions in order to minimize the effects of the patriarchy, often rechanneling energies that once were put toward direct political activism. Of course, at some level all feminist liturgy, including separatist liturgy, was political; whether it promoted worship of the goddess or simply asserted the rights of women to assume religious leadership, it stood in direct opposition to male-dominated faith traditions.

But evidence suggests that the majority of Catholic feminist liturgies in the seventies were not separatist. We will not understand the nature of these liturgies if we continue to associate feminist faith practice and ritual with cultural feminism alone. Separatist goals, and the influence of cultural feminism, were certainly present in the Catholic feminist movement of the seventies, but they were not yet dominant. As the cwsf eucharistic liturgy suggests, Catholic feminist liturgies of the seventies retained a liberal feminist orientation. Many were designed explicitly as a form of public political protest, a means of bringing feminist spirituality to bear on the institutional church. By the emergence of the Women-Church movement in the early to mideighties, however, feminist liturgies would reflect the desire of feminists to carve out a separate space along the church's margins and bring to an end fruitless struggles with the institutional church. What came first is worth investigating because the development of a deliberately political liturgy, embedded with cultural feminist elements, can tell us a great deal about the process by which Catholic feminists reconciled Catholicism and feminism in the first decade of organizational activism.

It makes sense that these feminists, as Catholic women, would use communal sacred ritual as a form of protest as well as a means of discerning the relationship between Catholicism and feminism. Catholic prayer and liturgy, usually in communal forms, were where many Catholic women (particularly women religious and former women religious) felt their identities most firmly grounded. As feminist consciousness grew within these women, they became increasingly uncomfortable with male-centered liturgy, but they continued to use Catholic liturgy, in adapted forms, to make sense of their changing identities.

Catholic feminists made liturgy the site of much of their activism because it was where they were most confident, comfortable, and creative; it was uniquely their own. Every feeling, every frustration, every compromise found expression in Catholic feminist liturgy, making it an ideal lens through which to view the movement's development. In ritual, Catholic feminists tried to root their feminism in the Gospels, bemoaned and celebrated their Catholic tradition, affirmed self-worth and the power of women, rejoiced in and limited feminist consciousness, linked their activism to secular feminists, took risks and steps toward radicalization, celebrated and legitimized calls to ministry, commissioned their leaders, disclosed their anger and pain, and protested Catholic and secular acts of discrimination.

But liturgy was also a vital center of activism because Catholic feminists, being largely women of faith who named God as central to their existence, had a powerful need to define feminism as something holy. Feminist sister Helen Wright once speculated that Catholic priests were getting nervous from fear that feminists were trying to "baptize the women's lib movement."[1] In fact, that is exactly what Catholic feminists were doing. If they could not make feminism holy, they could not be feminists. So part of the process of integrating a Catholic feminist identity was linking feminism to the vast array of Catholic sacred symbols, reshaping those symbols to fit their new consciousness when necessary. They also sacralized what were, for them, new symbols, gleaned from ecumenical exploration, goddess worship, women's history, and encounters with people and ideas from ethnic groups, classes, and nationalities other than their own, all of which helped inform their feminist consciousness and their plans for church renewal. Knowing the tensions between feminism and the church, they created a space where it was acceptable to view both feminism and Catholicism as expressions of God, easing the ongoing process of choosing among beliefs and commitments that appeared to be in contradiction. And because so many of their liturgies were also political, Catholic feminists believed they were advancing the feminist cause as they sacralized it.

This process of sacralization can be viewed from two different angles: the process of bringing their unique feminist consciousness to Catholic ritual, during which feminist and Catholic symbols intermingled in worship; and the process of integrating Catholicism into feminist protest, by which Catholic feminists used elements of Catholic ritual to protest sexism within and outside the institutional church. The liturgies reveal that Catholic feminists allowed faith and feminism to influence and shape each other in sacred space, facilitating the growth of Catholic feminist consciousness on the individual and organizational levels and ultimately challenging understandings of worship, protest, and holiness.

My analysis of these liturgies from both angles relies on unpublished archival evidence of liturgies planned and organized by Catholic feminist groups around the country rather than on model liturgies published by feminists at the time.[2] Because of the nature of liturgical celebrations, evidence is scattered and often incomplete. For example, to piece together "Healing a Wounded Church," a major public liturgy celebrated in February 1977 to protest the Vatican's recent teaching against women's ordination, one would need to pull together the liturgy handout in the files of Chicago Catholic Women in Chicago, the homily in the records of the NAWR in South Bend, and a full description of the central rite in a press release from the WOC collection in Milwaukee.[3] Unless planners wrote materials to guide worshippers through the celebration, and someone preserved it, no evidence from that liturgy would likely survive. Nevertheless, the papers of Catholic feminist organizations and individuals are surprisingly rich with evidence of more than eighty feminist liturgies, public and private, celebrated throughout the seventies by laywomen, women religious, laymen, and clergy. Each liturgy included in this study was explicitly feminist, designed to advance the liberation of women or to express support for it. Archival records were augmented by the recollections of my oral history subjects, most of whom participated in Catholic feminist liturgy in the seventies. Let us begin our exploration of Catholic feminist liturgy by first delving into its origins.

ORIGINS AND PARAMETERS

Catholic feminist liturgy was a unique product of the Catholic feminists' movement, but its development was influenced by several other movements, from the liturgical movement and Catholic renewal to secular feminism and the feminist spirituality movement. To begin with the Catholic influences, the use of liturgy as a tool for reform was not a new concept in American Catholicism, but the conscious merging of feminism and liturgy was. The liturgical movement to revitalize Catholic liturgy began in the United States in the twenties but found itself in the spotlight once the liturgical changes mandated by the Second Vatican Council (1962–65) required implementation. The council sparked renewed interest in liturgical experimentation; indeed, reformers viewed a new approach to liturgy as central to the church's renewal. Liturgical reformers hoped that Catholics would find a more relevant, just, and authentic church through new interpretations of eucharistic liturgy. Other reformers in the renewal movement agreed that new experiences of community through liturgy were vital to the church's ongoing development.

Beginning in 1966, directly following the council, reformers eager to bring the council to life experimented with liturgies in communities outside the traditional parish format. These reformers, disgruntled over the hierarchy's slow and cautious implementation of council mandates, decided to experiment in small underground church communities, so-called because news of the liturgical celebrations elicited crackdowns from the hierarchy. The underground church phenomenon, widespread across the United States between 1966 and 1970, provided a forum for modeling a renewed vision of church, liturgical experimentation, and protest and for teasing out the compromises necessary if reformers desired to remain within a flawed church. The underground movement also allowed unprecedented participation by women in the celebration of the Eucharist. Well before women served as liturgical ministers in parishes, women in the underground church served in every liturgical ministry except consecrating the Eucharist.[4]

Yet the underground church should not be considered a consciousness-raising (CR) vehicle for women, although it might have been populated by self-identified feminists.[5] As feminist liturgist Marjorie Procter-Smith has pointed out, the liturgical movement, in which the underground had its roots, differed significantly from the feminist liturgical movement because it sought reform by looking to "the church's liturgical practices of the past," whereas feminists looked at the church's androcentric past with deep suspicion.[6] However, the underground paved the way for a reform movement using separate, small community liturgies for worship, renewal, movement development, and protest. In addition, the most influential minds of the emerging Catholic feminist movement were well aware of the underground. Both Rosemary Radford Ruether and Mary Daly wrote about the underground phenomenon, and Elizabeth Farians participated in the only conference on the underground in 1968 in the midst of her work on the NOW Task Force. She claimed at the time that "women do much better in the underground church than in the established church. That's why they are leaving the establishment and going into the Underground."[7]

But a feminist liturgical movement did not emerge until the Catholic feminist movement became organizationally viable in the early seventies. Two groups, the "new nuns" and the women of the Grail, were crucial in this development because they had within their ranks many liturgical specialists, communities of women with liturgical experience, and they were committed to prayer and liturgy as instruments for communal worship and personal development. These women provided some of the first forums for feminist liturgical experimentation.

Catholic women also needed feminist principles and tools—most especially CR—gained from "secular" feminists to help articulate this new and distinct form of liturgical (and feminist) expression. CR inspired Catholic women, lay and religious, to come together in small groups outside of traditional Catholic institutions to share their experiences of being women within the church. Women religious recognized the power of CR early in the seventies, and the major national organizations for women religious encouraged its spread. It should not be at all surprising that such women would add spiritual and eventually liturgical components to such gatherings.

The flowering of Catholic feminist liturgy at mid-decade also owes much to the advent of cultural feminism, a new trend in the movement beginning around the same time as Catholic feminist liturgy. By 1975, cultural feminism had eclipsed radical feminism in the United States, placing new emphasis on the separate communal celebration of women's space and culture and the building of a network of women's institutions as opposed to radical political agitation for liberation.[8] Catholic feminism was heavily influenced by this development. In particular, Catholic feminist liturgy has much in common with the feminist spirituality movement, a form of cultural feminism focused on women's spirituality that also was coming into its own at mid-decade.

The term "feminist spirituality movement" encompasses myriad forms of goddess worship, neopaganism, and earth/woman-centered worship communities. "Feminist spirituality movement" and "feminist spirituality" are fluid terms, reflecting efforts by spiritual feminists to be inclusive and collaborative. But the concepts can mean very different things to different practitioners and to scholars as well. For example, Catholic feminist theologian Sandra Schneiders defines feminist spirituality as a form of religious expression that includes spiritual feminists from outside patriarchal religion as well as those who retain ties to their faith traditions; her main stipulation for inclusion is that these women have a fully raised feminist consciousness.[9] Sociologist Cynthia Eller, on the other hand, defines the feminist spirituality movement as open to feminists who remain in their traditions but maintains it is distinctly non-Christian (and at times, anti-Christian). "There are Christian and Jewish feminists who consider themselves a part of feminist spirituality, and there is no effort made to exclude such women," she argues. "But though feminist spirituality reaches into synagogues and churches, and parallel movements are happening there, the center is firmly outside, and indeed, sets itself in opposition to traditional religions."[10] With Eller, I would argue that the development of feminist spirituality within Catholic feminism is best considered a "parallel" movement, albeit one that shares much in common with women in the larger feminist spirituality movement.

Catholic feminist liturgy in the seventies shared a similar demographic with the feminist spirituality movement; its participants were generally white, female, middle class, and well educated. In fact, the feminist spirituality movement welcomed many former Catholic feminists into its fold in the midseventies and beyond, so a large number were well-versed in both movements. Several of the major beliefs found in spiritual feminism could be witnessed in Catholic feminist spirituality as well. Most spiritual feminists could agree with Sandra Schneiders's definition of a shared feminist spirituality: "The essence of feminist spirituality, then, is a reclaiming of female power beginning with the likeness of women to the divine, the rehabilitation of the bodily as the very locus of that divine likeness, and the right of women to participate in the shaping of religion and culture, i.e., of the realm of 'spirit.' "[11]

Moreover, Catholic feminists shared spiritual feminists' rejection of patriarchal dualities (i.e., body/spirit), a strong emphasis on memory and imagination, and the desire to reclaim women's past experience.[12] So too, the two groups shared a belief that spirituality is a powerful tool for bringing about change in the cosmos. Nonspiritual feminists often leveled the accusation that spiritual feminists were apolitical, content to retreat into a cocoon of their own making. But it would be a mistake to characterize all spiritual feminists in this way. Like Catholic feminists, they viewed prayer as a form of feminist activism.[13]

Catholic feminist liturgies, particularly those designated as women-only, contained elements that would not be out of place among spiritual feminist rituals. Often these elements were borrowed directly from the feminist spirituality movement or cultural feminists. A striking example can be found in a ritual from the first Women's Ordination Conference in 1975. Cynthia Eller notes that spiritual feminists often began their rituals by "casting the circle," demarcating sacred space and time separate from nonritual space and time. Sacred, or "mythic," time is considered timeless, truly a time apart. Language used at the Detroit conference's blessing ritual is strikingly similar. The leader began, ". . . we draw apart from our historic time symbolized by our change of space and mood, to enter into that mythic time where the central truth of our liberating redemption is both believed and experienced."[14] Catholic women often borrowed such symbols with ease, as in a 1980 prayer service in memory of "Our Foremothers—The Witches."[15] It was also not unusual to see trappings of cultural feminism in Catholic feminist liturgies. Catholic feminist songbooks and liturgy handouts often included the music of Cris Williamson, for example, a lesbian recording artist on the newly founded all-female Olivia Records label.

Catholic feminist spirituality benefited from opening itself to cultural feminism, ecumenism, and goddess spirituality, but it was distinct in the seventies and should not be considered an offshoot of the larger feminist spirituality movement. As far back as 1969–70 Catholic feminists like those in the Deaconess Movement were using spirituality to give their feminism expression and to provide support for their activism. Moreover, the first Catholic feminist protests, devised by Elizabeth Farians as early as 1970, were liturgical in nature. Catholic women—especially women religious—had their own rich history of liturgical experimentation, development, and participation from which to draw. Catholic feminists practiced a spirituality that was increasingly ecumenical but still identifiable as Catholic; liturgies were often eucharistic and contained many elements from the Catholic Mass or devotional practice. Mary appeared frequently in these liturgies, but the goddess rarely did.

Finally, Catholic feminist spirituality was less separatist and far more overtly political than the feminist spirituality movement. Many liturgies in the seventies, particularly at mid-decade, appeared to be open to men, and liturgical gatherings were designed as public protests into the early eighties. Catholic feminists in this period believed they could offer new models for a renewed church as they demanded liberation within the institution. By directing so much of their energy toward protest and reform in the seventies, even to criticize it, they were still strongly tied to the institutional church.

The very first Catholic feminist demonstration was a liturgical protest against clerical sexism and abuse of power. As was mentioned in chapter 3, on Easter Sunday 1969, Elizabeth Farians and the NOW Task Force supported a protest at a Catholic parish in Milwaukee. In previous weeks, the pastor had threatened to deny Communion to any woman who did not cover her head. In response, fifteen women from the parish put on the biggest, gaudiest hats they could find, and as they knelt to receive Communion, they took the hats off and placed them on the rail in front of the sputtering pastor. Although his anger was palpable, he did not deny the women the Eucharist. Elizabeth Farians did not attend the service, but she did handle the media and distribute flyers outside the church for the protest she titled the "Easter Bonnet Rebellion." In the following year, Farians planned liturgies in conjunction with the national women's strike of August 1970.

Once Catholic feminist liturgies began, whether for worship or for protest, they spread quickly. Evidence suggests that Catholic theological schools and Catholic colleges provided early spaces and communities for such liturgies, as did established prayer centers for women, such as the Grail. By 1972–73, liturgies at the LCWR and the NAWR national meetings took on a feminist tone, and SJIA advocated liturgical protest. Catholic feminists were on the move by 1974, building larger networks and meeting face-to-face to organize the movement. Feminists often included prayer and liturgy in such meetings to build a sense of community, witness the power of women's liberation, and provide a common focus on God. Also in 1974, *Sister-celebrations: Nine Worship Experiences*, an influential collection of feminist liturgies from a variety of Christian and Jewish traditions, edited by the Catholic feminist Arlene Swidler, was published. These liturgies served as models for women's groups interested in celebrating and innovating liturgy. By 1975, prayer and liturgy had become major components of nearly every Catholic feminist organization in the country.

Before we can discuss these liturgies in any depth, we must examine what Catholic feminists themselves meant by "liturgy" and, perhaps more vitally, "Eucharist." In the sixties and early seventies the word "liturgy" referred to the Mass; thus feminists often referred to the noneucharistic celebrations they designed as "para-liturgies."[16] However, they gradually adopted the term "liturgy" for these services as well, particularly because they wished to validate worship not sanctioned or celebrated by the institutional church.

Parsing the term "Eucharist" is much trickier. Many liturgies, especially prior to 1977, were clearly eucharistic; they were led by priests and followed the basic format of the Mass. However, the majority of liturgies documented in archival sources were not designed as masses. Of these, most were not eucharistic in character. These liturgies were more along the lines of prayer services whose design followed the needs of the particular community, occasion, and theme.

A minority of documented liturgies (and many more revealed through oral history sources) did feature a central Eucharist or eucharistic themes but without a male presider. Some groups of women substituted new symbols, such as apples, or milk and honey for the bread and wine or wrote new prayers in place of the standard canon. Other women celebrated eucharistic liturgies that followed the basic format of the Mass. One could inquire whether the participants in these liturgies believed they were in fact consecrating the Eucharist, but this line of inquiry, which tries to establish whether or not these liturgies were "illicit" or if the participants believed they were involved in an illicit act, misses the point, as this researcher discovered after interviewing numerous Catholic feminists.

Whether a liturgy was licit or not was of little concern for Catholic feminists who participated in eucharistic liturgies with female or no presiders. Their goal was to redefine the meaning of Eucharist altogether, to create a different model for eucharistic worship that rejected the clerical, hierarchical, and patriarchal elements of the Catholic Mass. According to Ada María Isasi-Díaz and Maureen Hickey Reiff, both of whom actively participated in such liturgies in the seventies, many if not most participants believed that what they were celebrating *was* Eucharist. If they avoided using the sanctioned words of consecration, it was not so much that they feared crossing a line into forbidden territory but rather that they found other forms far more meaningful and less painful. "Mass" was associated with the institution. But Eucharist did not have to be defined by the ritual words uttered by a male priesthood; it could be celebrated as an act of worship, love, and fellowship among women. If you believed, as these women did, that you shared equally in the life and mission of the church by virtue of baptism, then Eucharist need not require an ordained priest, male or female.

Yet Isasi-Díaz also recalled that Catholic feminists rarely raised the question of consecration, leaving it to individual participants to decide whether the group had indeed consecrated the Eucharist or merely blessed and shared bread symbolic of the Eucharist.[17] This tendency to avoid the subject suggests that not all Catholic feminists held the same beliefs on the matter. Reiff remembers that consecration as defined by the institutional church had no meaning for her anymore, so there was little need to discuss definitions of transubstantiation.[18] Undoubtedly, more conservative feminists would have shared in the fellowship of women without believing they had compromised their beliefs in the sanctity of Eucharist because they never considered that consecration had taken place. Ada María Isasi-Díaz believes this omission was in part political. If the issue was avoided by letting each woman believe what she would, participants could celebrate together without divisiveness. You can hear Isasi-Díaz's desire to keep the peace in a 1976 memo to her friend Rosalie Muschal-Reinhardt about an upcoming liturgy at a woc core commission meeting: "Please Ro, nothing controversial."[19]

Finally, even as feminists celebrated eucharistic liturgies among themselves, some feared making such liturgies public. In the mid- to late seventies, when a majority of women in the movement supported efforts to work for change within the institutional church, celebrating large, public eucharistic liturgies without male priests was too risky. Excommunication would not help them reach out to the nation's bishops. So Catholic feminists simultaneously practiced a new way of being church, of celebrating Eucharist that did not require the institution as they worked from within in hopes of renewing the church to the point where it could shed its reliance on rigid hierarchy and clericalism. This dual position, commonly held by Catholic feminists in the mid- to late seventies, caused considerable tension as we shall see.

Feminist liturgies, whatever their type, shared common characteristics, such as spoken and silent prayer, music, homilies and reflections, readings from scripture and secular, often feminist, sources. Liturgists adapted parts of the Catholic Mass to reflect feminist ideals, producing feminist versions of the penitential rite, the prayers of the faithful, the creed, and preface to the eucharistic prayer along with feminist adaptations of the Magnificat, litanies, and blessings.[20] Feminist liturgies often included men, both ordained and lay, who supported the movement, although women usually assumed leadership. When priests presided at a feminist Eucharist, their role was usually minimized. All types of feminist liturgies could be used as protest liturgies, although public protests were more likely to be noneucharistic. Often these noneucharistic liturgies were prayer services, led by women, and structured around readings, music, prayer, and occasionally dramatic pageantry and dance. Others were more like the Mass without the consecration. Another popular form was the public vigil, held to mark a specific event or anniversary.

Regardless of its format, Catholic feminist liturgy retained its primary function, that of all liturgy, to facilitate the encounter between God and community.[21] Catholic feminists used liturgy to bless, protest, discern, play, yell, serve, love, and celebrate. But ultimately faith, the desire to worship God in community, and the commitment to building God's kingdom on earth, drew them to liturgical planning and·practice. As Catholics, liturgy and the sacraments structured life and gave it meaning. For Catholic feminists, the need for communal spirituality was a constant.

BRINGING FEMINISM INTO CATHOLIC RITUAL

When Catholic feminists participated in and created their own liturgies, they were engaged in two different processes: bringing Catholic faith and practice into feminist protest and bringing feminism into Catholic ritual. The latter reveals Catholic feminists' efforts to reconceptualize Catholicism and, indeed, the very nature of holiness itself. Most Catholic women who came of age at midcentury had a very gendered conception of holiness (and the unholy). One feminist's story about women and liturgy in the late fifties shows how the gendered nature of holiness became ingrained. One day at Joan Workmaster's Catholic women's college, a large group of young women gathered for daily Mass. On Sundays, the young sons of the college's caretaker acted as altar servers, but on that day no boys were available, so no one served the priest. A woman religious had prepared the sanctuary for the service and had then taken her place in the sacristy, a room off to the side, attached to the sanctuary.

The only man in attendance was the priest, brought into the college regularly to celebrate the Eucharist. At Communion the priest, an elderly man recovering from heart surgery and suffering from severe glaucoma, came down the sanctuary steps on his way to the Communion rail where the congregation knelt to receive the Eucharist. The gate to the rail had been shut against the congregation before the consecration began. On his way down the steps he missed one and dropped the vessel containing the consecrated hosts, scattering them across the floor. The unfortunate priest dropped to his knees, fumbling to pick up the precious hosts that he could not see; the sister in the sacristy called out directions softly, ("a little to your right, father") until he had collected them all.

No one from the congregation or the sacristy moved. Workmaster, who dates her feminism to the early sixties, remembered feeling a mixture of anger, sadness, and perplexity as she and her classmates looked on in silence, helpless. She never questioned the restrictions that would have allowed a young boy to rush to the priest's aid but that kept her frozen in her seat. Perhaps if we were braver, she recalled, we would have stepped forward and walked through the sanctuary gates. But they were "so convinced of their second-class citizenship," they did nothing.[22] Both men and women were taught to revere the Eucharist; every Catholic child knew that hosts on the floor were a desecration. But none of the women believed that they should show their reverence by assisting the priest. They could not move, because ancient blood taboos dictated that women were unclean and could not approach the altar or touch the host. Inside the sanctuary, women were unholy.

It is true that laymen also could not touch the host, but at the time Workmaster believed that a layman would not have hesitated. As the Vatican later claimed in its 1976 "Declaration on the Question of the Admission of Women to the Ministerial Priesthood," ruling against women priests, something about maleness gave men the exclusive power to stand in the place of Christ. Men were literally elevated and separate; they belonged in an area of the church restricted to their use. For Workmaster and her classmates, women belonged in the pews where they showed their holiness through silent prayer. Following the eternal woman model, holy women were humble, obedient, and self-sacrificing. They were virgins, martyrs, or neither-virgins-nor-martyrs. Holy women bowed their heads and kept silent; they certainly did not storm the sanctuary gates.

But in just a few short years, Catholic feminists would destroy the gender demarcations of Catholic liturgy, redefining holiness for themselves. The first step was proclaiming the sacredness of women. In every way possible, feminists declared that women were holy—their bodies by dancing in sacred space, their intellects by preaching homilies, their vocations by blessing women in ministry, their friendships by celebrating sisterhood, and their foremothers by remembering women's history. Sensitive to the importance of sacred language, Catholic feminists branded exclusive language as unholy, rewriting texts to include women. "Blessed is *she* who comes in the name of the Lord," they said, revolutionizing the Sanctus.[23] They named outspokenness as a holy act, honoring women who refused to be silent. In feminist liturgy, no physical or spiritual barriers said "men only," except—for some—the act of consecrating the Eucharist. And by the late seventies the Eucharist had become the center of intense debate within the Catholic feminist community, precisely because many considered it the ultimate symbol of exclusion.

In the use of space, leadership, and language, feminists tried to live what they called a discipleship of equals. Catholic feminists demonstrated their new understanding of holiness not by replacing men with women in the sanctuary, but by avoiding use of the sanctuary altogether, instead sitting in circles on level ground. If a priest presided, he sat with them, and all worshipers stood around the altar. Catholic feminists also rejected the idea that sacred liturgy should be handed down to communities by male experts. On the contrary, they argued that women could find God in the communal planning process. Reflecting their ties to feminist theory and liberation theology, feminist liturgists valued praxis, the "creative actualization" of liturgy through a collective, practical process of trial and error emerging from individuals and the community.[24] In a very intimate way, then, they placed their female selves into the heart of the liturgies by rooting them in their own experiences of faith as well as oppression.

Just as these feminists sought to validate the sacredness of women, they also tried to affirm the holiness of feminism by explicitly introducing the concept of feminism into Catholic liturgy. They did so not only as an effort to challenge sexism in Catholic worship, but also because they recognized that prayer and liturgy could help Catholic feminists negotiate their divided loyalties. Patricia Hughes, a leader in woc, expressed it succinctly: "If we experience ourselves as living along an ecclesiastical San Andreas Fault, then, I suggest, we are to pray for its healing."[25] How better to affirm these two parts of a woman's identity than to sacralize both in worship with one's community?

Consider "A Liturgy of Liberation" celebrated at the University of Wisconsin's Catholic center in 1974, and its attempt to weave feminism into the fabric of the Catholic Mass. Its title announces the planners' intentions, to celebrate women's liberation in the context of Catholic worship, and participants returned to the theme often throughout the Mass. During the penitential rite, here termed the rite of reconciliation, the celebrant prayed for all women "who in your church and in your world have so often been ignored, patronized, and denied full expression of their gifts and have likewise denied one another." The first reading, Isaiah 61:1–2, spoke of the prophet anointed by the Lord and sent to bring liberty to the captives. The second reading, usually reserved for the epistle, was replaced by a lengthy excerpt from Mary Daly's article "After the Death of God the Father."[26] In the Gospel reading (Luke 4:16–30, which repeats the Isaiah passage above), the congregation heard that "no prophet is ever accepted in his own country." The preface to the consecration began with a blessing upon feminists: "We give you thanks for all who strive to release men and women from bondage . . . . Give clear purpose, imagination, and perseverance to those who in marriage and family life are rethinking traditional roles and seeking fresh vitality." The Mass's closing prayer asked the congregants to affirm that "becoming more fully human means less weeping and more raising my voice against dehumanizing forces." By weaving feminism into the Mass—explicitly drawing parallels to the Gospels—Catholic feminists made it visible and sacred, providing the ritual a form of validation that the institutional church refused to offer.[27]

Like the earliest Catholic feminist writers of the sixties who pursued a dual strategy of scrutinizing Catholic tradition for misogyny while also searching for redeeming facets of the same tradition, feminists in the seventies brought a similar approach to liturgy, confronting and honoring different aspects of the tradition to suit their own purposes. In 1973, for example, a group of feminists designed a Mass in response to a seminary study day themed "How to Make Our Tradition Work for Us." To begin the liturgy, each prayer outlined a church father's misogynist teaching ("From the tradition of Tertullian, who called women 'the devil's gateway' ") followed by the response, "Free us, O Lord."[28]

Catholic feminists rewrote all parts of the Mass, including the consecration, to rid them of sexist elements and to affirm feminism. But they did so without rejecting the tradition wholesale. A group celebrating a "feminist agape service" in 1979 lifted apples and wine in blessing, paralleling eucharistic consecration: "This is the apple of knowledge, the risk and gift of consciousness-raising, through which our eyes are opened to oppression and injustice."[29] This adaptation is particularly pointed when you consider that the participants were affirming Eve and her act of defiance (chosen as the symbol of feminist consciousness) in the manner that Catholics used to remember Christ's redemption of humanity from Adam and Eve's sin. Yet this service was not anti-Christian or anti-Catholic. In the "Blessings on Apples and Wine" organizers proclaimed, "Thanks to Jesus Christ we have all, women and men, workers and owners, been given a chance to restore again that good earth of milk and honey which is our promised inheritance and to live together in Peace and Justice." The worshippers also prayed a distinctly Catholic prayer, the litany, albeit one that included such saints as the abolitionist Sarah Grimké and the early-twentieth-century radical Emma Goldman.

But the best and most common example of feminists turning Catholic androcentric tradition into messages of liberation was feminist reinterpretations of Mary.[30] Unlike Catholic feminists of the sixties, feminists of the seventies were removed from eternal woman rhetoric and therefore were less ambivalent about Mary, adopting her as a symbol of courage, faith, and even liberation. A member of SJIA-US went so far as to christen her "Our Lady Queen of Feminists."[31]

But feminists were not inclined to adopt the Blessed Mother of their childhoods as a symbol of liberation; her image required reinterpretation. For instance, the psalm used in the 1973 seminary study day Mass cited above was an original poem based on the concept of Mary's fiat (*fiat mihi*):

> . . . You answered alone
> you did not run
> to Joseph or Anne
> or the temple men
>
> Fiat. It may be done to me.
>
> you answered alone
> yet you are the one they claim as a model
> to keep us from
>
> answering
> alone.
>
> Fiat. It may be done to me.[32]

The author interposed the first two words of Mary's fiat ("may it" to "it may"). Instead of submission, Mary's words now connoted permission. Contrary to a traditional reading of Mary's fiat as passive, feminists claimed Mary as a heroine who took her destiny into her own hands.

No prayer had more resonance for Catholic feminists than the Magnificat, Mary's prayer to God during her visit to her cousin Elizabeth. Feminists often incorporated the Magnificat in their liturgies, a woman's prayer for justice with no permanent place in the Catholic Mass. The traditional prayer from Luke 1:46–55, reads:

> My soul magnifies the Lord, and my spirit rejoices in God my Savior, for he has looked with favor on the lowliness of his servant. Surely, from now on all generations will call me blessed; for the Mighty One has done great things for me, and holy is his name. His mercy is for those who fear him from generation to generation. He has shown strength with his arm; he has scattered the proud in the thoughts of their hearts. He has brought down the powerful from their thrones and lifted up the lowly; he has

filled the hungry with good things, and sent the rich away empty. He has helped his servant Israel, in remembrance of his mercy, according to the promise he made to our ancestors, to Abraham and to his descendants forever.

The prayer was used by feminists in its traditional form, or adapted to eliminate exclusive language, or rewritten to stress further liberation and justice. A liturgy from the 1978 LCWR national assembly showcased the latter emphases. Taking on Mary's voice and turning it into a cry of liberation, the assembly prayed, "My soul sees the land of freedom and my spirit will be delivered from fear. . . . we shall become fully human as awaited by generations before us who were sacrificed."

The LCWR's use of the Magnificat also illustrates Catholic feminists' concern with social justice, a concept that, as we have seen, was at the heart of many Catholic feminists' self-understanding. Clearly Catholic feminist liturgies had more purposes than affirming feminism or challenging the hierarchy. This ancient prayer is a song of joy and praise to God but also a powerful affirmation of justice: "He has shown strength with his arm; he has scattered the proud. . . . He has brought down the powerful from their thrones and lifted up the lowly." The LCWR divided its Magnificat into sections, designating parts to be read by women and men representing the First and Third Worlds. First and Third World men read the original versions while the women of each group read the revisions. The First World group prayed the words of liberation and rejoicing; the Third World group spoke the prayer of justice. All concluded the prayer by dedicating their lives to the ministry of social justice: "We are women and men freed by Christ. We stretch out our hands to all our brothers and sisters especially the oppressed, the poor; and we pledge ourselves to equality, dignity, freedom for all persons in a world which will become the kingdom when all people will be free."[33] Catholic feminists from across the spectrum linked personal liberation with social justice, to inspire action. Liturgy provided infinite possibilities to establish these links and inspire women to build the kingdom on earth.

Catholic feminist liturgy could also make concrete the relationship between feminist consciousness and personal calls to ministry. Many women discovered both at the same time; others became feminists after ministry was denied them. Either way, both the call and the awareness of a woman's right to pursue that call were labeled as holy. One 1976 liturgy entitled

"Seeking Wholeness" at the Paulist Center Community in Boston offered Catherine of Siena and Mary Magdalene as models of women unsure of their own worth who found their dignity when asked by God to minister in the world. Readings, reflections, and prayers encouraged the gathered women to envision themselves as God's servants called, like Mary and Catherine, "to share new life and to participate with [Christ] in bringing new life to others."[34]

One of feminist liturgy's most important functions in this period, particularly after 1975, was to validate women's calls to ordained ministry. By the mid- to late seventies, women graduating from divinity schools and diaconate programs expressed pain at being prepared to minister in a church that would not receive them. The more liberal programs tried to include women in special liturgies or mention them in ordination ceremonies. Occasionally during the ceremony an ordinand would speak out against the injustice of excluding women or recognize the women seminarians present. While well-intentioned, these occasions often caused additional pain because they illustrated women's exclusion within the context of communal prayer. Since the church had no liturgies to bless these women, feminists created liturgies of their own.

The Detroit woc conference in 1975 celebrated "The Love of Christ Leaves Us No Choice: A Liturgy of Blessing," the first major liturgy designed to acknowledge and bless women called to priesthood. Others followed, some within congregations of women religious in commissioning one of their own sisters, others for mixed groups of laywomen and women religious. In 1976, when psychologist and feminist woman religious Fran Ferder began her project to interview one hundred women who sought ordination, the names were presented to her and her team in the context of a eucharistic liturgy. Women with calls were often given special roles in liturgies, as in the case of the Mass held to open woc's new national office in 1977; aspirants were given holy water and asked to bless the office.[35] Yet the Mass was still celebrated by Bill Callahan, a priest with strong ties to Catholic feminists in the Washington, D.C., area, where the office was located.

But soon the decision of whether or not to have a priest presider would cause considerable tension in the movement and reveal unresolved ambivalence toward the institutional church. Did celebrating the Eucharist with a male presider indicate a lack of feminist consciousness or collusion with the institution? How could feminists receive the Eucharist when the androcentric nature of the ritual made their stomachs churn? Should feminists model sisterhood by holding separatist liturgies? Reactions to these issues help explain why many feminists eventually chose to cut ties with the institutional church and/or the Catholic feminist movement; these debates will be discussed in the following section.

But overall, it's surprising how regularly Catholic feminists affirmed their commitment to the institutional church. They did so not by pledging support to the bishops, but by reaffirming their commitment to the renewal process. The liturgies of the first WOC conference are a case in point. Planners designed the liturgies as part of the task force's larger objectives for the conference: "to bring the theological issue of ordination of women to public discussion and prayer in the Roman Catholic Church."[36] In the "Liturgy of Blessing" a reader proclaimed, "Tonight we anticipate the season of Advent in a celebration of the Word living in us as Church. . . . We celebrate as a church in process, engendering the future."[37] The commitment to renewal, a "church in process," was celebrated throughout the weekend.

With this affirmation of Catholic feminists' commitment to renewal, the planning process and the liturgies themselves showed that conference organizers tried to include the hierarchy and a mixed group of women and men in the conference liturgies. In addition, by being nonconfrontational and relatively conservative, they signaled their desire to work within the existing system and transform the church from the inside out. The liturgy committee decided to celebrate a Sunday Mass, "Sure as the Dawn Is His Coming," instead of a noneucharistic liturgy presided over by women. To illustrate further their commitment to renewal, they invited Jean Jadot, the apostolic delegate, to celebrate. When he refused, they asked the NCCB, and when the bishops declined, the committee chose a supportive priest who, nevertheless, insisted on preserving liturgical norms, including exclusive language. For the large ceremony of blessing on Saturday evening, they ritualized the call to ministry by having the congregants bless each aspirant. Collins revealed that they specifically avoided any gesture that looked like the laying on of hands because they did not want the ritual to appear as a "pseudo-ordination."[38]

The majority of liturgies from the seventies, including the protest liturgies, expressed either an explicit or implicit desire to continue the struggle for liberation within the church, as with the following prayer from a vigil protest on the steps of the U.S. Catholic Conference headquarters, the home of the NCCB in Washington, D.C., on the occasion of the National ERA March in 1977: "We are trying to understand. We are trying to live out your call to us. Touch our hearts. Take away our fears and those of our bishops, our priests, and our brothers and sisters among the people. May we loosen our fastened tradition of unequal sharing of responsibility and ministry in our church, so that your Spirit may work in freedom, to bring forth new treasures of love and understanding. We ask this in your name, O Lord."[39] This prayer was typical in that participants simultaneously expressed their loyalty, criticized the church, and admitted their own limitations. Such a combination indicates the flexibility of liturgical worship and its capacity to express the complex beliefs of Catholic feminists.

BRINGING CATHOLIC RITUAL INTO FEMINIST PROTEST

The September 1979 issue of *Rising Up*, newsletter of the Catholic feminist lobbying group Catholics Act for ERA, featured Susan B. Anthony on its cover—not the suffragist, but her great-niece and namesake. The modern Susan B. Anthony was not only an ardent supporter of the Equal Rights Amendment, she was also a devout Catholic. Anthony told the newsletter's readers that, in addition to her extensive lobbying activities, she regularly prayed and fasted for an extension of the deadline to ratify the amendment. She noted that the vote for extension fell on the feast of the Assumption, a Marian feast day, and so Anthony stayed after Mass to pray the Litany of the Virgin, a prayer referring to Mary as the "mirror of justice." Susan B. Anthony encouraged everyone to take action: "Let us leave no prayer unprayed, no forum uncovered, no legislator unvisited, until we gain the equality promised us of old."[40] In the midst of her public activism for an ostensibly secular cause, Anthony could not contain her Catholic worldview, nor did she think she needed to; on the contrary, she believed it would help the cause. So did the editors of the newsletter, who chose the second Susan B. Anthony as a symbol precisely because she explicitly linked her Catholicism and her feminist activism.

Just as Catholic feminists tried to integrate feminism into Catholicism through liturgy, they also did the reverse: use Catholic liturgy to shape their identities as feminists. Nowhere was that more apparent than in protest liturgy, when Catholic feminists revealed their joint identities in public activism. From the midseventies through 1980, the movement chose a form of protest unique to its own traditions and agendas. The political demonstration of choice for this movement was not the sit-in or the protest march, but liturgy: masses, vigils, and prayer services. These served

Marjorie Tuite at a liturgical protest (Courtesy of the Women and Leadership Archives, Loyola University Chicago: Marjorie Tuite Papers)

multiple purposes, from self-expression, consciousness-raising and publicity to building sisterhood, confronting the hierarchy, and connecting with the larger feminist movement. That they chose these forms indicates that Catholic feminists believed their protest was most powerful when it was linked to their faith tradition and thus was most indicative of who they were. Therefore, public protest liturgy gives us another opportunity to examine joint Catholic-feminist identities.

But first, a clarification: while liturgy was the preferred form of public protest for Catholic feminists, it should be remembered that most Catholic feminist activism was not organized public protest. Most such activism took the form of organizational meetings, lobbying activities, networking, planning, letter writing, speech making, and theological research and writing. Not every Catholic feminist would have participated in these liturgies, either, although most probably did at one time or another. Moreover, there is no way of knowing what proportion of Catholic feminist liturgies was designed for public protest. Yet the majority of Catholic feminists' public protests took some liturgical form, be it prayers, ritual, or Mass. Through liturgy they rallied for the ERA and protested the Vatican's "Declaration" against women's ordination and Pope John Paul II's visit in 1979. On several occasions, Catholic feminist liturgies did turn into protests after activists were denied access to a Catholic church. "They probably wouldn't have let Jesus in either," someone remarked at one such event.[41]

So what can protest liturgy tell us about Catholic feminists' feminist identity? First of all, their choice to express themselves through liturgy in public forums indicates their belief that feminism was flexible enough to encompass such activism. There is no evidence to suggest that Catholic feminists doubted the fact that they were feminists or that their particular brand of activism was unacceptable to the larger movement. In fact, they seemed certain that feminism benefited from this liturgical approach, an approach they helped to innovate but that was shared by other feminist women of faith in the seventies.

Catholic feminists also contributed to the larger feminist agenda by publicly challenging the institutional Catholic Church, one of the greatest enemies of the larger movement. But for them this was not enough. They also needed to demonstrate that they had a right to call for and participate in the reform of their own tradition, a right they demanded throughout the seventies. They demonstrated to other feminists that reform was a viable option, and in their view of feminism, feminists need not cede their rights to reform by leaving their traditions behind. Obviously, many did leave the institution behind, but the ones who stayed were quite vocal on this point until the late seventies.

Catholic feminists also believed they aided the cause by publicly praying for an end to oppression. Their faith tradition taught them that prayer had power, and so they naturally believed that prayer could advance a feminist agenda and could rally other women to the movement. Therefore, they regularly exhorted feminists to offer prayers for the success of the movement. "We must pray together" a member of the feminist group Chicago Catholic Women suggested. "Women in [the] Gospel[s] acted in faith in face of overwhelming defeat, despair, and received miracles in return."[42] When the Women's Rights Committee of the National Association of Laymen initially met, their first order of business was to plan a liturgy "with the success of the Feminist movement as its special intention. It occurred to us that we have done everything but pray for ourselves."[43] Catholic feminists were believers and thought they could contribute to the movement by entreating God (who they believed was feminist anyway) to bless their struggle.

Catholic feminists also realized that one of their primary tasks as feminists, and one of the ways they contributed best to the movement, was consciousness-raising among Catholic women. Those who promoted CR figured out quite early that protest liturgy was one of the most powerful tools for raising the consciousness of Catholic women. They knew that Catholic liturgical symbols were deeply engrained and rich with meaning and that, if manipulated even slightly, they could provoke a powerful response that went straight to the heart of Catholic women.

Take for example a liturgy at the 1976 NAWR national assembly. This liturgy, called simply "The Liturgy of the Word" (the label traditionally given to the first half of the Mass), was attended by laywomen and women religious and was designed both as a protest and a CR experience. Three women (including Anita Caspary, leader of the Los Angeles IHM community that became a noncanonical community in 1968) presided at the liturgy and were specifically labeled celebrants. Planners used inclusive language throughout and facilitated a shared homily, but otherwise this was a standard eucharistic celebration. At the offertory, members of the congregation brought up the gifts of bread and wine and laid them on the altar, the celebrant said the preface to the eucharistic prayer, and the congregation followed it with the Sanctus (Holy, Holy, Holy . . .). Then a dramatic silence; the liturgy had ended.

Caspary explained the silence after the liturgy: "We didn't intend the silence to be so long after the offering. But it extended and seemed to have such weight and brought such sorrow. I didn't expect the silence to become so great with longing for a completion of the ceremony; I didn't expect it to be such a sad experience." Just by stopping the Mass at the point when women were forbidden to participate, the organizers opened an abyss of sadness and pain perhaps never recognized before. Even Caspary, who by then was long familiar with institutional oppression and feminist responses to it, was shocked by the power of this liturgy to move Catholic women.[44] This was consciousness-raising based in cultural understanding. Some of these women, most of them women religious, may have felt uncomfortable or unwelcome in typically middle-class CR sessions focusing on marriage, family, and sexuality. Even laywomen who would have fit into such traditional CR groups still benefited from efforts to reach them through the language of religion. Catholic women understood that Catholicism was more than an impediment to justice; it might also be the key to unlocking a feminist consciousness within women who considered themselves women of faith.

The feminism revealed by these Catholic feminist protest liturgies was complex and contradicts a one-dimensional portrayal of feminist motivations and sensibilities. One would be forgiven for being confused by their rhetoric. In the same service Catholic feminists might rail against the institutional church, speak about the power of sisterhood, earnestly proclaim their desire for reconciliation with the hierarchy, and pray for forgiveness of their own sins. The conflicting desires for separation and reconciliation, celebration and mourning, were often in tension within these women. These themes will arise many times in the following chapters as we follow the movement's transition in the latter half of the decade.

But no matter their inner turmoil, it seems clear that Catholicism was the language they usually chose to express themselves in public, and it should be made clear that they did so without mockery. Perhaps some believed this liturgical language would help them find common ground with members of the hierarchy; others thought their use of it might provoke those in power; still others supposed it could best express their conflicted emotions, inspire them, provide a community, or bring them a measure of solace. But I have yet to find evidence of Catholic feminists using Catholic symbols in a way that was insincere or intentionally sacrilegious. They might have used Catholic liturgical forms with great fury to illustrate the hierarchy's hypocrisy, such as the "Creed of Anger" chanted at a Washington, D.C., liturgy in 1977 to protest the "Declaration" against women's ordination, but they did so as believers who had no desire to be profane.

Actually, their protests were more often quiet, prayerful affairs and surprisingly nonconfrontational. The majority of the liturgies did not appear to have been designed to shock. Catholic feminist protesters often made a point of saying that their focus was prayer, not confrontation. An organizer of the New York WOC demonstration at the time of the pope's 1979 U.S. visit remarked that the press was "disappointed by our uncontroversial attitude. . . . we were simply testifying in solidarity with the eucharistic ministers excluded from the papal ceremonies."[45]

Yet the quietness of their protests should not obscure the power dynamics underlying these demonstrations. By adopting liturgical forms, Catholic feminists asserted their rights. The institutional church denied their right to celebrate liturgy when it restricted the priesthood to men; therefore, the simple act of celebrating liturgy in public was political and, for many, exhilarating. "Tonight we are witnessing that we have that firm sense of conviction; as we stand together, strong, united, with courage, we call for action on behalf of justice for women in the church," a group of Iowa Catholic feminists proclaimed at a liturgy in 1979. Later, they lifted their arms to pronounce a blessing over their cause and themselves. If the church denied them its blessing, then they would take that power into their hands.[46]

Their liturgies also reveal a very strong desire to connect with the larger feminist movement, including and especially secular feminists. Recall Catholics Act for ERA's effort to connect itself with Susan B. Anthony, one of the mothers of American feminism. Many of the protest liturgies seemed designed to connect the sacredness of the liturgy, for example, with the collective memory of the secular movement. The Boston chapter of WOC celebrated such a protest liturgy to mark the pope's 1979 visit. Boston WOC mixed scripture with women's history, producing a new version of the Declaration of Sentiments, the document written for the first American women's rights convention in 1848. They read Isaiah next to Susan Brownmiller next to Adrienne Rich, sang the Song of Miriam next to Cris Williamson's "Song of the Soul" and the old women's labor protest ballad "Bread and Roses." Most significantly, they blessed and broke bread together as participants chanted a feminist litany including Miriam and Priscilla, Anne Hutchinson, Phyllis Wheatley, Sojourner Truth, Elizabeth Cady Stanton, Susan B. Anthony, Harriet Tubman, Fannie Lou Hamer, and the American Catholic saint Elizabeth Seton. Just as in the case of the feminist agape in 1979, they asked for the blessing of feminists during an act of consecration that sacralized feminism.[47]

However, the process of bringing Catholicism into feminist protest also illustrates how torn many of these women felt when they believed they had to choose, even symbolically, between feminism and the church. This, too, was an aspect of their feminist identity, the feeling of being torn asunder. For some, liturgy only deepened this "ecclesiastical San Andreas Fault." The conflict among and within Catholic feminists over eucharistic liturgies best demonstrates this tension.

The Eucharist posed an enormous problem for Catholic feminists. It was the central symbol and ritual of the Catholic faith and therefore held a great

woc liturgy, 1978 national conference, Baltimore, Maryland
(Courtesy of the Marquette University Archives)

deal of meaning for most of these women, some of whom attended Mass every day. Long familiar with Catholic teaching, they would have understood Eucharist as more than the symbol of Christ's redemption of humanity. It was also the ultimate symbol of unity in the Catholic faith, the purpose of gathering community together (literally, "communion"). So, too, the act of consecrating the Eucharist encouraged the preservation of memory and shared history ("Do this in memory of me"). Beyond that, Eucharist was also associated with sustenance. The absence of it led many believers to describe their longing for it as a deep hunger. Anita Caspary, leader of the liturgical CR that cut the Mass in half, believed the exercise worked precisely because without the Eucharist, "the emptiness you're left with is traumatic."

Yet many feminists came to view the Mass, and particularly the consecration, as an androcentric ritual, focused on and performed by a man. Most feminists objected to gender-exclusive language and the all-male priesthood, but some also reacted against the Christocentric nature of the celebration. Regardless, the advent of feminist consciousness could make sitting through the Mass an unbearably painful exercise. Even those whose yearning for the Eucharist was acute when they stayed away could not find peace when they attended. The ultimate symbol of unity became a site for broken-ness and division.

This could be viewed as a personal, spiritual problem, but it was also a deeply political one as the seventies progressed. At both the 1975 and the 1978 WOC conference conflict ensued over the question of whether to cele-brate the Eucharist with a male presider (allowing for the sense of unity that the Eucharist was meant to provide and including their male allies in the movement) or plan a noneucharistic liturgy for women only (which might be exclusive but perhaps more empowering for women). Bound up in these debates was a question of radicalism. What was too radical? What was not radical enough? Having a male priest introduce themes of liberation into the eucharistic prayer? Creating a separate liturgy for women only? Having feminists say an adapted form of the consecration with different words or elements? Encouraging nonordained women to consecrate the Eucharist? For a large group of ideologically diverse women whose goals ranged from female empowerment to dialoguing with Roman Catholic bishops, these were not easy questions to answer.

Disagreement over feminist eucharistic liturgies arose before the first feminist protest liturgies were even celebrated. In 1968, Rosemary Rad-ford Ruether sent a memo to Elizabeth Farians outlining some ideas for a proposed ecumenical, liturgical protest against sexism in the Christian churches, although there would "be an emphasis on the Catholic situation as the worst example of them all." Ruether suggested burning offensive pages from canon law in a censor, the traditional vessel for incense (fore-shadowing Farians's "Pink and Ash" demonstration several years later), followed by "a very simple concelebrated agape with an ordained Protestant woman and two Catholic women theologians." Farians objected to this last aspect of the proposal, however. "The burning is just *rite*," she replied, "but I think the agape or eucharist might be counter-productive. We might be accused of 'using' the sacred." Arlene Swidler agreed, wondering if "the communion part seems self-destructive."[48]

As the seventies progressed and Catholic feminists became both more practiced in liturgy and more radicalized, Catholic feminists developed a number of different, often ad hoc options for handling these internal and external conflicts, and not all succeeded in calming tensions. New York WOC struggled over whether or not to have a Mass for its protest of the pope's visit. In the end they chose a Mass, because they did not know how to "replace the greatest sign of Love."[49] A year earlier, a group of feminists at the 1978 woc convention designed their own all-female liturgy to take place at the same time as the planned all-conference eucharistic liturgy, a move designed in part to press the issue. This choice over liturgy forced women to make what at least one feminist believed was a symbolic choice between women and the institutional church.[50]

As we have seen, liturgy could also magnify the distance between feminism and institutional Catholicism and among feminists on a political continuum between loyal opposition and radicalism. Tensions over liturgy could force Catholic feminists to decide which side of the fault line they should be on. However, liturgy proved to be more unifying and empowering than divisive and destructive. It could and did facilitate the healing of the fault lines running through Catholic feminists' identities. It provided a means of sacralizing this new feminist consciousness they were experiencing, so they might weigh feminism as an aspect of faith, not an enemy of it. Liturgy strengthened communities of women and made their determination visible to the world through public protest. Ultimately, liturgy provided the space where feminists could challenge, compromise, commune, and create as they nurtured the faith that gave them strength and their lives purpose.

7

a matter of
conversion

Said simply, it's a matter of conversion. . . . Their words and our wounds, our words
and their wounds . . . words and wounds uniting us in a call for conversion. But who
are *we* and who are *they*? And when we speak this language of division, when we
need to name the enemy, then, most especially then, are we not crying out for
conversion?
—Patricia Hughes "Healing a Wounded Church"

When I first came across the above passage, an excerpt from a homily given
by the Catholic feminist Patricia Hughes, I found it perplexing.[1] Hughes's
stress on mutual conversion and reconciliation for "we" (Catholic feminists) and "they" (the Roman Catholic hierarchy) was not unusual rhetoric
for a Catholic feminist. Such an approach would have fit in quite well at the
first women's ordination conference in 1975, when reconciliation and renewal were dominant themes. What caught my attention, however, was not
what Hughes said, but *when* she said it. Hughes preached this homily at a
Chicago prayer service entitled "Healing a Wounded Church," held on
February 27, 1977, when American Catholic feminists gathered to protest
the Vatican's definitive prohibition of women's ordination, the "Declaration
on the Question of the Admission of Women to the Ministerial Priesthood,"
an encyclical read in Rome in October 1976.

In fact, I soon discovered that Hughes's response was not unique. In the
year following the release of the "Declaration," American Catholic feminists

confronted the document with an awkward, hybrid rhetoric of rage and reconciliation coupled with renewed calls for dialogue. After running into the wall of definitive Catholic teaching, Catholic feminists continued to offer themselves for what could only be a very one-sided conversation. While we might expect the women of the Catholic feminist movement to begin distancing themselves from the institutional church immediately after the release of the "Declaration"—a document many found not simply illogical and unjust, but insulting—the movement as a whole clearly did not do so. Why would these feminists rush to counsel reconciliation with a church that had, in their view, just proved the extent of its indifference to women's concerns? Moreover, how are we to understand this phenomenon when it seemed to pass so quickly? The widespread commitment to reconciliation and dialogue in 1977 stands in stark contrast to the final two years of the decade, when the movement began to abandon the rhetoric of reconciliation and members of the movement's leadership openly questioned continued affiliation with the institutional church.

The 1976 release of the "Declaration" (and feminists' response to it) can be read as a pivotal event between the two women's ordination conferences of the seventies, both markers of the movement's attitude at the time. The largely hopeful and united Detroit conference in 1975 was followed in 1978 by a second conference marked by disparate approaches and increased radicalism. A major question in the history of American Catholic feminism, then, is how and why the movement changed so dramatically in three years. Reading the "Declaration" as the pivot point between the two conferences answers the question because it gives the opportunity to analyze the development of religious feminist consciousness in detail, both in individuals and organizations. The process of feminist consciousness, the negotiation among competing worldviews and desires, was on display on a grand scale in the year following the release of the "Declaration" as Catholic feminists attempted to balance commitments to church renewal with an overwhelming sense of betrayal.

What it tells us is that many Catholic feminists were indeed undergoing a process that would lead them away from the institutional church. But the experiences of that year remind us that we need to take their negotiation process seriously. The leaders of the Catholic feminist movement were reluctant to cut ties with the institution. In Detroit they had revealed an abiding love for the church, a love that compelled them to keep trying to reconcile with the institution and to convert the hierarchy to a feminist worldview. When Catholic feminists cried out for reconciliation, they sought more than peace between the church and feminism; they sought a personal reconciliation of their loves and commitments when events indicated they had to choose one over the other. Having always maintained that Catholicism and feminism were derived from the same source in the Gospels, they refused to do so. In time, the refusal to choose became untenable for many, and large numbers pulled away from the institution. But the initial impulse demonstrates the strong hope that one could embrace both a feminist consciousness and a full commitment to the Catholic Church without sacrificing either.

At the Detroit conference, the assembly collectively expressed what they wanted for the church and priesthood. In the two years that followed that meeting, the growing movement created strategies to achieve those goals. As we have already seen, the development of liturgy as a means of protesting church sexism, sacralizing feminism, and creating supportive communities for women was one of these strategies. Other strategies were financial, such as the formation of the CWSF to support women in seminaries. In addition, WOC and the Quixote Center, an organization for justice activism, tried unsuccessfully for years to get women to buy "funny money" (adorned with a picture of St. Therese of the Little Flower who aspired to the priesthood) from the organizations and drop it into their parish collections in lieu of a regular contribution. Still other strategies focused on ecumenical cooperation among religious feminists; many Catholic feminist activists (and certainly activist/scholars) worked extensively with religious feminists outside of Catholicism through such groups as NCAN's Institute for Women Today, Church Women United, the NOW Task Force on Women and Religion, and the Women's Caucus of the American Academy of Religion.

But by far the most prominent strategy for fulfilling Catholic feminist goals was "dialogue," the commitment to connect with members of the hierarchy and convert them to the feminist cause. Having invested considerable energy in the dialogue strategy, movement leaders were unlikely to abandon it quickly, even after receiving news about the "Declaration." The continued use of the dialogue strategy helps explain the extraordinary, if temporary, response to the Vatican teaching. In turn, the pain feminists felt as they processed the document explains why so many pulled away from the institution in the years following.

THE DIALOGUE STRATEGY

To better understand the dialogue strategy, we must begin by defining terms. In theory, "dialogue" is a process by which parties from differing groups meet together to listen to each others' perspectives and share their own in an atmosphere of tolerance and mutual respect.[2] In doing so, the parties may not be convinced by each others' way of thinking, but they hopefully gain a sense of their opponent's humanity, easing feelings of antagonism and the threat of violence. Dialogue is also, by its nature, open-ended and nonbinding.

Dialogue was vital to Catholic feminists' self-understanding as activists. By committing themselves to the dialogue process, Catholic feminists hoped to show that they were open and honest, committed to free exchange and egalitarianism. Sitting down at the dialogue table demonstrated their belief that power should be shared. Through dialogue they registered their desire to engage with the church, including the hierarchical institution, but also their determination to have their voices heard. They would attempt to convert the male Catholic leadership to women's liberation not only through confrontation—which still played a major role in the movement—but through rational dialogue and strategic kindness. Dialogue also fit well with a praxis model because it affirmed the value of individual experience; in this period, leaders in the movement believed that making personal contact with members of the hierarchy for the purpose of sharing one's experience of being female in the church could have a transformative effect.

So they believed dialogue gave them the opportunity to be good feminists and good Christians at the same time. This explains, then, their preoccupation with the concept. In the papers of Catholic feminist individuals and organizations throughout the seventies, but particularly 1975–78, references to dialogue are ubiquitous. Catholic feminists were determined to make contact with the bishops and be heard. In 1975, SJIA urged its members to take the organization's materials to their local diocese offices and have a "heart-to-heart" with their bishop. "We . . . attempt to dialogue with Bishops whenever and where ever possible," the group stated in that year's promotional material, although they admitted that "so far we can report no outward signs of inward conversion." After the Detroit conference, WOC urged attendees to take what they had learned back to their dioceses and to visit their local bishops. Catharine Stewart-Roache, a lay feminist and aspiring deacon, assured WOC she was doing her part to dialogue with her archbishop, Roberto Sanchez of Santa Fe. "He was very warm," she reported. "He's really learning to hug and that's what we need."[3]

When dialogue did occur, it could be successful. Feminists and bishops could reach the point of friendship, or at least mutual understanding, if not hugging. Dialogue seemed the perfect strategy in theory, but in practice it looked much different. Roache's experience with Sanchez was not typical. Keep in mind that while discussion of dialogue was frequent, actual dialogue was fairly rare. Because the American hierarchy was extremely slow to meet with feminists, the *attempt* to dialogue became much more significant than any dialogue itself. In practice, then, the dialogue strategy more closely resembled a protest action, more about feminists publicly beating on the doors of power, insisting on their desire and right to dialogue, rather than actually sitting down at a table with bishops.

For this reason the dialogue strategy was distasteful to some feminists who questioned the efficacy of putting so much energy into bishops (who were unlikely to respond) instead of into strengthening sisterhood. Recall the internal struggles of NCAN on this issue, when members took Margaret Ellen Traxler to task for getting into wrangles with bishops. Some feminists were unenthusiastic about dialogue because they considered themselves far better educated in theology (and certainly in feminist theory) than most bishops. Moreover, feminists who had been active reformers in the late sixties had seen dialogue with members of the hierarchy fail on a whole host of issues related to church renewal in the immediate postconciliar period. Certainly those who had been involved in the short-lived Joint Committee would have been highly skeptical of attempts to even get bishops to come to the table.

They were wise to be skeptical. Even when bishops came to the table, participants often felt as if they were speaking a different language. A review of the hierarchy's approach to women at mid-decade helps to explain the problem. In 1974, the Vatican's Study Commission on Woman in Society and in the Church, the first such commission ever created, released its report after three years of study. Although the commission concluded it was possible to "adopt all that is positive in contemporary efforts for the 'liberation' of women," it persisted in promoting complementarity and was steeped in eternal woman rhetoric. Since it originally defined its task as studying woman's role "on the basis of the radical equality of men and women but always in light of the ways in which they differ from and complement each other," the results were perhaps not surprising.[4] Pope Paul VI highlighted the growing chasm between Catholic feminists and the Vatican with conservative speeches in 1975 and 1976 on the subject of women. Feminists found some positive aspects to these speeches, particularly an indication that the pope was willing to talk about women's equality. But Paul VI ended his 1976 address by warning against feminists who wanted to ignore women's responsibilities in the home and who pushed an egalitarianism that "takes no notice of what is suitable and what is not suitable for women."[5] By this time, such rhetoric was so outdated for feminists that they had difficulty communicating with the hierarchy.

Dialogue, when it did occur, was riskier than all parties might expect, despite it being nonbinding. The very process of dialogue raised expectations that the church's national hierarchy was unable to meet. In turn, these unmet expectations drove women away from the institutional church. So, too, untimely displays of absolute power by members of the hierarchy (such as the release of the "Declaration"), though consistent with conservative conceptions of authority and obedience, frequently undermined the progress and goodwill engendered by dialogue. This led to a deep sense of betrayal among feminists. In this, the hierarchy was acting according to its nature: hierarchically. One must ask if it was only a matter of time before the best intentions of egalitarian dialogue ran headlong into the rights of authority that, however dormant, do not disappear.

But lest all blame for failed dialogue be left at the feet of the hierarchy, it should be said that many feminists' conceptions of dialogue were not balanced, thereby undermining the entire purpose of the exercise. While feminists spoke of dialogue as an opportunity to both listen and be heard, often their unspoken goal was the conversion of those in authority to a reformist understanding of the church and a feminist outlook. Therefore, "dialogue" was often more about feminists gaining the opportunity to be heard than seeking the chance to listen. A glaring example of this conception can be found in the proceedings of the Detroit conference. The section that included the conference talks was titled "One Part of the Dialogue."[6] Detroit was a gathering where feminists spoke to their own. They may have hoped that bishops would read the talks, but even if bishops did read them this does not constitute dialogue. In the late seventies and early eighties, when formal dialogues were established between woc and the nccb committee on women, women participants commented that the sessions were one-sided, more like "teach-ins" than occasions for mutual sharing.[7] While it is the responsibility of the powerful to listen to their people, the process is not a dialogue if it is one-sided. No doubt the assembled bishops were well aware that their purpose in these dialogues was to listen, absorb, and convert. In time, dialogue might have become more mutual as trust was built between the groups, but the dialogue process was derailed by heavy-handed members of the hierarchy who did not view dialogue as an alternative to hierarchical authority.

THE POLITICS OF DIALOGUE

By early 1976, plans were well under way to make WOC a permanent organization. Enthusiasm was high (although funds were low), and emerging leaders across the country began piecing the organization together. Its structure was nonhierarchical, directed by a national board called the core commission and run from an office that moved to whoever was willing to take up the job of office manager (from Kansas, to Washington, D.C., to Rochester, New York, within four years). Its goal was the ordination of women into a renewed priestly ministry in the Catholic Church. The new organization hoped to organize local groups into WOC chapters while staging national conferences every few years. Its leaders retained from the Detroit conference a commitment to reform and an interest in dialogue.

But WOC was not the only organization to form in the wake of the Detroit conference, nor the only group of women determined to implement the dialogue strategy. The movement was busy reorganizing itself in this period, both nationally and locally, and was eager to implement the ideas from the women's ordination conference on a variety of levels. To explore the dialogue strategy, and track the burgeoning organizational movement, we'll follow three emerging leaders who helped set the movement's determinedly optimistic tone and cement commitment to the dialogue strategy: Ada María Isasi-Díaz, Rosalie Muschal-Reinhardt, and Donna Quinn. All three were on the core commission of WOC, Isasi-Díaz and Muschal-Reinhardt would take over running WOC's national office in 1978, and Quinn would organize and lead the Women of the Church Coalition (WCC), a new umbrella organization to unite the movement's organizations, in 1978. In the midseventies, each experienced considerable frustration with dialogue, or more accurately the lack of it, but doggedly refused to abandon the effort.

Ada María Isasi-Díaz, an activist and theologian, was born in 1943 in Havana, Cuba. Daughter of a housewife and the manager of a large sugar-processing plant, Ada María grew-up in a large, stable, and loving middle-class family. Her attachment to Catholicism was strong as a child. Like so many other women in the movement she longed to be an altar girl but had to be content with playing Mass at home. (Because her brother José was an altar boy, Ada María took the part of the priest so that he could give the Latin responses). At one point she decided she wanted to be a saint but was devastated when one of her brothers told her she was too fat to qualify. She was vindicated when she discovered that Saint Therese of Lisieux had a chubby face, and so the young Ada María decided she could be a saint too. As she grew older she developed a typical teenager's zeal and began attending daily Mass. Because she was often the only one there, she was allowed to give the responses and ring the bells.

She remembers being at that time very centered in the moral tradition of the church. But she also recalls that for her, faith was always connected with a desire to associate with and help those in poverty. Early on, she had a sense of the value of the poor and common folk. Her mother used to chide her for spending hours chatting with Ilda, a local woman who came in to help with the large household. She struggled with how to "get [her] life involved with the poor." By the time she was a teenager, she expressed an interest in religious life because, as she phrased it, "if you were interested in religion and the poor in 1960 you became a nun."

But Ada María was not destined to be a nun in Cuba. In 1960, her father was known to have been critical of Fidel Castro's regime, which included the nationalization of the sugar processing plants across the country. When her father was away, Castro's men came to the house in the middle of the night, terrorizing the eighteen-year-old Ada María and her family. Shortly thereafter, Ada María left for the United States as a political refugee. She began school at the College of New Rochelle in New York and by 1964 had taken her first vows as an Ursaline sister.

In 1967, Ada María, now very much a "new nun," took up an assignment helping to implement Vatican II reforms in Lima, Peru. She recalls that she left very much with the "old missionary mindset" but found herself transformed by the experience of working among Lima's poor for three years. "They taught me to read the Gospel," she remembers. She also remembers the leniency of the Catholic hierarchy in Peru, which allowed her to participate in various forms of ministry that would have been denied her in the United States. Her desire to stretch boundaries extended to her own order. She described herself as being one of the "shock troops" pushing the New Rochelle Ursalines toward change, causing "huge" battles with older sisters in her New York community (although her relationship with her immediate community in Lima was strong). "In their books I was not a good nun," she remarked. "I wasn't obedient." In 1969, after eight years as an Ursaline, her superiors denied her request to make final vows, and Ada María was forced to leave the convent.

In the short term, this sudden change in plans caused major problems for Isasi-Díaz; as a refugee her papers were irregular (she had traveled to Peru on a falsified Cuban passport) and now had great difficulty getting back into the United States. It had long-term consequences as well, as Isasi-Díaz fell into a lasting depression and for five years struggled to find work and purpose. She bounced from working as a junior high teacher in New Orleans to working as a tutor as she traveled around Spain with her sister for a year and a half, always with barely sufficient funds. She reached her low point when she moved to Rochester in 1974 to be near family and could not find work. Overqualified for every available job, she lied to get a position at Sears, "the only job I ever hated."

It was at this nadir that Isasi-Díaz attended the Detroit ordination conference. Barely able to pay her way, she shared a car ride to the conference and acted as a group facilitator to help offset expenses. She was young, open, and had been drifting; the conference gave her immediate purpose and a strong national community. At the conference she met her lifelong close friend and colleague Rosalie Muschal-Reinhardt and Marjorie Tuite, the woman who was to have the most influence on her activism in this period. Recall how Isasi-Díaz was so enthralled by the conference that she never once looked out a window the entire weekend. The conference, preoccupied with themes of social justice—for women and the poor—was an ideal place for Ada María to find direction. It was here, too, that she affirmed her own call to priestly ministry in the "Liturgy of Blessing," although she faced the future with uncertainty. "I stood up for ordination—convinced that I might be able to serve thus," yet she was "afraid that I might be embarking on something that might fail."[8]

Ada María Isasi-Díaz believes she was "immensely blessed to have been formed by the movement." It became her "home, school, vocation." Ada María says she was "born a feminist" in Detroit; she also asserts, however, that "the church made me a feminist." She explains that although she dates her consciousness to the conference, her experiences in Peru primed her for this identification. The Catholic community there affirmed her forays into ministry and leadership and particularly her service to poor communities. It was the church that first helped her combine leadership and service in her adult life. Now that she had a consciousness of her own oppression within the institutional church, she would help to confront and transform it.

Driven by her enthusiasm, that process began as soon as she returned to Rochester. With a small group of women from the area who also attended the conference, Isasi-Díaz formed the Rochester Regional Task Force on Women in the Church (RRTF). RRTF had two official goals, "reinterpretation of ministry in the church community" and "full participation of women (both laywomen and sisters) in the church community at all levels." The group's unofficial goals were providing a meeting place where local women could experience feminist liturgy and community and support women working in ministry. The group also made an effort to reach out to women by speaking at parish councils around the diocese. But their official goals seemed to have been kept at the forefront. At their first meeting they outlined a strategy to achieve those goals, which included, "modeling and dialoguing with anyone, anywhere."[9]

One of the first things the RRTF did was to inform the Diocese of Rochester of its goals, request official recognition, and ask for the bishop's support. This request was not naive. Rochester boasted one of the most liberal bishops in the country, Joseph Hogan. Ada María was well aware of this because at the time she was working at a diocesan parish and was allowed to give homilies every other Sunday. Hogan did recognize the organization, appointed a liaison to the group, and offered his assistance. According to Isasi-Díaz, "He expressly told us that he does not see us as a threat and that he will be happy to be in contact with us and help us. . . . I think we can count on Bishop Hogan believing in and backing our cause" at the United States Catholic Conference.[10] Hogan was supportive, at least on the local level, interceding on the group's behalf when RRTF had difficulty with the editor of the diocesan paper, for example. RRTF also became involved with diocesan liturgical conferences and had some influence there. Isasi-Díaz calls RRTF's work "very fruitful."

But even Joseph Hogan had his limits. RRTF began a long and involved lobbying effort with the diocese to create an office for women's concerns. Dialogues were established, and Isasi-Díaz made her case. When the RRTF proposal was reviewed by the diocesan committee, they asked the group to "tone down" the language which they found too feminist and unnecessarily inflammatory. Isasi-Díaz attempted to compromise but balked when they suggested that the new office be titled the office of "Social Justice." Exhausted by the wrangling, she nevertheless wrote to RRTF colleagues, "I will . . . continue to push, ask, beg, smile, frown, demand, plead."[11]

Isasi-Díaz would not give up, in part, because she had reason to believe that Hogan could be influenced; at the very least he would engage in dialogue with RRTF. But in general, she was optimistic by nature. Her correspondence in this period is striking for how often she used the word "hope," a word she usually wrote in capital letters for added emphasis. Like Mary Lynch before her, Isasi-Díaz expressed at times the belief that God was behind their work and that therefore they would succeed. As she wrote to her friend Rosalie Muschal-Reinhardt in 1976, "with Jesus by us, who can hinder or stop us Rosalie? Really . . . he empowers me, you, us, and I will continue to say that I joyfully believe God is with us and nothing except selfishness will stop us."

But was she really so optimistic as to believe that the hierarchy would convert so easily? Remember how she reacted to her blessing at the ordination conference: at that point she was genuinely afraid of failure. When asked why she put "hope" in capital letters, Ada María says now that it was her "hyperbolic way of keeping hope alive in myself and others." She needed the boost because experience trying to dialogue with the Catholic hierarchy beyond the Diocese of Rochester soon tempered her optimism. When she helped establish RRTF she was "Pollyanna-ish," she now judges, having the impression that "other bishops were like Joe." Here is a prime example of dialogue raising expectations that were unlikely to be met on a larger scale. At the time she believed that "it was a matter of [the bishops] being enlightened by the scholarship—it had to happen! The realization that it wouldn't was very painful."

Isasi-Díaz came to the conclusion that she could not trust the bishops, but she continued to try to reach them. Dialogue remained a primary strategy for Isasi-Díaz, influencing not only RRTF, but also the national WOC. Isasi-Díaz was one of the original core commission members and later became the group's first regional coordinator when she and Rosalie Muschal-Reinhardt moved the national office to Rochester in 1978. In this capacity she traveled throughout the country meeting with local groups and budding Catholic feminists. For many of these women, she was their primary contact with the national movement, so her effort to build hope among the base was vital. Meanwhile, Isasi-Díaz was on her way to earning a master's degree in history and certification to teach. Her schedule was intense, as was the pressure to keep the organization relevant (and more pressingly, solvent).

She feared burnout—a real fear, as she watched other activists drop out of the movement for that reason—but she could not, or would not, stop. As she learned from her mother very early on, "to struggle is to live."[12]

Rosalie Muschal-Reinhardt was born in 1933 in Trenton, New Jersey, and grew up near a large extended family in an interracial neighborhood. Her parents were atypical for their day. Her mother was a "strong woman" who always worked outside the home, and her father willingly shared the house-work. She remembers that he never tried to put limits on her, encouraging her to use the gifts God gave her. According to Rosalie, one of those early gifts was a passion for justice (and a talent for activism). In eighth grade she led a student walkout to protest the bad food in the school cafeteria.

But if Rosalie was encouraged to question injustice, she also was a strong Catholic who was taught not to question the church. As she explains, "there was a time when I thought the institutional church and the Gospel were the same." Her commitment to the church as she understood it led her to enter a Sisters of Mercy convent right after high school in 1950. Rosalie only stayed in the convent for a year, but her stories of convent life are unlike those of most women who leave the convent after a short stay. She was not driven away by cold relationships and harsh rules. On the contrary, Rosalie says wholeheartedly that she loved her time in the convent.

Her description of the convent is reminiscent of an adult's fond memo-ries of summer camp. She tells stories of postulants short sheeting each other, surreptitiously rearranging the statuary to scare members of the com-munity, and eating contraband food in the bathtubs. She loved being with the other women and learning about her faith tradition (even though she was starting to question it). She also loved the cook's spectacular baked beans. In the end she decided she was not called to be a woman religious; among other problems, she just could not understand intellectually why postulants would have to wear bridal gowns when making their first vows. She also disliked the strict hierarchy in the community. She left without rancor and attended the induction ceremony as a member of the congrega-tion (where a member of the community presented her with a large jar of the baked beans).

Rosalie went on to attend Rider College, where she met Al Reinhardt, the love of her life, whom she married in 1955. She had fears when she found out he was not Catholic, but she visited the confessional where a thoughtful priest urged her to marry the man she loved, regardless of his affiliation. (She later found out that her confessor was a very conservative Catholic bishop. She made a point of thanking him more than twenty years later while lobbying at an NCCB meeting.) With this positive response, and after much soul-searching, Rosalie decided to marry Al without asking him to convert. This gesture convinced him that he truly loved her and she him. In 1957, Rosalie gave birth to her son Alfred, the first of four children. After his birth, Rosalie said her first "no" to the Catholic Church: she refused to be "churched." In Catholic practice, women were supposed to receive a special blessing from the priest after they gave birth, a ritual cleansing meant to purify them for reentry into the church building. Not understanding how she was somehow tainted by participating in the act of creation, she said no.

Despite this act of rebellion, Rosalie remained staunchly committed to the church. She was so excited by Vatican II that she anxiously awaited the arrival of her local Catholic paper every week to get the lowdown on events in Rome. Around the same time she began traveling to parishes, educating rank-and-file Catholics on the council changes. Rosalie was so involved in the Catholic community at this point that Al would say to friends that on any given night he never knew if he was going to come home to a convent or a rectory. By 1965, though, she was aware enough of women's place in the institution that she ceased contributing monetarily to the church; in fact, she never gave the church money again. "Why contribute to your own oppression?" she asks.

In 1967, Muschal-Reinhardt began a master's program in religious education at Colgate-Rochester Divinity School, a Protestant seminary in Rochester, a program she would not complete until 1974. A professor there told her she was priestly material and that she should seek ordination. But at the time she truly believed that "this is not my place in the church." By 1974, however, Rosalie was more attuned to systemic injustice in the church and decided to seek a master's of divinity from the Jesuit School of Theology in Chicago, a path practically unheard of for a married Catholic woman.

It was in Chicago that Rosalie became a self-identified feminist. She was led to feminism not by a feminist mentor (unlikely at that institution), but by sitting for hours in a library carrel reading the early church fathers. She grew so angry at the misogyny she found there, overwhelmed by the feeling of being "betrayed at home." Yet her discovery of patriarchy was also something of a relief. If sexism was a result of patriarchy it must be a man-made creation and did not originate with God. With God absolved, she took up the mantle of a religious feminist.

The anger she found in divinity school turned into a passion for the

Rosalie Muschal-Reinhardt at a woc meeting in 1978 (Courtesy of the Women and Leadership Archives, Loyola University Chicago: Chicago Catholic Women Records, Addendum I)

women's movement, and Rosalie acted on that passion with typical gusto. The year she entered divinity school she joined the first ordination conference task force, the local group Chicago Catholic Women, SJIA-US, and the Dupage County chapter of NOW. By 1976 she had been a facilitator at the Detroit conference, represented the women seeking ordination at that gathering, joined WOC's first core commission, and served as a regional vice president in SJIA. She accomplished this with four children under the age of eighteen while pursuing a degree full-time.

I have described Muschal-Reinhardt's background in detail because it helps explain the sensibility she brought to the movement in the midseventies. To this point she had showed an ambivalence toward the institution not because she failed to make up her mind about it, but because she recognized that it had the capacity to be both life-giving and harmful to women. This approach made her ideally suited to promoting the dialogue strategy. In spite of her anger, experience taught her that there was good in the church, that bishops were human beings who could be reached and led to conversion. Besides, her interest in dialogue extended well back to the sixties when she conducted ecumenical dialogues with religious women in

Spencerport, New York. She even wrote a weekly column for the local paper at that time called "Dialogue."

In an interview conducted twenty years after Muschal-Reinhardt finally chose to cut ties with the institutional church, she still described dialogue as fundamental: "Dialogue is to love as blood is to the body." To Rosalie, dialogue was a sign of love—for God, for humanity, for the church. More than that, she chose the path of dialogue because it became a crucial aspect of her new identity as a feminist woman of faith. She made her transition to feminist consciousness while working toward her divinity degree, and at the end of this process in 1977, in her master's thesis, she described how reconciliation and dialogue had become intertwined with her new sense of self:

> I, woman, Rosalie, through the grace of God, and through my experiences of human love began to forgive the tradition. Through this process of forgiveness, reconciliation, a new power stirred within me. I was able to claim my own authority from my own experiences and encounter with the tradition in a model of dialogue and mutuality. No longer was the power of authority one-sided; it became equalized in the process. I was able to love more, love my experience, love the tradition. This new level of love empowered me to strive more courageously for liberation of the tradition of my own and of all women and men. In the process, I became more me, a new creation.[13]

Like Ada María, she concluded that "It is in the radical attribute of hope, that I dare to begin."

Muschal-Reinhardt was heavily involved with the movement's attempts to dialogue on a national level with the American bishops throughout the latter half of the seventies, lobbying at the NCCB's annual meetings, attending the bishops' national conferences, participating in official dialogues between WOC and the NCCB's committee on women. These experiences were spotty. Rosalie hoped to make personal connections with bishops, something she saw bear fruit over the eight years she participated in dialogue. She believes that some of them grew more relaxed, less concerned with hierarchy and marks of status, and began to be more honest. "They truly believed they loved us by putting us on a pedestal," she remembered. She believes feminists made some headway in convincing them otherwise. Through dialogue efforts, feminists were able to identify bishops who were supportive. Besides Joseph Hogan these included Charles Buswell of Colorado, Frank Murphy of Baltimore, Thomas Gumbleton of Detroit, Roberto Sanchez of Santa Fe, Amedee Proulx of Maine, Carroll T. Dozier of Memphis, and Maurice Dingman of Des Moines among others.

Like Ada María, Rosalie hoped to educate the bishops she met, teaching them a new way to approach women and theology. Rosalie was convinced that the prohibition of women's ordination rendered women's baptism deficient, made them auxiliary members of the church, and labeled them diminished persons. "Bishops who do NOT accept the incarnational theology that all persons are redeemed in Jesus the Christ must answer the question, 'Are we women then not redeemed?' Those Bishops who believe that women are equal before God must be a sign to their brother Bishops."[14] She poured energy into befriending and teaching members of the American hierarchy, that she might help them see the vision of an egalitarian church she so fervently embraced. What modest success she achieved had little impact, however, as she was soon to learn. "We were under the false impression that bishops had power," she said. "They didn't."[15]

Rosalie Muschal-Reinhardt was strongly influenced in this period by her association with a third activist. In October 1974, Dominican sister Donna Quinn was sitting in an Association of Chicago Priests meeting when she looked around her and asked, "Where is the *women's* group in Chicago?" In December she attended Mary Lynch's meeting to form the ordination conference task force, of which she became a member, and issued a general invitation for Catholic women in Chicago to organize. The result was Chicago Catholic Women (CCW), one of the most prominent of the local Catholic feminist organizations.

Donna Quinn was born July 26, 1937, in Chicago, making her a generation younger than Margaret Ellen Traxler, who was a major influence on Quinn. She joined the Sinsanawa Dominicans at a young age, taking her final vows in 1960. Quinn could easily be classified as one of the "new nuns." In 1968, she made her own modified habit and veil, adapted from a commercial dress pattern. Soon she neglected to wear her veil, as on one occasion in 1969 when her superior told her she needed to put her veil on before she sat down to dinner. Since Quinn had begun to question whether "a veil on my head made me more of a person," she refused; around this time she "became more and more mouthy."[16]

In 1974, she moved from Milwaukee to Chicago to teach math and history at a predominantly African American all-girls high school. Not long

Donna Quinn at a ccw meeting (Courtesy of the Women and Leadership Archives, Loyola University Chicago: Chicago Catholic Women Records, Addendum I)

after, she started Chicago Catholic Women, leaving full-time employment to build the organization. She supported herself through a variety of part-time jobs that included teaching a course on bedside manners to hospital workers at a local community college, working as a staff member at the Eighth Day Center for Justice, and teaching a course for deacons' wives. Quinn believed she "was not asked back" to this last job because she was too outspoken on the issue of women's ordination.[17]

Quinn played a vital role in the Catholic women's movement from the midseventies onward and exemplified the trajectory of the movement, partly because she helped shape it. She began as a renewal-focused reformist in 1974, starting ccw and keeping its focus on institutional change. She also served on the original ordination conference task force and the first woc task force. Quinn was also a member of ncan (she served as executive director in the early eighties) and now. In 1977, her reformist viewpoint reached its zenith when she founded the wcc, which, as noted above, was created to bring all American Catholic feminist organizations under one umbrella group, playing the role Elizabeth Farians initiated and then relinquished in the early seventies. Quinn's early reformist mindset was sustained by the belief that "this is my church, this is my tradition. I love this church. I want to change it so that it will reflect a moral atmosphere and have an integrity of its own because it is mine."

But her love of the church could not withstand its continued discrimination against women. The more she battled the hierarchy, the more she identified with the feminist movement.[18] When asked in a 2001 interview what she had to accept or reject in both Catholicism and feminism to integrate the two, she explained that ultimately she was unable to sustain this integration and came to identify solely with feminism. "I have never rejected anything in the feminist movement," she said. "I've always said that I love the word 'feminism,' I have put that first. . . . I'm just happy that my space on this earth, my time on this earth was given to making this feminist movement more known. We really are somebodies as women on this earth, and if the Catholic Church and tradition didn't respect that, that was their loss."[19]

But as Quinn built CCW in the midseventies, she approached reform with great zeal. The new organization included some of the most prominent Catholic feminists in America, such as Patty Crowley (cofounder of the Christian Family Movement), Rosalie Muschal-Reinhardt, Maureen Hickey Reiff (who would later become a leader in NAWR and the Women-Church movement), Marjorie Tuite (prominent theologian and activist on feminist causes and issues of justice in Latin America), and Rosemary Radford Ruether. Nearly a quarter of the original 1975 ordination conference task force were CCW members.[20]

From the first, Quinn conceived of CCW as an example of laywomen and women religious working together and sharing leadership. A moving story that Donna Quinn tells is central to this self-understanding. In CCW's first year, the archdiocese sent its communications director to observe a meeting; in the course of the meeting he asked how many present were laywomen. Knowing that women religious were classified as laity under canon law, everyone raised her hand. The priest grew frustrated: "No, no, no, I mean, how many are sisters?" Everyone raised her hand again.[21]

The story reflects how deeply Quinn desired this ideal of sisterhood, but the reality was not so simple. Quinn was very sensitive to the hostilities between laywomen and women religious but insisted that the groups could build a sisterhood together. While Quinn's effort was a good start, her wishful thinking did not yet reflect reality. Rosalie Muschal-Reinhardt

Unidentified participant at a CCW vigil in support of the ERA (Courtesy of the Women and Leadership Archives, Loyola University Chicago: Chicago Catholic Women Records, Addendum I)

remembers that when she was in CCW, Donna Quinn "dragged her to every meeting" to prove there were laywomen in the movement. Maureen Hickey Reiff argues that Quinn's expansiveness toward laywomen could often be thwarted by her need to retain control of the group. "It was very much Donna's baby," she said.[22]

Nevertheless, CCW was a strong activist presence in Chicago. Like RRTF, CCW worked on local issues of discrimination against women, but unlike Isasi-Díaz's positive relationship with Bishop Hogan, CCW experienced only resistance from Cardinal John Cody. CCW conducted studies, both on the archdiocesan and parish levels, to determine how many women served in decision-making positions, from vicar of religious (the head of all men and women religious in the diocese) to the marriage tribunal to the smallest parish's finance committee.[23] The organization demanded an affirmative action hiring policy and used the CCW office as a clearinghouse for information on archdiocesan job listings (because of this, the archdiocese sent a memo to all parishes disavowing any connection to Donna Quinn). CCW insisted that the archdiocese include the names of its female leadership and employees in its yearly directory.[24] CCW also attempted consciousness-raising in the archdiocese. Group meetings regularly featured speakers on feminist issues, often from among its own ranks. CCW was determined to branch out beyond its own membership, however, and tried to connect with predominantly lay parish women's groups by offering traveling workshops on subjects ranging from women's ordination to women in the church today to reconciliation and by organizing consciousness-raising groups.

From the beginning, however, CCW wanted to press for dialogue on a national scale. They had their opportunity when the NCCB announced a national conference on the state of the American church in honor of the bicentennial titled "A Call to Action: Liberty and Justice for All." Finding this title a promising start, CCW set to work wrangling a seat for itself at the bishops dialogue table. "A Call to Action" was the first major test of Catholic feminists' relationship to the institutional church after the Detroit ordination conference. The NCCB's plan was ambitious; they conducted a series of hearings throughout the country in 1975, taking testimony from Catholics at all levels on issues concerning the church. The NCCB then used these testimonies to set the agenda for the conference, at which lay, religious, clergy, and organizational delegates would gather to discuss the church, its mission, and its commitment to social justice. As an attempt to listen to the voice of the faithful, the bicentennial hearings and the "Call to Action" conference were unprecedented in the history of the American Catholic Church. Catholic feminists were determined to be part of this process, viewing it as an excellent opportunity, and indeed an invitation, to dialogue.

The bishops' sudden interest in democracy had its limits, as CCW was quick to discover. CCW inquired as to who would represent women at the Archdiocese of Chicago's hearing in preparation for the regional hearing in St. Paul. The program identified only one woman giving testimony (a lay-woman listed under her husband's name). Organizers told CCW that a priest would represent both clergy and women religious. Outraged, CCW unsuccessfully lobbied the chancery for representation and then decided to hold its own hearing. When Donna Quinn, the group's director, took the collected testimonies to St. Paul and tried to present them, a monsignor literally screamed his disapproval from the podium microphone. CCW members later titled their testimony "The Experience of Powerlessness in the

CCW pro-ERA vigil (Courtesy of the Women and Leadership Archives, Loyola University Chicago: Chicago Catholic Women Records, Addendum I)

Church."[25] By the fall of 1976, CCW was not surprised to find itself left off of Chicago's official delegate list and planned a meeting directly before the conference, inviting the entire Chicago delegation to attend (prompting yet another in a long line of angry letters from Cardinal Cody's office disavowing CCW). Undeterred, most of CCW's leadership headed to the conference anyway.

Ada María Isasi-Díaz and Rosalie Muschal-Reinhardt also were determined to be at "A Call to Action." Isasi-Díaz wrangled a vote by being appointed Rochester's delegate from the diocese's Hispanic office. True to form, she and RRTF informed the bishops that they would be praying for them and fasting as the bishops prepared for the conference. Rosalie Muschal-Reinhardt sought entry and a vote as WOC's representative. She joined forces with the representative of the *Wanderer*, the nation's most conservative Catholic publication, to lobby for a vote. In the end, she was pleased that democracy seemed to work when both were named voting delegates. Donna Quinn, Patricia Hughes, Nadine Foley, and others were all on hand as unofficial delegates to help shape the resolutions, including one supporting women's ordination. Other resolutions included recommendations in support of an affirmative action plan, an end to sexist language in church documents and liturgy, diocesan and parish structures to facilitate women's leadership, the revision of canon law to eliminate sex discrimination, and female altar servers.

"A Call to Action" was not the conference the NCCB bargained for; many conservatives would probably have applied the word "fiasco" to the proceedings. Although bishops controlled their own delegate pools, the conference took a very liberal bent from the beginning, due to the large number of organizational delegates with voting rights and lobbyists who were allowed to participate in discussions and the drafting of resolutions. In the end, these resolutions were far to the left of any NCCB policies and, as such influential Catholics as Joseph Bernardin and Andrew Greeley pointed out, the "people in the pews."[26] The resolutions on women were the best examples of this phenomenon.

After the conference, Muschal-Reinhardt wrote a euphoric letter to WOC's core commission, opening with the salutation, "Rejoice and be glad—I bring you good news!" She jumped from topic to topic as if she could barely contain her excitement, thanking a lengthy list of Catholic feminists from WOC, LCWR, NAWR, Las Hermanas, NBSC, CCW, and Priests for Equality, emphasizing their substantive contributions to the process as well as their solidarity. But women's solidarity was not the only cause of Muschal-Reinhardt's excitement; she was enthusiastic about being part of the dialogue process and working with the bishops: "The real gift of Detroit (in my opinion) was the PROCESS. We cannot go back. Bishops admitted how freed up they were from being in a small group working through the issues, compromising, agreeing, disagreeing. The Process was the first gift of Detroit—and therefore, the structure is changed." Feminists received strong support from their bishop friends, especially Bishop Charles Buswell, who presented the resolution on women's ordination.[27]

Despite the difficulty many women experienced participating in the regional hearings, as well as the backlash from Catholics who believed the conference was unrepresentative, Catholic feminists were buoyed by "A Call to Action." It appeared that dialogue could actually work. Thus, the movement was unprepared for the disaster that was about to strike. Just two months after the conference ended, the Vatican promulgated its definitive teaching prohibiting women's ordination.

The Vatican's Congregation for the Doctrine of the Faith (CDF) released its "Declaration on the Question of the Admission of Women to the Ministerial Priesthood" in January 1977, three months after it was approved by the pope in Rome. In 1965, the Vatican had renamed its "congregation" responsible for safeguarding Catholic faith and moral doctrine because it feared that the organization's previous, thirteenth-century name, the Holy Office of the Inquisition, provoked negative connotations.[28] So it was not the frightening holy office of old, but the new CDF that released its final doctrinal judgment on the issue of women's ordination: "The Sacred Congregation for the Doctrine of the Faith judges it necessary to recall that the Church, in fidelity to the example of the Lord, does not consider herself authorized to admit women to priestly ordination." Befitting its new, gentler image, the CDF acknowledged that its "Declaration" would "perhaps cause some pain" but tried to soften the blow by pointing out that the positive value of the doctrine would be proven in the long run, "since it can be of help in deepening understanding of the respective roles of men and of women." In the final analysis, the CDF assured women, "The greatest in the kingdom of heaven are not the ministers but the saints."

The CDF offered in its "Declaration" a series of arguments designed to address each major point on either side of the question. It relied heavily on the "constant tradition" of the church, claiming that, aside from a few heretical sects in the first centuries, the church from Christ and the apostles through the present day had never doubted its refusal to ordain women. One of the CDF's major arguments was its most controversial, the belief that an ordained priest must bear a "natural resemblance" to Christ to fulfill the priestly function.

According to the CDF, if a woman were a priest "it would be difficult to see in the minister the image of Christ." Moreover, the CDF asserted that "the Incarnation of the Word took place according to the male sex: this is indeed a question of fact, and this fact, while not implying an alleged natural superiority of man over woman, cannot be disassociated from the economy of salvation: it is, indeed, in harmony with the entirety of God's plan as God Himself has revealed it, and of which the mystery of the Covenant is the nucleus." The CDF concluded that some women might feel an "attraction" to the priesthood, but "however noble and understandable . . . it still does not suffice for a genuine vocation. In fact, a vocation cannot be reduced to a mere personal attraction, which can remain purely subjective." On the contrary, a true vocation could only be authenticated by the church, which already knew women could not be priests since "Christ chose 'those he wanted' (Mark 3:13)."[29]

Not surprisingly, Catholic feminists found little comfort in this statement. Some could not hold back their rage. Ann Patrick Ware spoke for many in a nearly stream-of-consciousness reaction to the "Declaration" that sarcastically underscored the church's betrayal of women: "The church, I read, 'does not consider herself authorized to admit women to priestly ordination.' I can't help wondering, if 'she' did feel 'herself' so authorized, how would 'she' know? I smile feebly at the little special touch of irony: 'Given in Rome, at the Sacred Congregation for the Doctrine of the Faith, on October 15, 1976, the feast of St. Teresa of Avila.' Fathers, how could you?"[30]

Catholic feminists were universally angered by the document. They immediately identified the "natural resemblance" argument as the least theologically sound and the most offensive; most protests against the "Declaration" centered around this argument. Catholic feminists' rebuttal concerned women's place in salvation. "If the maleness of the Incarnation excludes women from priesthood," woc asked, "does it not also exclude women from Salvation?"[31] There is only one baptism for male and female, they argued. Is not every person called, through his or her baptism, to resemble Christ?

But what would be the movement's response after years of stressing its commitment to the institution? Undoubtedly the document's release caused individuals to leave the institutional church and the movement. The document was too painful and too infuriating for this not to have happened, although their departure is difficult to document. Anecdotal evidence from interviews suggests that some participants did consider this to be their last straw. But the movement's leaders did not leave. Instead, they chose to apply the strategies they had been developing over the previous two years to this volatile situation. As we have seen, they responded to this catastrophe liturgically, finding power and solace in feminist communal worship. They also applied their dominant strategy of dialogue, even though it seemed unsuited to the situation at hand. The document had emerged not from the nccb, but the Vatican. The nccb might have been unresponsive to feminists in the past, but at least feminists had the opportunity to make contact; the Vatican was a citadel by comparison, with little need to allow feminists access. American Catholic feminists would find it difficult to teach members of the curia to hug.

Leaders of the movement organizations understood this and instead turned to large-scale protest action for the first time. To begin, each major Catholic feminist organization released a strong public statement against the "Declaration." Never an organization to mince words, NCAN announced in its response (titled "Dismay at the Bad Theology of the Vatican Declaration and a Call for Women's Groups to Join Together") that it was "appalled" at the "Freudian theology . . . spewing forth from the Vatican."[32]

Yet each organization, including the radical NCAN, expressed its loyalty to the church and its intention to continue dialogue. NCAN ended its "Dismay" with the hope that all feminist groups could share the goal of "finding a home for feminine expression of Christ's mission in the Church." WOC and the LCWR initially went so far as to say they welcomed the document. In what should probably be interpreted as bold attempts at spin control, each organization praised the document because it rejected women's natural subordination and affirmed gender equality.

WOC insisted that, "far from 'closing the door' on the discussion, it is apparent that the language and argument of the Declaration invite responsible research and discussion."[33] Most groups, as in the case of the RRTF, "wish[ed] to respond in the spirit of continuing dialogue between the Church community and the Church magisterium."[34] These releases should be treated with care, as they were crafted for public consumption and do not necessarily reflect the true feelings of Catholic feminists in the movement. However, while the releases may not reflect the depths of feminists' anger, they do indicate that activists in the major national and local organizations were still unwilling to sever ties to the institutional church.

In reaffirming the dialogue strategy, Catholic feminists followed their instincts as well as their established strategy. But they also tried new strategies; following the press releases, WOC began organizing the movement's first national protest action, inviting every Catholic feminist organization, national and local, to protest the "Declaration" by holding a public prayer vigil on the theme of "Healing" one month following the document's release, preferably at the nearest cathedral. When feminists were refused access, a common occurrence, they drew additional media attention by holding their vigils on the cathedral steps.[35] Many of the vigils focused more on prayer than protest. Ada María Isasi-Díaz asked WOC not to use the term "demonstration" for the vigils, and for her own part she emphasized the liturgical nature of the RRTF vigil. An isolated activist in rural Louisiana wrote to her bishop for permission to observe the vigil by praying alone in the cathedral; it was granted.

Several other groups tried to affirm their commitment to the church even before the vigils took place. Chicago WOC's previgil press release featured a prominent statement of loyalty from Maureen Hickey Reiff, identified as a "former President of the Mothers Club of St. Victor Parish": "I am among those women who have decided to remain in the Church, even now. We hope our fidelity will be a power for renewal. . . . This means making justice and love the primary laws of the Kingdom. This is the Church we are going to pray with, and in, and for."[36] Mary Beth Onk, another WOC organizer, wrote a letter to her archbishop when he denied her group access to the cathedral, even though their vigil was only silent prayer. She wrote that many would choose to see the vigils only as angry demonstrations, "and how sad indeed, Archbishop, for there will be many faith-filled men and women praying with conviction for a church they dearly love."

Organizers wanted the vigils to be more than "angry demonstrations," but they certainly saw anger as an appropriate response to the "Declaration," and many vigils reflected that. In fact, it was through liturgy that the hybrid rhetoric of rage and reconciliation was most often expressed. Feminists created spaces in the vigils to ritualize both impulses; the sacred, supportive character of the events revealed both the depth of feminists' commitments to the church and the rawness of their emotions. But no matter how much rage they vented, Catholic feminists ended by affirming their loyalty to the institution. In the vigils, anger was nearly always tempered by the caveat of reconciliation.

Two of the major vigils, that of the Washington, D.C., WOC affiliate and a joint vigil for Chicago WOC and CCW, demonstrate this phenomenon. Catholic feminists in Washington chose to pray and protest on the steps of the cathedral after the archdiocese forbade them entry. Their worship consisted of a "three part healing liturgy of Recognition, Anger and Support." The liturgy's highlight was a dramatic scene enacted by Georgia Fuller, the Episcopalian head of the NOW Task Force on Women and Religion, and two members of Priests for Equality. Both groups had strong ties with Washington WOC and the closely affiliated Quixote Center. In this scene, a woman bent over with her burden of injustice sought healing from two clergyman. When they each turned her away, she was "healed instead by a woman imaging Jesus." After being healed, the first woman took bread and wine, silently raised them in blessing, and distributed them to the participants. Next, the worshippers joined in a "Creed of Anger," chanted a round of "Woe to you, scribes and Pharisees," and then offered their neighbor absolution and a blessing.

The Washington woc vigil showcased a rare, if not unprecedented, public display of Catholic women's rage. But the vigil may be more notable for its claiming of priestly power for women. The vigil explicitly invited women to claim the power of consecration and absolution, even though the group only chose to pantomime the sacraments of Eucharist and reconciliation. Notably, although priests were present, they were not asked to celebrate the Eucharist. Washington woc's liturgy was by far the most radical of the protests, and it demonstrates that the "Declaration" did have a transformative, radicalizing effect on the group.

Yet after the liturgy, Washington woc distributed the following statement of love and loyalty: "Ending on a high note of praise and joy, the liturgy sent participants out to work for justice at all levels. The message was loud and clear. The women love the Church. They will no longer remain silent. They will not go away. They will continue to minister and work for a renewed ministry in the Roman Catholic Church."[37] For the organizers, rage and reconciliation were not inconsistent. If anything, their rage only demonstrated the distance between feminists and the hierarchy and, therefore, the greater need for healing.

Similar themes emerged in the Chicago vigil, "Healing a Wounded Church," although the anger was much more subdued and the stress on mutual conversion more prominent. These women expressed rage in their "Rite of Betrayal and Forgiveness," but they then called "all persons present to forgive the leaders of the Church and to ask God that this time of suffering might bring new life." Patricia Hughes's homily explicitly asked feminists not to dwell on their anger; for Hughes, anger brought divisiveness and was a sign that feminists, too, were in need of conversion. In the "Rite of Conversion and Restoration," the organizers reminded worshippers, "By recalling that *God* is bringing about conversion, we do not become so disillusioned that we abandon the struggle."[38]

For nearly a year after the vigil protests, feminists continued to seek reconciliation through dialogue with the hierarchy.[39] In its 1977 Lenten prayer calendar, Chicago woc and ccw assigned each day a prayer of reconciliation and the name and address of an American bishop.[40] The woc core commission chose to distribute the calendar throughout the country. A 1977 Christian Feminists newsletter proclaimed that the "highlight of the year" was when Archbishop Jean Jadot, the papal delegate to the United States, came to one of their meetings and listened to their concerns about the "Declaration." By April, the NAWR leadership wondered "if we have adequately tried to dialogue with our Bishops on the content of the declaration and its meaning to women of the Church." Therefore they recommended that individual sisters seek out their bishops to convince them that the subject was not closed.

Dialogue still dominated the movement's agenda. Organizers planned their next major protest for the NCCB's annual meeting scheduled for May 1977 in Chicago. Donna Quinn and Rosalie Muschal-Reinhardt were determined that, in this year of the "Declaration," feminists' voices would be heard. They reserved a room at the Palmer House Hotel, site of the NCCB meeting, and invited LCWR, NAWR, NCAN, SJIA, WOC, the Institute for Women Today, the Christian Feminists, Las Hermanas, NBSC, the National Sisters Vocation Conference, and Priests for Equality to send representatives. This was the meeting that resulted in the formation of the WCC under the leadership of Donna Quinn.

The organizers participated in some street demonstrations, but their chief goal was expressed in their invitation to the bishops to "dialogue with us." In the same spirit, WOC called on its membership to pray and fast during the three-day meeting to "keep ['A Call to Action'] alive."[41] Very few bishops accepted the invitation to dialogue, but these women were not easily deterred. Rosalie Muschal-Reinhardt said of her chance encounters with bishops at the meeting, "I think it was important to meet them on elevators, and I loved the reactions to 'I'm Rosalie Muschal-Reinhardt with WOC'—they were ALWAYS polite—some were so affirming, some neutral and some—well, their eyes went blank—we smiled at them the hardest."[42]

Muschal-Reinhardt threw herself whole-heartedly behind dialogue, and few were better suited to the task. Shortly after the NCCB meeting, Muschal-Reinhardt wrote a passionate letter to her friends in which she asserted, "WE BELONG HERE AND HERE WE WILL STAY UNTIL HEARTS OF STONE ARE TURNED TO HEARTS OF FLESH." But the organizer was well aware of feminists' painful position in the year following the "Declaration," and in the same letter she admitted that she had to ask herself why she was genuinely happy to be at the meeting among the bishops. "It seems to me, Rosalie, you are happy with crumbs," she said to herself. Then she asked, "why do I stay here?" meaning, why did she stay in the church? She continued, "The answer came tumbling out of me—because I love the church and I believe Jesus can help me and my sisters. And so I realized I am not happy with leftovers or crumbs—but this is the process—leftovers will lead to the table of the wonderful God."[43]

As her evocative metaphor suggests, Muschal-Reinhardt clearly recognized the limitations, and even the debasing dimensions, of the dialogue strategy and, indeed, of committing herself to staying in the church. Yet this realization did not lead Muschal-Reinhardt to distance herself from the institution; she admitted she would continue to accept the scraps from the hierarchy's table so long as it got her to the altar. The desperation embedded in this statement reveals that Muschal-Reinhardt's—and by extension the movement's—strategies for integrating deepening feminist consciousness with loyalty to the institutional church were showing signs of serious strain. Muschal-Reinhardt's self-awareness foreshadowed what was to come.

8

sustained
ambivalence

I must admit . . . as I am frustrated more and more, my commitment to Catholicism is decreasing. My commitment to Christ is and will always be strong, but as it comes in conflict with the abuse of power in the church hierarchy, my respect for the formal church diminishes.
—Patricia K. Durbeck, personal correspondence

In 1975, after an exhilarating experience at the Detroit conference, Catharine Stewart-Roache made it a personal responsibility to convert Archbishop Roberto Sanchez, her bishop, to a belief in women's ordination. She pursued dialogue and in the process of training in the Santa Fe Archdiocese diaconate program came to know and like him. Liberal, and more responsive than most, Archbishop Sanchez worked with the female diaconate candidates, agreeing to let them make a public statement of purpose when their male colleagues presented themselves for ordination candidacy in 1977. The five women declared their intention to "faithfully serve Christ and the Church which is his body," asking for the prayers of all present that women might one day be ordained. Sanchez replied, "The Church joyfully accepts your statement of purpose. May God who began the good work in you bring it to completion."[1]

Yet Stewart-Roache experienced growing uncertainty as her own pain over being refused ordination came to the fore. Her poem, "The Body of Christ," which tells the story of a woman presiding at Mass, indicated Stewart-Roache's ambivalence. The female priest recites the creed: "I believe in the giver of life / I believe in the church / and I look for. cry for. yearn for. / resurrection." But she approaches the altar "unhealed, without joy," hesitating at the consecration:

> Could she celebrate this broken body of Christ?
> celebrate this incomplete body of the lord?
> celebrate when a part of this body said:
>
> no
> unworthy
> unfit
> unacceptable matter.
>
> she put the bread down slowly.
> painfully.
> the eyes of her sisters expected more: expected all.[2]

Stewart-Roache expressed the key Catholic feminist dilemma of the late seventies: she identified the sacraments as the source of her peace, and the institutional church as the source of her pain, yet could not divorce one from the other and so remained caught between the two.

Stewart-Roache reached a turning point in 1978, a "moment of broken-ness," as she later described that time. In an official request to Sanchez for ordination, her tone was full of dignity but also resigned and devoid of hope. "I have been a Catholic all my life," she said, "and it seems to me that we are far from the reign of God in this moment of brokenness. . . . This broken-ness means that an important way of releasing the power of God within me is being denied me and the community which desires my ordination and service."[3] In her awareness of her own oppression she did not reject God, her call, or her community; it was the institutional church that was broken.

Prior to 1978, the movement tried to integrate faith and feminism with-out questioning its loyalty to the institutional church. The dominant theme was SJIA's confident "We are feminists BECAUSE we are Catholic." This stance led Catholic feminists to adopt the dual strategies of conversion and dialogue. Yet as Catharine Stewart-Roache's experience suggests, these strat-egies were beginning to prove untenable with the hierarchy's increased re-sistance and feminists' deepening understanding of their own oppression.

In the process of integrating feminism into preexisting Catholic world-views, 1978 marked a turning point. Numerous factors suggest that the movement began to distance itself from the institution, including feminists' growing willingness to admit internal struggles between loyalty and the desire for greater distance, to express intense pain, and to consider a plurality of options in response to the institution. Catholic feminists also showed increased radicalization in protest activity and ideology and grew markedly more involved with secular feminists and other feminist women of faith. For some individuals, these developments led to a permanent break with the church and the end of their self-identification as Catholic feminists. Others sought a new way to be Catholic and feminist, a means of committing to reform, cherishing the life-giving aspects of the tradition, and celebrating sisterhood without subjecting oneself to the institutional church's soul-killing abuse of power.

Before I understood the nature of the movement's transition in this period, I asked my interview subjects what I considered to be very straightforward questions: Did you choose to leave the church? If so, why and when? A few came down vigorously on one side or another, even citing the dates when they made these choices. Most, however, offered more enigmatic responses. "I didn't leave the church," feminist theologian Mary Hunt replied. "The church left me." She went on to argue that most of the women active in the movement never left at all; they simply continued enacting church in ways consistent with their beliefs, and if the institution could not get behind them, it was the one that pulled away. Rosalie Muschal-Reinhardt told how she eventually abandoned the institution to its own devices but insists she remains firmly a part of "the church." Maureen Hickey Reiff explained that the last time she belonged to a parish was in the early eighties, yet she still calls herself Catholic "because it's in my bone marrow." Donna Quinn sounds as if she "left" the church decades ago, so fervent is her criticism of the institution, but she is still a committed member of her religious community. The terminology of "staying" and "leaving" has proven inadequate. How then are we to understand these responses?[4]

Recent scholarship on feminist women of faith in general, and American Catholic women specifically, is illuminating on this issue. Religious studies scholar Mary Farrell Bednarowski argues that at the end of the twentieth century feminist women of faith chose a "willed ambivalence, a sustained, and cultivated ambivalence" as a creative means of taking stands against oppression while still staying open to reform and that this approach allowed these feminists to flourish "on the margins without losing sight of the center."[5] In other words, they sought a location, often termed "the margins," that allowed them to be their true selves without being crushed by the institution, on the one hand, or abandon a fundamental aspect of themselves—their faith rooted in Catholic theology and sacramentalism, their heritage as Catholics, and their understanding of the ideal church—on the other hand. A position on the margins also allowed women to declare that they had faith in the idea of church, and hoped for its conversion, but that they were unwilling to subject themselves to oppression any longer.

Following Bednarowski, I have come to call this position "sustained ambivalence," a state that can be creative, as she argues, and long-term, but also painful. The literature on American Catholic women supports this construct. Note the terminology a variety of scholars have used to describe Catholic feminists. Psychologist Sheila Pew Albert refers to Catholic feminists in the nineties as "revolutionary loyalists," while Miriam Therese Winter argues that in the same period Catholic women were "defecting in place." Mary Jo Weaver said of feminist women religious that they were "inside outsiders."[6] Far from abandoning "the church" en masse, many tried to find a way to leave and stay at the same time. All of these terms indicate a similar phenomenon: these women deliberately tried to carve out a new space to accommodate a new way of being feminist women of faith. If they could no longer trust the institution, they would distance themselves from it as much as they could while finding a new way to "be church" that was truer to their vision of what an egalitarian Christian community should be.

The purpose of this study is not to describe how sustained ambivalence manifested itself, since it was more a phenomenon of the post-1980 period. Rather, this chapter argues that sustained ambivalence is a development rooted in time, specifically in the period 1978–80. Indeed, 1978 seems to have marked the historical origins of this phenomenon for Catholic feminists, predating the worst of the Vatican's crackdowns against Catholic feminists in the early to mideighties. Initially returning to the rhetoric of reconciliation following release of the "Declaration" in 1977, Catholic feminists began to ease away from such rhetoric and to lose their hopeful tone. They talked more and more frequently about their anger and pain; they openly discussed whether or not the institutional church was redeemable. Such shifts were accompanied by an increased identification with the larger feminist movement. In the same period, the movement was fraught with tension over strategic and ideological disagreements, indicating the change that was to come. Catholic feminists also began to lay a theological foundation for this new position of sustained ambivalence as they practiced ministering to each other and worshipping together. In the stories of organizations and individuals, we see the move to the margins beginning.

ACKNOWLEDGING AMBIVALENCE

As we have already seen, the shift toward sustained ambivalence was not sudden. There was no one single moment following release of the "Declaration" when the movement switched over, abandoning vocal loyal opposition for a location on the margins. Therefore, much of the activity that took place in 1978–80 was consistent with earlier patterns of thought and behavior. The organizations of feminist women religious, including NCAN, LCWR, and NAWR, continued to espouse a feminist activism inspired by and focused on social justice. The only organization of the three to change substantially in character was NAWR, which invited laywomen into its ranks and became steadily more radicalized as the decade progressed.

WOC also pursued an agenda similar to that adopted before the "Declaration." Under the leadership of Rosalie Muschal-Reinhardt and Ada María Isasi-Díaz, who by 1978 were running the national office out of Rochester, WOC put much effort into building local and regional groups. Unfortunately, a great deal of energy was expended to keep the group financially solvent; WOC was perilously close to going under most of the time due to lack of funds. WOC also continued to pursue the dialogue strategy. As of 1979, WOC had sponsored a series of dialogue sessions with the NCCB's committee on women in the church, local groups were still reporting visits to their bishops, WOC was continuing to lobby at the bishops' meetings, and one of the group's major initiatives was a petition drive asking the hierarchy to reject the "second argument" of the "Declaration," that is, that women cannot "image" Christ. In addition, the umbrella organization Women of the Church Coalition continued its lobbying work to gain women more representation at the NCCB.

Finally, the last years of the decade saw a series of protests at ordination ceremonies conducted by some of the more adventurous feminists within the movement. Participants picketed outside cathedrals, wore armbands, stood up from the pews when the names of the ordinands were read. These protests were quite radical by Catholic feminist standards, but even so the women who participated continued to work from a dialogue mindset. They were still engaging with the institutional church in an effort to be heard.

In some ways, then, the last two years of the decade seem like business as usual for the Catholic feminist organizations, but clearly something made this period different. Tensions within organizations, particularly woc, began to show. Most of these tensions originated from ideological disagreements, indicating that significant change was occurring, and it was not uniform. The nature of these disagreements—debates about how closely feminists should be tied to the institutional church—suggests the swing toward a more ambivalent position, as does the fact that talk of leaving the church coexisted with ongoing efforts to dialogue with bishops. However, one need not look to organizations alone to see this change occurring.

Women paid the price for this brokenness, according to Catholic feminists, and their eagerness to discuss it marks a change. Women's pain at the hands of the church became a major theme in the writings of Catholic feminists across the movement between 1978 and 1980, and it is significant evidence that they were beginning a large-scale rethinking of their position vis-à-vis the church. Catholic feminists could not seem to talk often enough about the depth of their suffering and the violence the church had inflicted on them. The betrayals of the "Declaration" were undoubtedly connected to this change. Around this time, Catholic feminists began referring to themselves metaphorically as battered or raped women and the church as their abuser. Not surprising, since he was viewed as the chief abuser, Pope John Paul II's visit to the United States in 1979 inspired a flood of this rhetoric, from a protest song sheet titled "Songs for the Wounded" to a poem, "Kiss Boy Babies Only," by Ritamary Bradley:

> . . . O Kiss boy babies only, John Paul Two.
> Plant purple tenderness on no girl child.
> Reverse King Herod's rule and let the sword of death descend
> Sharp, irreversible upon
> Girl children only . . . and cut them off from life.
> For life flows, as you teach, from bread of Christ.
> Broken upon the table of the Lord.[7]

Indeed, Catholic feminists were so preoccupied with pain in 1979 that they chose to commemorate the anniversary of the release of the "Declaration" instead of celebrating a positive anniversary like that of the first women's ordination conference. At one such prayer service in Baltimore, the assembled feminists prayed, "We are the church—we have a baptism to receive—we are in anguish til it is over."[8]

Few of these feminists seemed to consider that such excessive talk of pain brought with it an emphasis on victimization as well as promoted a seeming preoccupation with the self. For example, a group protesting an ordination ceremony in 1979 issued the following statement: "The pain we feel over ordination is a share in the all too plentiful pain which is widespread among the poor and marginalized, the sick and old, women and physically disabled, Third World and Black people, gay and lonely folks."[9] Earlier in the decade, Catholic feminists might have used this concept to argue that their pain made them more aware of the needs of others. Here, however, the protesters simply added themselves to the list of the marginalized. I do not wish to imply that this new self-centeredness was detrimental to the movement. Feminists consider the acknowledgment of pain in one's self and one's sisters (and the willingness to name the abuser) to be a major step toward a deepening feminist consciousness. It should be pointed out, however, that this language differs substantially from an earlier emphasis on the pursuit of social justice for the sake of self and others that rarely dwelt on the self as victim.

This rhetoric did help reinforce a sense of greater sisterhood as more and more women shared in the pain of betrayal and the grief they felt as they became more and more disconnected from the church they loved. The preoccupation with suffering clearly had an emotional impact on movement participants, particularly those in leadership. Verbalizing their distress signaled to themselves and others the move to a position of ambivalence and the willingness to seek alternative means of being church with their sisters.

These shifting approaches within the movement as a whole first became evident in November 1978, when Catholic feminists met for the second women's ordination conference in Baltimore, Maryland. The Baltimore conference was similar to the one held in 1975 in Detroit in that it combined speakers, small-group sessions, and liturgy, and it took as its theme "New Women, New Church, New Priestly Ministry." Additional goals were to develop "deeper conscientization," "to place the issue of sexism firmly within and related to an analysis of society that includes oppressions of race and class," and "to clarify and sharpen the meaning of feminism." Attendance topped two thousand, and laywomen were better represented. Like the first conference, the second looms large in the memories of those who participated. But the conferences were markedly different in character and tone. If Detroit showed the movement's surprising unity, Baltimore revealed

Participants at the opening ceremonies of the 1978 WOC national conference in Baltimore, Maryland (Courtesy of the Marquette University Archives)

its discord. Catholic feminists discovered that as individuals they had responded differently to the events between 1975 and 1978, and no longer were they in the same place as activists, Catholics, or feminists anymore.

The weekend started on a dramatic, unified note when conference participants gathered for a stirring liturgical protest at the harbor. Following the service, feminists marched along the waterfront connected to each other by long plastic chains symbolizing their oppression. But this sense of unity did not last. Participants came to the conference from strikingly divergent positions, ranging from those who still advocated dialogue to advocates of exodus from the institution to rank-and-file members who just wanted ordination, and they were shocked by the mounting tensions in the movement. Mary Luke Tobin, feminist, social justice activist, and revered figure in the movement opened the conference with her own view of why participants had come to Baltimore: "You have come—there is no mistake about it—you have come because of love for the Church, because you wish to call the

Church to its best." She indicated her continued faith in dialogue, suggesting that if John Paul II wanted to explore women's mission in the church, "perhaps we might urge him, respectfully, to invite us to a personal dialogue with him."[10]

But Tobin's talk of love, respect, and dialogue seemed out of step with the mood of the conference. Conference talks and casual conversation revealed that a significant portion of the participants rejected the rhetoric of loyal opposition that predominated at the Detroit conference and were eager to see what would replace it. Two speakers who sensed this change, but reacted differently to it, reveal the range of opinion in Baltimore.

Fran Ferder, a Franciscan sister, psychologist, and staff member of the Quixote center, had spent the previous year on the road interviewing one hundred women called to priesthood. In a talk on trends in the movement, Ferder commented that "some of us have become angry with God. They have stopped believing in the promised land. They no longer point the way to the holy. Some have withdrawn, left the church, pulled out of the structure. They've forgotten the vision. . . . They have grown weary of waiting. They have stopped praying. They have nothing to say about the gospel. . . . They're still willing to take up the sword and they are still willing to storm the Temple. But, when they get inside, they won't feel at home there, because they've lost touch with the sacred." She concluded that, in the struggle to live with the "oppressive reality" of the church, feminists must look "at what our marching means, at what our battle stands for, and at how our marching and our battle will renew priesthood."[11] Her talk echoed the feelings of many participants who worried that the tone of the conference was too anti-institution and noted what they considered to be a disturbing lack of prayerfulness at the conference.[12]

On the other end of the spectrum was Eileen Stenzel, a theologian and women's studies program director, who advocated radical separation. Rooted firmly in a feminist theoretical outlook, Stenzel argued that sisterhood "suggests . . . that feminist experience as radical discontinuity with prevailing normative structures contains the paradigms around which genuinely human communities can be understood." In other words, if women disengaged themselves from oppressive traditions they would "recover autonomy and power." In her view, then, Catholic feminists should pursue their own unique way of ministering to each other and their communities not as stopgap measures, but as legitimate and prophetic forms of ministry. She did not argue that Catholic feminists should stop seeking ordination but

Latina feminists in protest at the start of the 1978 WOC national conference
(Courtesy of the Marquette University Archives)

that the struggle for ordination "must be one which strengthens us to refuse the tradition on which ordination rests."[13]

Ordination itself proved to be a major point of contention at the conference. Catholic feminists began to split over the question of when they would accept ordination. Some concluded they would accept ordination as soon as it was offered, no matter if the priesthood had yet been transformed. To others, the eagerness of these women to be ordained seemed to indicate a lack of commitment to an egalitarian vision of the priesthood. In the minds of these skeptics, women who would be ordained at any cost would be easily co-opted by the establishment and, perhaps, even harbored secret tendencies toward clericalism. This debate proved extremely confusing for feminists who came to Baltimore seeking the unconditional affirmation that aspiring priests had received in Detroit, only to hear it implied from some quarters that their desire for priesthood was somehow suspect. The sense of confusion that resulted was so widespread that some journalists and feminists began referring to Baltimore as the "anti-ordination conference."[14] "I'm ambivalent about this [conference],"

Catholic feminist holding a banner paraphrasing Galatians 3:28 at the 1978 WOC national conference (Courtesy of the Women and Leadership Archives, Loyola University Chicago: Chicago Catholic Women Records, Addendum I)

one feminist woman religious stated. "I wonder if some of these people know what they're clapping for here."[15]

Postconference discussions in the media and letters to the WOC office reflect the changes revealed at Baltimore. A member of CCW commented that "the mood after Baltimore was for some militant and for others confused and frightening."[16] Billie Poon, a laywoman called to priesthood, called the conference "extremely painful." She remarked, "I could neither identify with nor support the anger and hostility that many of the women speakers displayed. I was disoriented and alienated by the spiritual poverty I felt in the Conference program. The fruits of Jesus were not particularly visible. Lots of ego trips were."[17]

On the other hand, theologian and conference speaker Mary Hunt wrote *Commonweal* to criticize a column claiming divisiveness at the conference. "The meeting was a unified event," she said, "progressing from union of purpose through variety of approaches to union of purpose with renewed, deepened understanding of differences." Rosalie Muschal-Reinhardt also brushed off talk of division. "I'm ecstatic!" she said by the end of the weekend. "This is the church, honey!"[18] Indeed, this was the final image the conference organizers hoped to project: unity in diversity. woc passed a conference resolution asking participants to affirm "the necessity of the difference among us and pledge ourselves to continue the dialogue with all those who have been disenfranchised." The resolution seems to have been an attempt to convince everyone that, indeed, the movement was still unified, when it appeared to be splitting apart.[19]

Although many rank-and-file Catholic feminists left Baltimore disappointed or confused, history shows that conference organizers and speakers were attuned to the movement's shifting mood (whether everyone was happy about that shift or not). Moreover, theologians at the conference were able to offer direction to the movement in the midst of this divisiveness. Two speakers in particular, Mary Hunt and Elisabeth Schüssler Fiorenza, pointed the way forward. Before discussing their considerable contribution to the movement's development in this period, however, it should be noted that theologians themselves came to be another source of tension. As more women emerged with advanced degrees in theology and took up leadership in the movement, some activists without such qualifications came to feel marginalized as well as suspicious of academic approaches that seemed to them to be overly hierarchical. The tension this caused was only just beginning at this point but would become so advanced that it was one factor in the major split that occurred in woc in the early eighties.[20]

Mary Hunt was born in 1951 in Syracuse, New York, one of three children in an Irish-Catholic family. She does not remember being particularly pious as a child, but she was heavily influenced by Catholic social teaching, especially on justice issues. She received her BA in theology/philosophy in 1972 from Marquette University, where she participated in the antiwar movement. She cites Dorothy Day as an early influence. Hunt came to feminist consciousness at Harvard Divinity School where she earned a master's in theology and where she was influenced by Rosemary Radford Ruether, a visiting scholar at the time. Ruether helped Hunt realize that ministry could be an option for her. What was born in the ecumenical atmosphere of Harvard was nurtured at the Seminary Quarter at Grailville. Hunt says of the experience that everyone left Grailville "as if we were shot out of guns." She would need that drive to complete her next undertaking, the simultaneous completion of a doctorate in systematic theology and a master of divinity. Hunt pursued the latter degree, in part, because she wanted to "challenge herself to have a pastoral side." She also says that her decision was largely political, not originating from some sort of mystical "call."

Like so many other Catholic feminists, Hunt's feminism grew out of her religious consciousness; she clearly stated that she came to feminism through her study of theology. Therefore, her feminism has always been intertwined with questions of justice, spirituality, and ministry. Furthermore, Hunt's feminism does not analyze women's oppression in isolation. From the beginning her feminist theology, what she referred to in 1978 as her "feminist liberation theology," has stressed interlocking oppressions on the basis of gender, race, class, and sexual preference. Having come out as a lesbian in 1972, Hunt was one of the first Catholic feminists to challenge a heteronormative perspective among Catholic feminists.

Mary Hunt was a Catholic feminist from the second generation with strong ties to Catholic spirituality and social teaching but not to the institutional church. Moreover, her feminist formation was within communities of ecumenical feminist academics, not within Catholic feminist organizations or religious communities. She did not mind being called Catholic, neither was she tempted to join another Christian denomination, but Hunt was never limited to a rigid conception of church or ministry. Her expansive vision of church, her drive, and her unique perspective left her well positioned to step forward as a leader in this transitional period when feminists began to distance themselves from the institutional church. Her Baltimore conference talk, a theological study that became the basis for her M.Div. thesis, was the launching point for Hunt's career as a leader in the movement. More important, her talk—what other feminists in the movement later referred to as her "finest hour"—offered Catholic feminists a new direction.[21]

Hunt's presentation, "Roman Catholic Ministry: Patriarchal Past, Feminist Future," was one of the conference's most popular talks, perhaps because it pointed the way to something new with a spirit of hopefulness. She insisted from the outset that she would not deal exclusively with ordination because she objected strongly to an "add women and stir" approach. When she announced that she was not interested in "the shrinking clerical pool," she was also stating that the "feminist future" she had in mind was well beyond the confines of the institutional church. "The paradigm of Church has shifted from that of a male-dominated transnational religious corporation based in Rome," she argued, "to that of a people's Church with a people's ministry, nurtured locally in parishes and base communities throughout the world." To assist this transition, feminists must move away from seeking "some form of ecclesiastical ERA" and instead "turn the power model upside down by giving those who have been excluded, women, Blacks, gay people, the poor, equal voice in the Church."

She described the ideal ministry as mutual, collegial, cooperative, and best envisioned as a kind of "creative loitering" in which ministers watched for and responded to basic needs. Hunt then went on to describe what it was like to attend the ordinations of her classmates. She witnessed the laying on of hands with distaste, feeling the pain of her own exclusion as well as disgust over the sense that the ceremony seemed more like the acceptance of men into an exclusive club rather than an invitation to ministry. "The old model is dead," she argued, and everything in her address urged women to move on. How this expanded vision of ministry fit within women's established relationships to the institutional church was unclear, but Hunt obviously hoped that women would seek new models and claim them as legitimate expressions of church. Whatever the ministry, she recommended "preparation, openness, and a sense of humor." "Forgiveness is possible," she concluded. "Hope is warranted."

But it was theologian Elisabeth Schüssler Fiorenza who articulated the concept of sustained ambivalence (although she did not use this term), offering the gathering a concrete alternative that more and more women would adopt in the coming decade. Schüssler Fiorenza's talk analyzed the "Pre-Conference Process," a series of small-group meetings held around the country in spring 1978, comprising five hundred people in fifty-three groups and designed to gauge the current thinking of Catholic feminists.[22] She concluded that the feminists in these groups fell into three distinct categories in their tack toward feminism: "While the first approach wants to complement male hierarchical structures with the qualities women can bring to ministry and the second approach wants to withdraw women's powers and abilities from church ministries in order not to be co-opted, the third approach insists on the conversion of the church as well as of women." In other words, position one represented those who wanted ordination without changing basic structures, and position two represented those on the verge of leaving the church altogether (or who had already left). Position three, which she endorsed, represented those willing to work to change church structures, albeit armed with both a "critical theology of liberation," an approach that rooted the church's refusal to ordain women in the male-dominated church's desire for power, and a willingness to witness prophetically by living the new concept of a liberated church now.

Schüssler Fiorenza was outlining the movement's future position, not its past strategy. In fact, she had been concerned beforehand that her talk would be too radical for her audience, but the response to it convinced her that she could claim to be speaking from the movement's center, not its radical fringe. In her analysis she argued that a church that was willing to "risk Christological heresy" to support its view could not be reasoned with theologically; it could only repent and be converted.[23] But she did not mean conversion through befriending bishops and dialogue, as had been the movement's primary strategy since the first conference: "It is . . . necessary that women stop pleading for ordination and justifying it in the face of sexist church traditions." On the contrary, she concluded, "Such a conversion from ecclesial sexism demands from us the courage to 'come out of the closet' and to make public that we as Christian women have power to image Jesus sacramentally, to break bread in community, to reconcile people with God and each other, to proclaim the truth and power of the Christian gospel."

She believed that women ministering, women celebrating liturgy, women being the church in ways conforming to their vision of the church as the people of God would bring about this conversion. She then specifically articulated the position of sustained ambivalence. "Instead of allowing themselves to be pushed out of a church so unjust and oppressive to women," she explained, "many of the respondents opt for a partial identification with the church." Catholic feminists would continue to engage in this struggle within the church, if only from the margins, because "the credibility of the Christian gospel and church is at stake."[24] She called on Catholic feminists to start a "spiritual hunger strike," that is, publicly refuse to participate in male-dominated liturgy, in analogy to the suffragist protests between 1917 and 1919. Marjorie Tuite, who planned the conference process, objected strongly to this statement, but Schüssler Fiorenza made it anyway.[25] The statement cost her an important job and caused a flood of protest letters to descend on the University of Notre Dame, where she was then employed.[26]

The talks were not the only forum where participants worked through questions about the movement's direction. The central tension of the conference found most vivid expression in the liturgies celebrated there. The key issue was whether to include a liturgy with a male presider—in other words, the Eucharist. In Detroit, the women who felt called to priesthood had affirmed the centrality of the Eucharist in their lives, but the interim had wrought changes in women's attitudes toward liturgy, and many in Baltimore concluded that they could no longer attend eucharistic celebrations. That same year but prior to the conference, Elizabeth Carroll, a theologian and former LCWR president, remarked, "Prayer today is a battleground. Public prayer, especially the Eucharist, becomes a locus of almost unbearable pain. The oppressive quality of a male priesthood . . . overwhelms me. The insensitivity to language which excludes women from the saving act of redemption makes it almost impossible for me to be at peace enough to receive the Eucharist."[27] In response to such feelings, conference organizers planned an elaborate eucharistic celebration for Saturday evening, diminishing the role of the presider as much as possible and highlighting the experiences of women from a variety of global perspectives. Bill Callahan, Jesuit founder of Priests for Equality, was invited to preside. According to Donna Quinn, Callahan was chosen because "he was the most laid-back [priest] we could think of and he wouldn't intrude."[28]

Near the start of the conference, however, flyers began to appear announcing an "alternative liturgy" for women only to be held at the same time as the larger eucharistic celebration. According to organizers it would be bilingual and include "a sharing of bread and wine free from relationships of domination and oppression."[29] These flyers suggest that the liturgy was a spontaneous act, but it was not. Barbara Zanotti, one of the most radical members of the WOC core commission, conceived of the event in advance, unbeknownst to the conference planning committee. Some movement veterans believe that Zanotti was deliberately trying to stir the pot, force the movement to confront the divisions growing within it, and to radicalize Catholic feminists.[30] The scheduling of the liturgy prevented participants from attending both; feminists struggling with shifting loyalties to church and feminism would have to make a very public choice.

For Donna Quinn, this choice became a crisis and a turning point. As a member of the WOC leadership team, Quinn felt she had to be true to the task force and to attend the liturgy as planned. Such a choice also affirmed her past position as a strong reformist. In retrospect, she viewed this decision as a breach of her integrity and a rejection of women, "and I always regretted that." In fact, from the remove of twenty-four years, regret brought tears to her eyes. "I knew that was the place to be, with the women who were trying to make a difference, in that small room. That's where I belonged."[31] From this point onward, Quinn backed away from institutional reform, encouraging women to devote their energy to building women's networks and openly celebrating liturgy without male presiders.[32]

Elisabeth Schüssler Fiorenza saw one of the flyers and on a whim decided to attend. She was a person who was generally skeptical of traditional or feminist liturgies badly done, but she chose to go although she feared she would find only a handful of women who "shared her theological perspective." When she arrived, however, she found that the room was full, and the celebration proved to be "one of the most moving liturgies of my life. Before my eyes and ears my theological convictions 'became flesh.'" This was the first time she attended a liturgy where the Eucharist was celebrated communally by women without a priest present as presider.[33]

Heightening the tension felt at Baltimore was the increasing pressure to choose. Although this choice took concrete form for Quinn and Schüssler Fiorenza, not everyone saw the options so clearly. The impression left by this conference was a lingering sense of ambivalence. The conference raised more questions than it could possibly resolve. Still, the feeling persisted that the movement had reached a turning point. Some participants— far more than the spattering of individuals who had made this choice earlier in the decade—were obviously ready to take a giant leap away from the church. Others seemed equally committed to renewal, while the majority seemed to be seeking a middle position from where they could stay or leave at the same time.

In the months immediately following the Baltimore conference, the woc core commission had to address these issues and succeeded in discussing them openly and honestly, even if they were not able to resolve very much. Rosemary Radford Ruether, not a member of the core commission but an informal advisor to the group, opened the debate with a letter to woc leadership written soon after the conference ended. She concretized the ambiguity of Baltimore by calling attention to two possible directions for woc: (1) "The purpose to ordain women into the priesthood of the Roman Catholic Church in some recognizable continuity with what those terms have meant historically"; and (2) "The purpose to renew the Church as a communitarian grass-roots egalitarian utopian redemptive non-sexist approximation of our particular vision of the Gospel."

While she remarked that "the second goal is lovely and I groove on it,"

Ruether ultimately concluded that it contradicted the first and "comes perilously close to sounding as though we are more interested in *abolishing* the priesthood than joining it." She argued that if the movement were to be committed to both renewal and ordination, it needed to adopt a pluralistic strategy based on a more "politically realistic" model and the recognition that most Christian denominations had reached women's ordination incrementally. As such, Ruether thought that retrenchment from the anti-institution tone of the conference was in order.

At the same time, she believed that the creation of separate, noninstitutional, sacramental women's faith communities built on a liberation theology "base community" model was a positive, legitimate step. But Ruether's affirmation of base communities came with a warning. If not approached with "theological reflection," and with a clear understanding of goals, the issue could be divisive, and bishops could splinter the movement and conquer.[34] With her vision of base communities, Ruether offered a position very close to that of Elisabeth Schüssler Fiorenza. Separate feminist communities could function as sites on the margins for Catholic feminists who wished to explore new ways of being both Catholic and feminist as they committed to renewing the institution.

In January 1979, two months after Baltimore, the core commission gathered to debrief and determine WOC's future goals. It was a very tense meeting, the process colored by both negative mail criticizing the conference's lack of direction and prayerfulness and the growing divide between local members and national leaders. According to Ada María Isasi-Díaz, "There is not a strong sense of feminism among our members. Feminism scares many of them. The strong feminists are hurting so much that they are unable to give time and space for growing to the women and men who are not there yet."[35] Each core commission member offered her or his vision for WOC's future. Some stressed the need to develop local chapters, noting the gulf between the national leadership and where the membership stood on the issues.[36] Others said that ordination had to remain the primary goal, capitalizing on momentum generated at the conference and joining other national organizations in the effort. Jamie Phelps, the only African American member, wondered if ordained white women would be any different from ordained white men, and she advocated paying attention to the needs of black Catholics. Everyone acknowledged the need to articulate a clear goal and strategy.

Soon all of the issues that had surfaced in Baltimore tumbled out onto the table, with Ruether's letter stimulating the debate. Questions were raised: "Is ordination first? Is Liberation first?" "Is woc against the Institution? Or is woc against the structures and systems of the Institution?" Some affirmed that woc should work from within structures and focus on expanding ministries at the parish level while encouraging base communities, as Ruether advocated. Others questioned identifying with the institution at all, saying that woc would be viewed as too conservative if it put energy behind expanding liturgical ministries and the diaconate and that it should instead support "a parallel structure of sacraments" emerging in women's communities.

The debate reached its zenith with an exchange between Barbara Zanotti, a feminist activist and leader of Boston woc, and Jamie Phelps, then head of the National Black Sisters Conference. Zanotti argued that woc must not "retrench," saying, "We must be bold; sexism is an urgent issue. woc must act from an integrative or feminist stance that it is a priesthood for and of the community." She asked that woc emphasize in its literature approval for women celebrating sacraments. Phelps challenged Zanotti: "Are those authentic sacraments? A woman cannot celebrate if she is not ordained by male bishops. When you set up a new altar, you set up a new church." She remarked also that black Catholics who left the church due to its racism "have not changed the main body. . . . Walking away will not challenge the parent body."

Zanotti replied that if the sacraments were controlled by sexism one had a duty to reclaim them. Phelps rejoined that traditionally such people would be excommunicated. Zanotti concluded that "woc is in communion with Rome; Rome is not in communion with us." When someone remarked that the nonsacramental life might have more to offer, the discussion abruptly ceased. As the minute-taker noted, "It was agreed that it was better not to explicate, if raised explicitly, we would have divided ourselves."

The meeting closed with a Mass "enabled" by Father Carroll Stuhlmueller, a core commission member. The group decided that its next major action would be reformist, a large petition campaign to lobby the NCCB for the removal of the "second argument" from the "Declaration." Barbara Zanotti was elected to the core leadership team. Clearly woc did not have a unified sense of where it was headed, but the issues at hand, the choices available, and the central ambivalence had been named.[37]

LIVING WITH AMBIVALENCE

At this point, we must pull back a moment and seek the larger picture. Yes, intraorganizational arguments do indicate tension and division. Yet I must listen to my interview subjects here and point out, as they did with surprising consistency, that Catholic feminists were also having a good time. When asked what they most wanted to be remembered about the movement's history, they frequently asked me to write about their close friendships, sense of excitement, and the amount of laughter that occurred at their meetings. The complexity of human nature is so apparent here because although these women could not stop talking about their pain, they also were experiencing great excitement and anticipation for what would come next. For many women, the process of coming to a deeper feminist consciousness was exhilarating as well as painful and confusing. Sisterhood was powerful, yes, but it could also be light-hearted.

I offer Marsie Sylvestro as a case in point. More than that, she illustrates the gradual move toward ministry on the margins. Marsie Sylvestro was born in New Haven, Connecticut, of the same generation as Mary Hunt. Family lore has it that baby Marsie used to egg on the other infants in the nursery and get them to cry. Sylvestro concludes, then, that she was born a feminist. She also says she "was a priest in my childhood." She regularly played Mass, decorating vestments with crayons and arranging her stuffed animals as the congregation. Like so many others, the sudden understanding that she could not be an altar girl left her extremely angry. Her mother was a powerful influence, urging her not to "let anyone say you can't do it because you're a girl."

Sylvestro attended a Catholic high school adjacent to the Yale University campus, and it proved to be the site for her development as an activist and feminist. She would sneak out of class to attend marches organized by Yale student feminists and was active in antiwar activities. But as was mentioned earlier, her feminism did not originate solely from secular sources. She vividly remembers one of the nuns taking her class to campus to hear Angela Davis speak. As it happened, Sylvestro also participated in home masses as a teenager with Dolly Pommerleau and Bill Callahan, who became major figures in the Catholic feminist movement.

Out of high school, Sylvestro joined the Sisters of Charity of our Lady Mother of Mercy, in retrospect because she was called to priesthood but at the time because she felt a commitment to religious life. She was most definitely a "new" nun, an archetypal version of the phenomenon in fact (though she always referred to herself in sixties' parlance as a "relevant nun"). A guitar-playing sister, her first musical composition was a song titled "Is Your Zeal for Real?" She even had a television show for children in New Haven called "A Brand-New Day." She left the convent in the early seventies, explaining that she "met a man across a crowded room." The relationship was short-lived, however, and by the midseventies Sylvestro identified as a lesbian after a relationship with a woman who also was a former nun. Meanwhile she was putting herself through college by working as a campus minister, first at the University of Detroit, and then at Manhattan College, and was emerging as a feminist activist with ties to both secular and Catholic feminism.

The Detroit conference helped Sylvestro recognize her call to priesthood and began her "formation" as a Catholic feminist. In her work as a campus minister she felt a great deal of freedom to push institutional boundaries. She celebrated the Eucharist with students and remembers that they would come to her for confession. "You are my priest," they would tell her. She always treated her work as her ministry, and she slowly came to believe that she need not wait for ordination. In this, Sylvestro was on the movement's cutting edge. "We were not asking permission to be priests," she insists. "We wanted recognition that we already were priests." Her intention was to give women the courage to embrace their gifts and to recognize the calls to priesthood in their vocations and daily lives.

Sylvestro became active in woc leadership in the last years of the decade. She says that woc helped her reclaim the joy of her childhood spirituality and gave her a genuine sense of excitement (she loved the strategizing that went on there). woc also led her to a new career and passion. At Baltimore Sylvestro attended the large eucharistic liturgy, in part because she wanted to support her old friend Bill Callahan, but she was extremely pained by the music, sung by a group of Jesuit seminarians. Livid, she went to Dolly Pommerleau, chair of the organizing committee, and demanded an explanation. Dolly looked at her and told her there was no women's liturgical music, and if she wanted it, she should go write it. From the call of a mentor, Sylvestro found the desire to write that music and went on to write some of the movement's most important songs in the eighties, including the anthem "Bless You, My Sister."

Sylvestro gained a lot from woc, but it gained as much in return from her. Sylvestro is serious about her activism, but she is also extremely funny, always ready with a raucous comment or dirty joke. Her humor brought needed levity to a group battling in the trenches. Stories abound, such as the one about Sylvestro and Rosalie Muschal-Reinhardt at an NCCB meeting in 1979. They encountered a salesman with a display of religious garb meant for the bishops. Muschal-Reinhardt commented that he would soon have to adjust his wares to accommodate women's entry into the priesthood. He replied that the day that happened, he would close up shop. When his back was turned, Marsie and Rosalie "liberated" a selection of ecclesiastical headgear, including a black berretta still in Marsie's possession. Sylvestro also performed at movement gatherings, adopting a series of personas. The most long-lived was a character named "Regina Coeli" (one of the Virgin Mary's titles). Sylvestro would emerge onstage in an elaborate Mary costume and perform a stand-up routine as the Blessed Mother. Her shtick included pulling a Raggedy Ann doll from her bag and proclaiming, "I always wanted a girl!"

Marsie Sylvestro was committed to a renewed priestly ministry rooted in the spirituality of her "Catholic heritage," but after several years in the WOC national office in the early eighties, she decided she was not willing to wait for the institution to catch up to her. She recalled that after getting a taste of ministry, she started to wonder why she needed anyone's permission to continue. She retained her ties with movement women and continued to minister within her own communities, which often retained a Catholic identification but were formed outside institutional boundaries. In the early eighties she helped found the Conference for Catholic Lesbians, for example. When asked why she ceased identifying with the institutional church she replied simply, "I left the abuser."[38]

Other signs showed that women's growing ambivalence was leading them to a new, more distant relationship to the institutional church. As noted in chapter 5, the radicalization of Catholic feminist liturgy was part of this shift. Another sign was increased involvement with secular feminists. Catholic feminists were never completely isolated from the larger movement, even in the early seventies. NCAN probably had the strongest ties to secular organizations, such as NOW. But in the late sixties and early seventies the larger movement was not welcoming to women who wanted to pursue feminism from a religious faith perspective. The head of NOW's Task Force on Women and Religion in 1977, an Episcopalian named Georgia Fuller, described the atmosphere of the feminist movement in the early seventies: "Yes, I was a closet Christian! For in the early seventies, god was indeed dead for feminists. . . . We left [churches]—and leaving brought us tremendous freedom. Leaving churches also brought us tremendous loneliness. . . . We thought that in leaving churches, we were leaving our spirituality. So we deceived ourselves by saying that spirituality was weak and passive. We had no need for spirituality. And we were wrong."[39] The Catholic feminist movement, optimistic, overtly Catholic, and focused on renewal, would not have thrived in this environment.

Catholic feminists also had little use for the internal debates that rocked secular feminism in the early to midseventies. The secular movement was marked by growing fault lines between liberals and radicals, "straights" and lesbians, as well as feuds over national leadership and extensive "trashing" of leaders.[40] Once the strand of feminist activity led by Mary Daly and Elizabeth Farians unraveled, Catholic feminists were almost universally liberal. Second, as the secular movement was rocked by Betty Friedan's denunciation of the "lavender menace" of lesbianism in the early seventies, the issue was just beginning to be discussed by Catholic feminists; prejudice lingered to the point that the movement was not a comfortable environment for lesbians, although they certainly existed in the movement's rank and file and its leadership.[41] Therefore, Catholic feminists generally ignored this debate until the mid to late seventies, when discussions of lesbian rights and the need to minister to lesbians emerged at about the same time.

By mid-decade, however, Catholic feminists were working extensively for the ERA, putting themselves in close contact with secular feminists. At the same time, Catholic feminists' ecumenical ties with other feminist women of faith increased. The first ordination conference signaled to the larger movement that Catholic feminists were now sufficiently organized to provide a significant presence in the church, and so feminists on both sides reached out to each other.

A high point was the National Women's Convention in Houston (1977), the first conference of its kind, including feminists representing a wide range of viewpoints and politics. According to Margaret Ellen Traxler, an official delegate, "It was without doubt the most exciting and inspiring experience of my life, and I have had many with which to compare!"[42] Annette Walters and Jacinta Mann, both leaders in NCAN, and Donna Quinn, a leader in NCAN, CCW, WCC, and WOC, shared her exhilaration. The Houston convention marked a rare opportunity for Catholic feminist leaders to experience solidarity with a broad spectrum of feminists.

WOC had ties to NOW, particularly through the Task Force on Women and

Religion, although the Quixote Center had a much closer working relationship with NOW. Many Catholic feminist women participated in local NOW chapters and in the national leadership. In 1979, the full-time leader of Wisconsin WOC, Mary Ann Ihm, cochaired NOW's brand new spirituality task force.[43] NOW and Catholic feminist leaders viewed each other with respect, as when NOW New York chose Rosalie Muschal-Reinhardt, "a living and vital feminist," as its conference keynote speaker in 1978.[44] Margaret Ellen Traxler said of NOW that same year: "I look to you and always have regarded you as the prophetic and redeeming wing of the Women's Movement and I always will regard you as that, come what may!"[45]

Yet, just as Catholic feminists were ambivalent about the institutional church, they also were ambivalent about the secular movement. Some, like Donna Quinn, embraced the movement wholeheartedly, but others sought a position on the margins of feminism as they had on the margins of the church. In a talk at the Baltimore WOC conference, Anne Carr chided Catholic feminists who distanced themselves from secular feminists for fear of being labeled "strident," calling their concern self-righteousness, stemming from the belief that their own cause was somehow "holier." Yet she argued that Catholic feminists should adopt a position on the margins of the movement, explaining that just as the church must "maintain a critical edge, a healthy abrasiveness in relation to its culture, but without complete withdrawal," Catholic feminists should assert their difference: "In affirming ourselves as Christian feminists and in offering the kind of reflection that our particular resources provide, we might make ourselves heard in new ways."[46]

The best example of Catholic feminists' ambivalence, both toward the institutional church and feminism, was abortion. The first fact about abortion that one notices when perusing the Catholic feminist archival record is its absence. If one were to take the archival record as pure fact, a researcher would be forgiven for thinking that Catholic feminists simply did not discuss the issue, even around the years of *Roe v. Wade*. For a variety of reasons, the majority of Catholic feminists found themselves caught among competing loyalties, beliefs, and strategies and therefore chose to avoid the subject as much as possible. Scattered correspondence, interviews, and the history of a very different kind of Catholic feminist organization tell the story.

First off, it should be noted that some Catholic feminists throughout the period of this study opposed abortion rights, disproving the claim that all American feminists supported abortion rights.[47] From the earliest years of the NOW Task Force, when hesitant women wrote to Elizabeth Farians asking if there was any place for pro-life feminists in the movement, some women made their opposition to abortion known. One example was Jacinta Mann, a member of NCAN and Houston delegate. As she told her own religious community, who were afraid that her participation in the convention was a statement in favor of abortion, "I have no intention of resigning as a delegate to Houston and losing my chance to keep Christ in the feminist movement. . . . Besides, it is a mistake to consider all feminists as abortionists. I am a feminist, but I am NOT 'soft on abortion' as I was recently accused of being."[48] Like many other women in the movement, raised Catholic, active in Catholic ministries, and steeped in the worldview of a woman religious, Mann simply could not support abortion on demand and was willing to say so publicly. Others like Kathleen Keating, head of NAWR in 1977, also declared opposition.[49]

Anecdotal evidence from interviews, though, suggests that a majority (but not an overwhelming majority) of feminists active in the Catholic movement were in favor of abortion rights. For example, the major feminist theologians, including Rosemary Radford Ruether and Elisabeth Schüssler Fiorenza, were publicly pro-choice, as was Donna Quinn. But unequivocal statements in favor of abortion rights were few and far between among organizational activists. More common were positions like that of Margaret Ellen Traxler. Directly after the Houston convention Traxler told the *Houston Chronicle*, "I am pro-life but I respect each person's conscience."[50] In other words, she was pro-choice. She tried to convince Jacinta Mann to "tell the world that we too support those women who are calling for women to control their own bodies."[51] But note how she distanced herself from the issue. She did not want to be one of the women who called for choice; she wanted to support the women who called for choice. Her confusing position did not prevent her from jumping into the middle of a fight on the issue, however.

In 1975, Traxler wrote to Betty Ford, congratulating the first lady on her handling of the abortion issue on the television news program *60 Minutes*. Ford had spoken against the Hyde Amendment, which would revoke federal funding for abortions, thereby affecting poor women disproportionately. Although Traxler had as yet taken no public stand on abortion, her strong belief in social justice led her to conclude that elite individuals had no right to make such a choice for poor women. Of all arguments for abortion rights, this was the one most likely to sway Catholic feminists or to provoke the moral dilemma between the sanctity of unborn human life and respect for the rights of women.[52] Traxler despised Congressman Henry Hyde so much that she referred to him in the Ford letter as a "fat ass" and then sent him a copy of the letter.[53] Hyde, in turn, sent a copy to several pro-life groups and to Traxler's superior. Traxler responded meekly to her superior's caution against making hasty judgments in anger but insisted to the end that "fat ass" was "the correct name for the man addressed."[54] NCAN was the first Catholic feminist organization to take a public stand in favor of a woman's right to choose. But even in 1982, when this statement was issued, it began "while we continue to oppose abortion, in principle, and in practice."[55]

But such voices were rare in the seventies. If the majority were pro-choice, why would they not say so publicly? And while the majority of the leadership seems to have been in favor of abortion rights, what of the rank and file? It would serve us well, at this point, to try to break out of the standard American paradigm for thinking about abortion by attempting to insert shades of gray into the discussion. Abortion was not an easy issue for these women, no matter what side of the argument they chose. Both Catholics and feminists viewed the decision as an obvious one, their conclusions diametrically opposed. So how was a Catholic feminist to approach it? As women committed to both feminism and Catholicism, it is likely that most viewed abortion as a significant moral dilemma (instead of a mortal sin, on the one hand, and a triumphant rallying cry, on the other). Certainly most did choose a stance, but some undoubtedly felt caught between the two positions. You can see this tension even in Margaret Ellen Traxler, usually so forthright and clearly committed. This is one reason for maintaining silence: to avoid alienating oneself from either the institutional church or one's feminist sisters.[56]

Other reasons were definitely strategic. Catholic feminist organizations relied on Catholic women for their funding, and these women certainly did not all share a pro-choice outlook. Organizations could not risk offending their base for a low-priority issue, so they avoided taking positions on abortion. Moreover, significant numbers of Catholic feminist activists worked for the institutional church as teachers, secretaries, ministers, associates, and so on. They, too, had great incentive to keep mum, as crackdowns by the international hierarchy would soon demonstrate. Remember, too, how committed many of these organizations were to dialogue. Any whiff of pro-choice rhetoric would have quickly derailed the dialogue strategy. According to Frances Kissling, long-time abortion-rights advocate and an observer of the Catholic feminist movement, "these were people of high integrity. If they engaged in discussion about abortion they would have to take a position." And taking a position would mean controversy and punishment.[57]

A fourth reason also compelled Catholic feminists to keep silent. The ERA became a major goal for many Catholic feminists in the mid to late seventies, and silence on the abortion issue was an important strategy in that battle. Ratification of the Equal Rights Amendment was a major focus of every American Catholic feminist group after 1972, when Congress sent the amendment to the states.[58] Maureen Fiedler, leader in the Quixote Center, was a major force in Catholic feminist work for the ERA, particularly after she cofounded and directed the group Catholics Act for ERA, a coalition designed to rally support among Catholics and counter opposition among bishops and the hierarchy. She worked extensively in Oklahoma, Nevada, Missouri, and Florida as well as in the battleground state, Illinois. When the Republican party removed the ERA from its 1980 platform, Fiedler chained herself to the doorway of the Republican National Committee's national headquarters. Fiedler was so determined to win Illinois for the ERA that as the ratification deadline loomed in 1982 she and six other women announced the "Women's Fast for Justice," eating nothing and drinking only water for thirty-seven days.[59]

Catholic feminists like Maureen Fiedler who worked for the ERA did so consciously as Catholics because they believed this would be their best contribution to the movement. Who better to convince large numbers of American Catholics, and in particular Catholic legislators, than women religious? Their arguments stressed two points in particular. The first was that ratifying the ERA was a virtual mandate of the Second Vatican Council.[60] The second, repeatedly argued by Catholic feminists in their attempts to support both Catholicism and feminism on issues that placed the two groups on opposite sides: abortion and the ERA were completely unrelated.[61] Fearing that Catholics connected abortion and ERA through the women's movement, Catholic feminists rushed to reassure reluctant Catholics that support for the ERA was not an endorsement of abortion rights. Here, too, the ambivalent position of Catholic feminists on abortion was in evidence. Most who used this argument did not claim to be opposed to abortion rights; usually they expressed no opinion at all, only their belief that abortion and ERA were unrelated and that, therefore, any Catholic, even the president of Notre Dame, could advocate ratification in good conscience.

This position could cause tension between Catholic and secular feminists. After receiving a pro-ERA form letter from NOW president Eleanor Smeal vigorously denouncing the NCCB for its abortion stand, a Catholic feminist commented angrily that "Eleanor Smeal told us in [the] first strategy meeting that abortion and lesbianism would be kept quite apart . . . from ERA." She decried Smeal's "McCarthyish . . . blatant religious bigotry." The writer seemed to be reacting more from the need to win over Catholics than the desire to denounce abortion and lesbianism, though she could very well have been opposed to both. By trying to separate abortion and ERA, a connection secular feminists desired to promote, Catholic feminists attempted to keep a foot in both camps.[62]

The final evidence for Catholic feminists' ambivalence on the question is the movement's treatment of Catholics for a Free Choice (CFFC). Formalized in 1973, CFFC was cofounded by three Catholic laywomen with the stated purpose of presenting a legitimate Catholic perspective on abortion that differed from that of the American hierarchy. From the beginning their protests were lively, their connections to the secular movement were very strong (their ties to the institution substantially less so), and their participation was not welcomed by the Catholic feminist movement. Although some leaders in the Catholic feminist movement were affiliated with CFFC, including Rosemary Ruether, Elisabeth Schüssler Fiorenza, Mary Hunt, and Donna Quinn, the organization was not invited into the WCC or represented at either of the women's ordination conferences in the seventies. CFFC leadership did not interact with other prominent Catholic feminist organizations; in fact, CFFC is rarely mentioned in the papers of any organization prior to the early eighties.

To be fair, the feminists in CFFC were very different from the majority of those in the Catholic feminist movement and were unlikely to have close ties with self-identified Catholic feminists, particularly with the more conservative feminist women religious. Those in the CFFC identified primarily with the secular movement and did not describe their feminism as originating in their faith tradition. However, when Frances Kissling accepted leadership of the organization in the early eighties she tried to establish ties with the Catholic movement but met with opposition. In 1983, she was invited to a planning session for the next major national conference, only to be asked to leave since not all groups represented were comfortable with her presence. She asked for fifteen minutes to address the group, which she spent telling them that they were acting more like the hierarchy than they were willing to admit.[63] As we shall see, CFFC was to play a major role in the Catholic feminist movement when, in 1984, the firestorm surrounding one of their protest actions marked a turning point for the movement.

Finally, another, very different form of ambivalence existed within the Catholic feminist movement in this period. Catholic feminist women of color often found themselves on the margins of both the church and the feminist movement, and while this could be the result of a personal choice, it often was simply the reality of a racist American and Catholic culture in the seventies. As was discussed in chapter 5, feminist women of color brought questions about race, ethnicity, and racism to the table as early as 1975. Shawn Copeland, representing the NBSC, and Maria Iglesias of Las Hermanas made dramatic statements at the first women's ordination conference, demanding to know if feminism would make white activists more attuned to the needs of black and Hispanic communities. Both the NBSC and Las Hermanas included avowed feminists within their ranks. From the start, however, both groups decided that ministry to and advocacy for their respective communities were of paramount concern, with feminism viewed as a secondary goal. Yet leaders in both would like to have seen blacks and Latinas better represented in Catholic feminist organizations and their concerns addressed.

The movement was overwhelmingly white and middle class, and the composition of the leadership reflected this. Several Catholic feminist theologians, notably Rosemary Radford Ruether, whose activism began in the civil rights movement, and Marjorie Tuite (one of the few leaders in the movement to "get it right" according to Jamie Phelps), had long articulated the relationship between racism and sexism in America, but on an organizational level, feminists had been slow to address the issue.[64] In response to the rising debate, Catholic feminist organizations from LCWR to NAWR to WOC attempted to confront issues of racism. To be fair, many Catholic feminists were just becoming cognizant of the need to confront these issues, but their efforts were never particularly successful. Often the issue of race arose when feminists tried to expand or improve their social justice ministry. It was not unusual for women in these organizations to discuss the needs of oppressed people and Catholic feminists' responsibility toward them. Yet, these listings of "the oppressed" often lumped everyone together in a jumble: minorities, prostitutes, the incarcerated, the poor, and the disabled. And although Catholic feminists could be articulate about "sex/race/class," the movement on a large scale rarely produced concrete plans to alleviate oppression rooted in the intersection of racism, sexism, and poverty.

When accused of racism, feminist women religious tried to diversify their organizations, but these efforts seemed stuck in "the worst kind of tokenism." WOC was a particularly glaring example of this tendency. In a 1977 memo, WOC officers discussed how a list of women had been "invited to represent a category," including "Hispanic (Caribbean), Hispanic (Chicana), Alienated, Black Laywoman, Native-American, Single, Prostitutes." They were also actively looking for women to fill "Lesbian, Prison, Divorced/Separated, and Native-Asian" slots. In interviews, both Shawn Copeland and Jamie Phelps expressed their frustration at being asked repeatedly to fill the "African-American" slot on the boards of Catholic feminist organizations. Although the organizations never stated the invitation in this way, that is how the women interpreted it since they were usually the only African Americans on the boards.[65]

Phelps, a woman religious and theologian, agreed to join the WOC core commission to explore the authenticity, scope, and validity of women's cry for ordination, and as we have seen she took an active role in challenging WOC leadership. She commented that "if I'm going to be a token, I'm going to get something out of it for the black community." Phelps acknowledges that the white leaders of WOC had much learning to do. "They were really pretty naive," she remembered. "They had not done a self-critique of their own white supremacy." She experienced racism in WOC and believed that many of the women still operated out of an assumption that people of color were inferior. Anecdotally, it seems clear that some Catholic feminists were very adept at talking about the theoretical underpinnings of racism but not so adept at seeing lingering racism in themselves. Phelps adds that she "does not impugn the good they did, but it was flawed."[66]

Ada María Isasi-Díaz credits Jamie Phelps and Yolanda Tarango, a prominent leader in Las Hermanas, with helping her recognize racism within the movement. In her case, she believes that it led some of the women in WOC leadership to consistently ignore her. Isasi-Díaz believes that some in WOC were uncomfortable with having a Latina as the face of the organization, even for a brief time. As a major leader from WOC's inception, she took the opportunity to caution the group repeatedly about tokenism. She acknowledges that woc worked very hard to gain minority representation, as did most of the groups. But they struggled, mainly because black and Latina feminists had many calls on their time and were not interested in being slot fillers. Also, though the leadership eagerly welcomed the chance to be diverse, Isasi-Díaz believes they would have grown very uncomfortable if they had ever recruited enough women of color that the whites were no longer a majority.[67]

These activists, then, experienced a marginalization and attendant ambivalence from a number of fronts, making their experience in the movement unique. In a letter welcoming a young Latina into the movement, Isasi-Díaz stated her belief that ordination was a real concern for Latinas (though some had suggested otherwise). Then she outlined what it was like to be a feminist woman of color in the church. As an example she recounted a conversation with the director of the Spanish apostolate in the Diocese of Rochester: "Do you want me to fight now against the Americans so that they will believe in my personhood and then in a few years have to turn around and fight with you so that you will accept me as a woman equal to you in all aspects?" Isasi-Díaz also recalls how Latino activists would accuse the Latina feminists in their midst of being corrupted by the Anglo women. The organization Las Hermanas flourished because it helped Latinas strengthen their feminism through sisterhood and consciousness-raising, confront sexism among men in their own communities (academic, activist, parish, and family), and challenge the church at the same time. As they were engaging and challenging on so many fronts, and since they encountered racism among some of their white "sisters," they chose an open but deliberately cautious stance toward the movement.

Shawn Copeland also tried to articulate the unique experience of being a black Catholic woman. woc asked her to craft one of the prayer services for the 1978 Baltimore conference. The result was "Your Daughters Shall Prophesy," an intensely personal prayer that reads like the message of an outsider who did not expect or need to be heeded. As she asserted at the beginning, "The Conveners and Planners of this conference have asked me to speak a word. I do so reluctantly. The word I speak comes to me from my God, from my ancestors, from my sojourn. The word I speak surrounds me, becomes me, penetrates me. The word I speak is *waiting*. Waiting. Waiting does *not* surrender the standard . . . submit defeat . . . suppress the call. . . . Waiting is the struggle for fidelity. For some, waiting is an abomination, an embarrassment, an anachronism: still, I ask you wait." Despite, or perhaps because of, her stance as observer, Copeland understood the tone of the conference, the urge to move on.

Copeland used her experience as a black Catholic woman to explain the virtue of waiting—in other words, of discernment. She tried to communicate to them that one finds "the gracious sovereign love and mercy of our God" in waiting. After all, "the gentle breeze calls tradition to *new* life in every age." She began and ended her prayer with these words: "I am a child born of the union of tradition and crisis. Sorrow is my grandmother, suffering and striving my aunts, begin anew my great-grandmother. I am the daughter of the Church: my name is waiting." She was asking those present to contemplate the contradictions in their culture and in themselves, to pray with their ambivalence, to "struggle for fidelity."

Her message may have been needed, but the conference was too busy running around in confusion, too much in a hurry, for her words to be heeded. In the coming decades, feminists from the NBSC and Las Hermanas, including Copeland, Phelps, Isasi-Díaz, and others, such as Tarango, went on to earn degrees in theology. With this knowledge, and their grounding in feminist and civil rights activism, they began to articulate new theologies rooted in the experiences of black and Hispanic Catholic women. They continued to carve out a place of prophetic witness on the margins of the movement.

THE END OF AN ERA

In many ways, the period 1978–80 was transitional, as Catholic feminists' pain, anger, and growing feminist consciousness led them toward a new way of being activists and of being church with one another. But two moments—one very public, one private—at the close of the seventies and the beginning of the eighties give us a good indication that the movement had indeed reached a turning point. The era when Catholic feminists could put their hope and energy into dialogue and reform was drawing to a close.

In autumn 1979, all eyes were on Pope John Paul II, soon to arrive for his first American visit as pope. Catholic communities across the country spent millions of dollars to welcome the pontiff to the United States, a point not overlooked by social justice–conscious Catholic feminists. So eager were American Catholics to welcome the pope that bishops willingly agreed to John Paul's many stipulations, including the demand that only priests could distribute Communion. In American cities across the country, WOC chapters planned major protest actions against this new pope who already seemed so hostile to both feminism and renewal.

In Houston, woc members left rocks at the door of the chancery, symbolizing that the church was giving them stones instead of bread, while singing a feminist version of the Catholic hymn "Immaculate Mary": "Immaculate Mary, We're branded since birth, to sit back and be led by all men on earth. Oh no, oh no, oh no Maria. No more, no more, Maria." In Des Moines, Catholic feminists marched under the banner "Equal Rites for Women" and prayed a feminist rewriting of the Magnificat, Mary's prayer of thanksgiving to God. New York woc staged an all-night vigil outside the United Nations, where the pope was to deliver an address. Boston woc celebrated an ecumenical liturgy the day before the pope's visit to that city, cosponsored by now and Dignity, an organization for gay and lesbian Catholics. The day of the pope's arrival, Boston woc held a large protest at which they declared their intention to initiate a "women's church in exile."[68] But the protest with the greatest impact took place in Washington, D.C., and to the surprise of feminists and Catholics alike, it originated not with woc, but with the lcwr.

On October 7, 1979, the atmosphere in the National Shrine of the Immaculate Conception in Washington, D.C., was tense. In Philadelphia the day before, Pope John Paul II had received a standing ovation from a crowd of seminarians, cheering his speech opposing women's ordination. Now he faced a cathedral full of American women religious, many steaming over his comments in Philadelphia. Scattered throughout the cathedral were fifty-three women religious wearing blue armbands. No one was sure what they were planning, and authorities were nervous. Organizers did not seem overly concerned about the chosen speakers, however. Theresa Kane, president of the lcwr (and head of the Sisters of Mercy of the Union) would offer a brief welcome on behalf of America's women religious, and then the Holy Father would give his address.

Kane had joined the lcwr in 1970, her first year as a Mercy provincial, just as the lcwr began to restructure itself and move to the left.[69] In 1973, lcwr emerged as a proponent of justice for women in the church, and by 1975 the group of superiors had developed and sponsored consciousness-raising groups for sisters across the country. Meanwhile, the lcwr maintained its role as chief mediator between American women religious and the Vatican, attempting to gain self-determination through diplomacy. According to Kane, the lcwr was "steeped" in women's rights issues between

1972 and 1979. By 1979, Kane felt herself to be a part of a national community of Catholic feminist women. When the opportunity arose to address the pope, she knew what she would do. "It was never a question of should I say it, but how," she remembered.[70]

In her speech, Kane first extended "greetings of profound respect, esteem and affection from women religious throughout this country." She then spoke briefly of the "valiant" women religious who helped build the American church and of sisters' renewal efforts after Vatican II, expressing their feelings of responsibility to the church. She praised the pope for his courage in speaking on behalf of the poor and oppressed worldwide; she pledged American sisters' solidarity with his efforts "to respond to the cry of the poor."

Kane's remarks then took an unexpected turn. She spoke of the suffering and pain experienced by American women and asked the pope to listen with compassion. Using the church's own documents to her advantage she delivered her controversial message:

> As women we have heard the powerful messages of our Church addressing the dignity and reverence for all persons. As women we have pondered these words. Our contemplation leads us to state that the Church in its struggle to be faithful to its call for reverence and dignity of all persons must respond by providing the possibility of women as persons being included in all ministries of our Church. I urge you, Your Holiness, to be open to and respond to the voices coming from the women of this country who are desirous of serving in and through the Church as fully participating members.[71]

Kane concluded her brief welcome by promising the prayers, support, and fidelity of America's women religious and by praying for Mary's blessing on him. This was all she had planned to do, but on the spur of the moment she approached John Paul II and knelt down before him for a blessing, which he gave.[72]

Kane's welcome walked a line made of spider's silk, so precarious was her balancing of opposing forces. At its heart, the welcome was both an outrageously courageous personal act of defiance and a deep expression of loyalty and love. Consider Kane's impromptu decision to kneel before the pope for his blessing, a move that could be considered the supreme act of submission, a questionable choice for a feminist. But from her opening paragraph Kane asserted her power as a woman by claiming her right to call

Theresa Kane welcomes
Pope John Paul II to the
National Shrine of the
Immaculate Conception
in 1979 (Courtesy of
the University of
Notre Dame Archives)

on Mary, by saying it was fitting that a woman's voice be heard in the shrine, by recalling the valiance of her sister forebears, and by openly judging the church according to its own standards. Directly before she knelt, she ended her welcome by assuming the power of blessing over him. She could be feminist in her call for justice for women and in her own assumption of authority, but she could also be Catholic in her references to Mary and the Magnificat, in her valuing of contemplation, in her respect for authority and tradition, in her concern for the poor, in her gentleness of spirit.

Kane was completely unprepared for the reaction, which was fast and highly polarized. Within the shrine many women religious cheered, led by the women in blue armbands who stood in protest during the pope's address; others writhed in shame that any sister could be so rude to the Holy Father. Within hours, news of the welcome spread across the country and around the globe. The story of a woman religious, in a suit, calling for women's ordination in the presence of the pope was of interest to more than just the Catholic community. For the first time, the issue of women's ordination was catapulted into the international secular media.

Catholic feminists from the most conservative to the most radical were universally thrilled, if not euphoric. For one brief moment after years of struggle they could finally claim a victory. They called Kane "courageous," "valiant," "strong," and "prophetic." Some drew explicit comparisons to the Virgin Mary; one letter opened effusively, "Blessed are you among women, women of today and of days to come and years and years to come. . . . Yours is a name to be esteemed, a name to be revered."[73] Catholic feminists had had so little to celebrate for so long. Their letters to her offered a well-spring of gratitude because a woman had stood up in the presence of the pope and spoken honestly. Over and over writers said, "thank you for saying it for me."[74]

Despite the joy of victory, however, Kane's address marks the culmination of an era, not the beginning of one. Kane's choice of action, her message to the pope, and the way she delivered it were all characteristic of the dialogue strategy, of the kind of loyal opposition common at mid-decade. This is not to say that loyal opposition disappeared completely from the movement, but it did recede in prominence and was less promoted among the movement's leadership. A Catholic feminist had reached the highest possible heights of dialogue; she had spoken her truth to the pope. There was nowhere else to go from there. The journey to the margins continued.

The second moment occurred the following summer. It was a private moment, marked by very few, and caused no public scandal or feminist euphoria. Nevertheless, it too suggests that a milestone in the movement had been passed. In July 1980, Rosalie Muschal-Reinhardt and her husband Al marked their twenty-fifth wedding anniversary. To celebrate the occasion they decided to hold a Mass in their home with friends and family, but in the end they held it on their own. Rosalie could not bring herself to ask a priest to preside. She felt too battered, too excluded, too tired to try to make peace with the institutional church anymore.

Rosalie Muschal-Reinhardt, the movement's most enthusiastic champion of dialogue, the woman who smiled at bishops in elevators, the most determined to stick with the church she loved, could no longer make the effort. In the following years she remained on the church's margins and settled into the long-term realities of sustained ambivalence. She maintained close ties with other movement women who made a variety of choices about their relationships to the institution. She taught in a Catholic school; she even joined a community of religious women as a lay associate. But she would no longer struggle with the institutional church. An era came to a close with her farewell, as only Rosalie could phrase it: "Goodbye, boys. You can have your church back."[75]

epilogue
1980 – 1986

Throughout your ministry, you remembered us while others
forgot. . . . Mary's son in bone and blood, we share this meal
at your invitation. We do this in memory of you.
—Kerry Maloney, "A Eucharistic Remembrance"

Late in my research I stumbled on a tantalizing photocopied document that
was stuck, randomly, in an archive folder. Titled simply the "Gospel of
Priscilla," it was a first-person narrative account of the women's journey to
Jesus's tomb and their attempts to share the good news of resurrection with
the other disciples.

The gospel story unfolds from a woman's perspective, telling the tale of a
group of grieving women setting out for the tomb of a loved one with oint-
ments and spices. Amazed to see the tomb empty and hear the voices of the
angels, they returned to the others with "a new joy growing in our hearts."
The male disciples scoffed at their news and sent Peter out to verify the
women's crazy story. When he returned without seeing angels or a glowing
light, the men "looked at us reproachfully, having disturbed their sorrow."

Dismissed, the women returned to the kitchen. "Our rejection by the
men saddened us," the author wrote, "but nothing could for long dampen
that joy growing out of the confusion in our hearts. 'He is risen!' we whispered and sang to one another as we went about our chores." As they
worked they told stories of Christ and his teachings, and when they stopped
to eat their midday meal they broke the bread they had just baked and

Catholic feminist protest from the early eighties (Courtesy of the Women and Leadership Archives, Loyola University Chicago: Chicago Catholic Women Records, Addendum I)

remembered what Christ had promised. "Our beloved Teacher, or friend, was with us, and we Knew that despite the fact that our story went against reason, it was the truth and nothing would ever be the same again."[1]

The "Gospel of Priscilla" encapsulates the mood of the early eighties for Catholic feminists. Like so many other of her sisters at this time, Priscilla felt spiritually and politically empowered. By placing herself in the story she named herself a disciple and encouraged other women to do the same. She was "doing" theology at the most fundamental level, confident that she was free to reenvision the story of Christ's resurrection from the perspective of her own experience. Not incidentally, she was also confident in her identity as a feminist woman of faith. Priscilla was "saddened" that the men would not join them, would not accept their revelation as truth, but she was happy to seek the company of women set apart. The women understood and trusted each other, and their sense of joy was unfettered. This gospel was proclaimed as part of a "Eucharistic remembrance," through which Catholic feminists consecrated bread and wine within the context of this sister-hood. "Throughout your ministry, you remembered us while others forgot,"

Panel discussing Women-Church in the early eighties (Courtesy of the Women and Leadership Archives, Loyola University Chicago)

they prayed. "Mary's son in bone and blood, we share this meal at your invitation. We do this in memory of you."[2]

In the spirit of the early eighties, these women were confident, bold, spiritually grounded in a theology they were creating for themselves, committed to sisterhood, and willing to distance themselves from the institutional church. The dominant themes of the seventies—the need to confront, to catch the hierarchy's attention, to be listened to, to renew—never disappeared from the Catholic feminist movement, but after Theresa Kane's welcome these goals decreased in importance, replaced by a focus on developing women's spiritual communities at the grass roots, independent of the institution. Attention shifted toward personal spiritual fulfillment, ecumenism, and renewal through models of just, nonpatriarchal Christian community.

But the "Gospel of Priscilla" suggests something else about the Catholic feminist community in the early eighties: they were also not all in agreement. A few minutes of searching on the Internet led me to a very startled Priscilla Ballou, the woman who wrote the piece in the early eighties as a member of Boston woc. (She was overjoyed to see her gospel story again, having lost her last copy of it decades earlier). She explained that a core group of women from Boston woc would begin each meeting with the Eucharist but only if those preparing the liturgies consented to it, and not all of them did. As Ballou remembered it, "There were differing degrees of comfort among the members of the group with celebrating [Eucharist] without benefit of officially ordained clergy."[3]

As internal divisions within the local and national WOC indicate, not all Catholic feminists viewed independent feminist spiritual communities as a positive development, fearing they would lead women away from the struggle for renewal. In recognition of these divisions, WOC elected not to hold a national conference in 1981 and promoted regional conferences instead. These regional conferences, particularly the "Women-Moving Church" conference in Washington D.C., proved to be incubators for a new branch of the movement. Further developing the themes she had raised at the 1978 Baltimore conference, theologian Elizabeth Schüssler Fiorenza introduced the concept of the "*ekklesia* of women" (women church) at the D.C. conference. She encouraged participants to view "the gathering of women as a free and decision-making assembly of God's people," a theme she would explore in her monumental 1983 book, *In Memory of Her: A Feminist Theological Reconstruction of Christian Origins.*[4]

Divisions persisted within the movement after the regional conferences. According to sociologist Tracey Memoree Thibodeau, around this time WOC broke into factions as questions of identity overshadowed those of strategy; under continued opposition from the institution, the power of the ordination issue to unite the movement faded. Such key leaders as Rosalie Muschal-Reinhardt and Ada María Isasi-Díaz left WOC's leadership. Soon, a faction emerged urging feminists to reevaluate their identification as Catholics. In Thibodeau's analysis, "when political opportunities closed, especially in relation to women's ordination, Catholic feminists opted for an exemplary approach. They turned inward, emphasizing the personal empowerment of Catholic women and the transformation of the self."[5]

Accordingly, 1983 saw the founding of WATER (the Women's Alliance for Theology, Ethics, and Ritual), a highly influential educational center for "justice-seeking people . . . a response to the need for serious theological, ethical, and liturgical development for and by women," founded by Catholic feminists Diann L. Neu and Mary Hunt.[6] Also in 1983, the Women of the Church Coalition, established in 1977, held a milestone conference under the leadership of Donna Quinn called "From Generation to Generation: Women Church Speaks." This conference transformed the WCC into Women-Church Convergence, a loose affiliation of grassroots Women-Church cell groups from across the country designed to support women's explorations of identity, the nature of church, and expressions of feminist spirituality through the creation of liturgy. Many preexisting Catholic feminist organizations affiliated with Women-Church.

In Women-Church, feminists experimented through praxis with a lived faith outside the bounds of patriarchy. According to Rosemary Radford Ruether, a major contributor to the theoretical underpinnings of Women-Church: "We must do more than protest against the old. We must begin to live the new humanity now. We must begin to incarnate the community of faith in the liberation of humanity from patriarchy in words and deed, in new words, new prayers, new symbols, and new praxis. This means that we need to form gathered communities to support us as we set out on our exodus from patriarchy."[7] Therefore, Women-Church was not simply a means of self-transformation; it was also a way of reenvisioning church from a position on the margins, aiming to avoid separatism while acknowledging that "we often cannot even continue to communicate within these traditional church institutions unless we have an alternative community of reference that nurtures and supports our being."[8]

Women-Church offered Catholic feminists options and a means of sustaining ambivalence. It embodied the insider/outsider position because it existed somewhere on the margins, exploring new conceptions of spirituality while retaining ties to Catholic ritual and theology. Participants in Women-Church used it either as their primary worship community (as a means of escaping the institution) or as a supplement to their primary parish community (a respite when women wearied of androcentric liturgy).

Although Women-Church captured much of the movement's attention and energy in the first half of the eighties, political activity did not cease, and members of Women-Church were not necessarily apolitical. Catholic feminists throughout the movement continued the struggle for ordination while launching a new campaign against exclusive language in Catholic liturgy and documents. Many Catholic feminists, including the influential Marjorie Tuite, continued to pursue social justice issues as feminists, most notably working to aid those suffering from war, poverty, and oppression in Central America.

But all Catholic feminist political activity in the eighties was overshadowed by the papacy of John Paul II and, not incidentally, the concurrent presidency of Ronald Reagan. Feminists viewed both as regressive administrations that threatened a whole host of liberal causes and beliefs, feminism the greatest among them. For Catholic feminists, John Paul II posed a threat because he appeared to be aggressively rolling back the reforms of Vatican II. Early in his papacy, the pope signaled his refusal to dialogue with feminists, and he began a series of crackdowns designed to keep feminists,

Catholic feminists protesting U.S. involvement in Central America in the early eighties (Courtesy of the Women and Leadership Archives, Loyola University Chicago: Chicago Catholic Women Records)

particularly women religious, in line (as he instigated a similar backlash against liberation theologians). The Sisters of Mercy, the most visibly feminist order of sisters, bore the brunt of Vatican attempts to control and silence American women religious in the early eighties. First, the Vatican successfully challenged the order's decision to allow tubal ligation in its hospitals by threatening sanctions against the order. Then Vatican officials notoriously forced three Mercy sisters, most notably Agnes Mary Mansour, to choose between their vocations and their positions in public office.

The worst days of repression began in 1984 when a group of men and women signed a *New York Times* advertisement sponsored by Catholics for a Free Choice, asserting that "a diversity of opinions" existed among Catholics on the issue of abortion. Among the signers were Rosemary Radford Ruether, Donna Quinn, Margaret Ellen Traxler, Maureen Fiedler, Mary Hunt, Frances Kissling, and Marjorie Tuite. The Vatican used the advertisement to provoke a showdown over feminism. They threatened the lay signers with a host of reprisals if they failed to recant, but the priests and religious in the group faced dismissal from their orders and defrocking. The

Supporters protesting the Vatican's treatment of Sister Agnes Mary Mansour (Courtesy of the University of Notre Dame Archives)

few priest signers quickly recanted, as did several sisters, but a group of women religious known as the Vatican 24 stood their ground.

The process took two years of negotiation among the signers, their congregational leadership, and the Vatican. In the end only two sisters, Barbara Ferraro and Patricia Hussey, resigned from their orders; the rest reached compromise positions allowing them to remain. Some Catholic feminists view the incident as a victory of sorts, citing the orders' refusal to summarily dismiss their sisters despite extreme pressure from the Vatican. Others believe sisters were compromised by leadership that failed to stand behind them.[9] Still others blame the women religious who did not leave their orders. In 1987, Mary Hunt and Frances Kissling wrote an analysis of the

Ada María Isasi-Díaz and Rosalie Muschal-Reinhardt at a reunion of Catholic feminists in 2006 (Courtesy of the author)

ongoing case against several of the signers. Their analysis revealed the intense feelings of distrust and betrayal among Catholic feminists that resulted from the case. The authors believed that when the vast majority of women religious in the Vatican 24 chose to negotiate a compromise rather than refuse to recant their positions, they betrayed the movement and the two women religious who stood their ground. The fact that most of the signers chose to compromise was actually consistent with the history of Catholic feminism in America. Catholic feminists had long resisted any pressure to choose between their loyalties to feminism and Catholicism. By 1987, however, Hunt and Kissling were prepared to reject those who appeared to choose institutional loyalties over sisterhood.[10]

Feminists can all agree, however, that the incident of the Vatican 24 demonstrated the extremes to which the Vatican would go to silence feminist opposition as well as the extent to which the church had retreated from Vatican II reforms. The church that in the sixties and early seventies inspired Catholic women to become feminists with its commitment to renewal now seemed determined to crush them. Little wonder that in the eighties so many retreated to the margins or simply said goodbye to the institutional church.

WHAT THEN IS THE legacy of these determined women and their quest for justice? The question is difficult to answer not only because some of the movement's initial and most visible goals were not reached, but because their goals changed over time. First, it must be noted that the movement these women began in the sixties survives, persisting in a variety of forms within what continues to be a hostile institutional climate. The Women's Ordination Conference, NCAN, LCWR, WATER, Women-Church, and other organizations founded during the movement's heyday continue to work for justice for women, often with a more pointedly global focus. The trend toward moving away from institutional reform still holds. For many of these groups, now that the sisterhoods are contracting and the movement's constituency is aging, the most pressing goal is recruiting the next generation of Catholic feminists into activism.

In recent years the movement, influenced by Catholic feminists in Europe, has begun to move in a strikingly new direction by ordaining its own women. The number of women with training for ordination either to priesthood or diaconate has increased steadily over the decades, and patience has grown thin. Whereas in earlier years many of these women would have sought ordination in a Protestant denomination, in recent years such organizations as the international group Roman Catholic WomenPriests have begun conducting their own ordination ceremonies for women they deem qualified. The group asserts that the women bishops who conduct these ceremonies were secretly ordained by Roman Catholic bishops and therefore claims apostolic succession for its priests. In one way, then, the group tries to redefine legitimacy by proceeding with ordinations against the explicit orders of the Vatican. Yet the group appears to subscribe to the belief that a woman needs the institutional blessing of succession to be legitimate.

Catholic feminists of the late seventies seemed to reject such an approach because they wanted a transformed priestly ministry without the trappings of clericalism. And, indeed, several feminists from that era who spoke with me were uneasy about these recent ceremonies for that very reason. Widely publicized images of women prostrating themselves to receive the blessings of apostolic succession seemed to them a step backward for women as well as a reformed priesthood. Yet the ceremonies have been endorsed by many Catholic feminists, including the Women's Ordination Conference. Will these ceremonies produce the new priestly ministry Catholic feminists hoped for? The question remains to be answered.

Perhaps the most obvious and lasting impact of the Catholic feminist movement has been in the academy, particularly in the discipline of theology. Feminist theologians, many of them Catholic, have helped to transform that discipline, its professional organizations, and the institutions in which they work. While striving for academic excellence, these theologians also view their work as ministry, seeking to reach a large audience of women and men with messages of justice and equality. Through their efforts, countless people have been empowered to "do theology" of their own, enriching the collective understanding of faith and justice.

An evaluation of the movement's impact on the larger feminist movement must be more measured. It is difficult to gauge this impact, but the fact that Catholic feminists have largely been left out of histories of American feminism is a good indication that their contributions have been undervalued. I suggest that the Catholic feminist legacy to the larger movement is threefold. First, the Catholic movement undeniably channeled thousands of otherwise unreached women into the feminist sisterhood. Second, from the earliest years of second-wave feminism, Catholic feminists were instrumental in helping secular feminists see that religious faith did not somehow make a feminist suspect. The examples of religious feminists, such as the activists discussed in this book, helped the larger movement come to respect spirituality and religious affiliation as a legitimate choice for a feminist, thereby broadening the understanding of feminism itself.

Third, as this book has argued, Catholic feminists illustrate for the larger movement the process of claiming a feminist identity when a woman has divided loyalties. These women's hesitancy to choose one side over the other does not necessarily indicate a lesser commitment. Rather, their process of negotiating among competing loyalties reminds us that, historically, feminists have not automatically abandoned who they are to conform to a constructed notion of what a feminist should be. All along, women were defining feminism for themselves, and that understanding of feminism made room for continued, if transformed, loyalties to patriarchal institutions.

Finally, we must turn to the movement's impact on the church itself. In the case of the institutional church, the question of legacy can be a depressing one. For those who hoped to see concrete changes within the priesthood, governance, and official teachings, the past few decades have been disheartening. Gains, such as the official acceptance of female altar servers, have been counteracted by setbacks, such as the Vatican pronouncement that not only is women's ordination prohibited, it can no longer even be *discussed*. Rollbacks of hard-won reforms continue to this day, to devastating effect.

But despite its failure to move the upper echelons of the institutional church, the movement's impact has been clear. Without making any major political gains, Catholic feminists slowly, quietly assumed leadership roles as pastoral associates, pastoral administrators, theologians, liturgists, directors of religious education, and seminary instructors. As the numbers of priestly vocations plummeted throughout the eighties and nineties, Catholic women, feminist or not, took up the slack and have helped shape the religious lives of countless Catholics in parishes across the country. None of these gains would have been possible without the movement's struggle in the sixties and seventies to open divinity schools and seminaries to women, to encourage women to follow their calls, to make connections between feminism and social justice, and to make liturgy their own.

On a more abstract level, Catholic feminism has helped change the way that American Catholics understand their identities as Catholics. Along with other reform movements in the sixties and seventies, Catholic feminists embraced the Vatican II ideal that the people do indeed constitute the church, and as such they have helped define what it is to be "Catholic." Their movement provided a means of making that vision concrete. Battered by patriarchy and the daily indignities of sexism in the church, Catholic feminists not only outlined a new vision for the church, they also claimed that this vision was legitimately Catholic by defining it as such. As "the church" they had a right to do so if they followed the precepts of justice. This is not "cafeteria-style" Catholicism, where Catholics pick and choose what they want to believe. This is a liberated Catholicism in which Catholic women understand that the unjust institutional power structure does not have the power to define them, or imprison them, or even reject them. Its ability to have "power over" has greatly diminished. In this view, the people of God have a right and an obligation to define what it means to be Catholic in the world, and Catholic feminists were, and remain, some of the most visible and strongest advocates of that view.

Finally, the movement freed thousands of women, if they so chose, to seek a new spiritual home that could fulfill the promise of justice, whatever that home might be. The women who left the institutional church did so for legitimate reasons, and the Catholic feminist movement helped many of these women transition through that difficult process without necessarily giving up those aspects of Catholicism that sustained them. The movement gave women options for forging new religious as well as feminist identities.

In the end, this holds true for Catholic feminists inside, outside, and on the margins of the church. The Catholic feminist movement provided the means of connecting women to what had formed and inspired them as they worked over time to confront and possibly reject a sexist church. In the process, they discovered that the commitment to both challenge and embrace their loyalties could be the most difficult, but also the most liberating, aspect of feminist consciousness.

notes

1. NCAN, press release, 1972, NCAN-R 2/2, MUA.

2. This analysis differs from other studies of Catholic feminism because it is an in-depth narrative and interpretive history focusing on the origins of Catholic second-wave feminism and its development over time. As it is the first substantive study of this subject, the historiography is severely limited. One monograph, Donna Stei-chen's *Ungodly Rage*, purports to be a history of the movement but is in reality an antifeminist polemic written by a conservative Catholic journalist. Several edited volumes and essay collections do include brief histories of the Catholic feminist movement. See Ebest and Ebest, *Reconciling Catholicism and Feminism?*; Rader, "Catholic Feminism," which provides an overview of the movement from a contem-porary perspective; and Rosemary Radford Ruether's overview in Ruether and Keller, *In Our Own Voices*. The literature also includes memoirs, such as Barbara Ferraro and Patricia Hussey's *No Turning Back*, Janet Kalven's *Women Breaking Boundaries*, and the fine analysis of Catholic women's narratives of "exodus" in Debra Campbell's *Graceful Exits*. My project complements these texts by providing historical context.

Only two studies of contemporary Catholic feminism provide a substantive anal-ysis of the movement's history in the period covered by my book, but each has limitations for current scholarship. Mary Fainsod Katzenstein's *Faithful and Fearless* argues that the dominant theme in Catholic feminism has been "discursive radical-ism," meaning that the movement developed mainly through words and images and eschewed public protest. My book challenges both of these conclusions. The second study, Mary Jo Weaver's oft-cited *New Catholic Women*, remains the most influential portrait of the movement to date. But because my study is not designed to analyze a contemporary movement, and has the benefit of thirty years' distance, my analy-sis of the movement's first twenty years—something Weaver only touched on—is more comprehensive. Other notable studies of the contemporary movement include Sandra Marie Schneider's *With Oil in Their Lamps* and Miriam Therese Winter, Adair Lummis, and Allison Stokes's *Defecting in Place*.

Most histories of Catholic women in the twentieth century written from a Catho-lic studies perspective either do not extend past the Vatican II period, for exam-ple, Robert Orsi's *Thank You, Saint Jude*, or do not address feminism in depth, as in Carmel McEnroy's *Guests in Their Own House*. In fact, the study of the post–Vatican II period in the United States is just beginning; I consider this work to be part of that larger project.

Moreover, most general histories of American second-wave feminism written prior to 2000 hardly mention religion, and when they do speak of Catholicism specifically, it is generally to blame Catholics for leading opposition to abortion rights. These titles are too numerous to name. The most in-depth study of feminism in this period is Alice Echols's *Daring to Be Bad*. My study offers a fascinating counterpoint to Echols's work, illustrating the differing approaches to feminism at the peak of American feminist activity.

Finally, religious studies scholar Ann Braude has spearheaded efforts to acknowledge the existence and contributions of religious feminists from a variety of faith traditions and to analyze their impact on the history of feminism. I also consider this study to be a contribution to that larger project. See her *Transforming the Faiths of Our Fathers*. For a recent monograph tracing the history of Evangelical feminism, see Cochran, *Evangelical Feminism*.

3. For an example of a historian who argues that secular feminism produced religious feminism, see Rosen, *World Split Open*, 263–65. Rosen argues that by 1975 "the women's movement had spilled over its banks, creating hundreds, then thousands of new tributaries, as it flooded the nation." One of these tributaries, in her view, was religious feminism, a movement that actually was under way at least a decade previous to 1975. Rosen also briefly mentions Catholic feminists, only to characterize them as women who left the church after waging "a war with the Vatican that they could not win." See also Brownmiller, *In Our Time*, 328.

4. Sandra Marie Schneiders, a scholar of contemporary Catholic feminism, also argues that Catholic feminism was "actually more indigenous to the Church itself than an import from the surrounding culture." See Schneiders, *With Oil in Their Lamps*, 62.

5. Shreve, *Women Together, Women Alone*, 53–55. For a more in-depth reading of "the click," see DuPlessis and Snitow, *Feminist Memoir Project*, 7–8. DuPlessis and Snitow suggest that these revelation stories have taken on the character of myth, a means of providing "shared meaning and experience" for feminists with the power also to exclude those who did not share in the conversion experience.

6. Any discussion of second-wave feminism must include what is bound to be a confusing discussion of terminology. Historians have adopted a variety of classifications for second-wave feminists; the most predominant are liberal feminist (or "reformist" or "egalitarian" or "equality") and radical feminist (or "revolutionary" or "liberationist"). Each of these terms includes myriad subgroupings. One historian breaks "radical" into three additional subsets, "radical feminism," "political lesbianism," and "feminist socialist radicalism" (or "Marxist"). See Castro, *American Feminism*, 66. From the midseventies onward, the term "cultural" feminist emerges. For a discussion of the distinction between "feminism" and "liberation" see Berkeley, *Women's Liberation Movement in America*, 53. For an excellent illustration of crossover in the lives of rank-and-file feminists, see Chafe, *Road to Equality*. See also Susan Brownmiller's movement memoir, in which she argues that reformers and radicals all referred to the movement as "women's liberation." She also notes that many radicals got their start in NOW. Brownmiller, *In Our Time*, 8.

7. This organization is now known as the National Assembly of Religious Women (NARW).

1. Sattler, "Why Female?"; emphasis in original.

2. Becker, "Rational Amusement"; see also Thomas, "Catholic Journalists."

3. For example, see Schneiders, *Beyond Patching*, 31. Schneiders argues that most Catholic feminists would date the beginning of the movement to 1968 and the publication of Mary Daly's *The Church and the Second Sex*. Schneiders also believes that secular feminism predated religious feminism in the second wave. It is striking that Catholic feminist authors who themselves wrote feminist works in the sixties do not in retrospect recognize the significance of these works. In the compilation *In Our Own Voices: Four Centuries of American Women's Religious Writing*, Rosemary Radford Ruether's overview of the Catholic feminist movement begins with the movement's origins in the fifties, mentions Vatican II and the birth control commission, then skips ahead to the early seventies. In an April 2001 book review, Sally Cunneen, who edited a 1968 volume that contained significant evidence of feminist thought, claimed that women did not begin raising their voices against church sexism until the early seventies. See Cunneen, "Spirit of Equality." For a similar approach from a non-Catholic see Rosen, *World Split Open*.

4. Joan Workmaster, interview by the author, 10 March 2003.

5. Marsie Sylvestro, interview by the author, 11 June 2006.

6. Murray, letter to the editor, 207.

7. Elizabeth Farians, oral history interview, May 1992, Tully-Crenshaw Feminist Oral History Project, M125, SLRIHU, 153.

8. Special thanks to Fritz Fleischmann for this insight.

9. On the relationship between civil rights and peace activism and second-wave feminism see Evans, *Personal Politics*, 35. Historians often cite Evans as the first to argue that the movement originated in the civil rights and peace movements. But they err in thinking that Evans believed these were the exclusive origins. In fact, Evans argued that most southern white women entered the civil rights movement through religion: "Most white women who participated in the early years of the civil rights movement tended to be southerners, and virtually without exception white southern women who joined the civil rights movement came to it first through the Church." Sociologist Barbara Ryan also argues against limiting the movement's origins to the civil rights and peace movements, suggesting that historians must consider the contributions of women activists working for legislative changes in the fifties and early sixties. See Ryan, *Dynamics of Change*, 40.

10. Farians, Tully Crenshaw interview, 71; Georgia Fuller, "A Tale of Journeying," 1 May 1977, CCW-R 5/2, WLA, 1; Pogrebin, "Anti-Semitism," 46. On attitudes toward Jewish feminism in the larger feminist movement, see also Hyman, "Jewish Feminism."

11. Cohen, *Sisterhood*, 201–2.

12. Catholic feminists did participate in the woman suffrage movement from the late nineteenth century to the ratification of the Nineteenth Amendment in 1920. For a number of reasons, including the church's vocal opposition to woman suffrage, and anti-Catholic bias among the movement's middle-class Protestant leadership, Catholic women did not participate in large numbers. Small groups of middle-class Catholic women in several eastern states formed Catholic suffrage societies. After the turn of the century, when working-class women joined the movement, working-class Catholic women involved in the labor movement also began to work for suffrage. However, although many of these women were critical about church leaders' condemnation of woman suffrage, they did not develop a larger critique concerning women's oppression in the church. See Kenneally, "A Question of Equality," 125–51.

13. Kalven, *Women Breaking Boundaries*, 78. Dolan, *American Catholic Experience*, 414.

14. Burns, *Disturbing the Peace*, 5–7.

15. Dwyer-McNulty, "Moving beyond the Home," 87.

16. Ibid., 87–88.

17. Ruether and Keller, *In Our Own Voices*, 28.

18. McNamara, *Sisters in Arms*, 628.

19. For an excellent history of the women auditors and their experiences of the council, see McEnroy, *Guests in Their Own House*.

20. Dolan, *American Catholic Experience*, 425.

21. "Buried Talents," 17.

22. Maron, "Mary Daly," 22.

23. For collected writings on the "New Feminism," see Schumacher, *Women in Christ*.

24. Becker, "Rational Amusement," 55–90.

25. Orsi, *Thank You, St Jude*, 93.

26. See ibid. for discussion of concern over female morality in this period. See Dolan, *American Catholic Experience*, for a history of Marian devotion in the first half of the twentieth century.

27. Le Fort, *Eternal Woman*, iii.

28. Bingemer, "Woman: Time and Eternity," 100.

29. Le Fort, *Eternal Woman*, 4.

30. Bingemer, "Woman: Time and Eternity," 105.

31. Le Fort, *Eternal Woman*, xv.

32. Ibid., 18.

33. Ibid., 8.

34. Ibid., 9.

35. Mueller, review of *The Eternal Woman*, 304.

36. Aubuchon, "Role of Woman," 2.

37. Dubay, "Wonder and Woman," 365.

38. McIntyre, "Nobility," 97.

39. Schmiedler, "Our Tainted Nature," 171,

40. See, for example, Gorres, "Women in Holy Orders?" 84–93.

41. Matthew 16:24.

42. John 12:24.

43. See Fisher, *Catholic Counter-Culture*.

44. Kersbergen, "Toward a Christian Concept," 9; "Search," 435.

45. Lacey, " 'Soul Size' Challenge," 158.

46. Yzermans, "Hand," 43.

47. Aubuchon, "Role of Woman," 3; "To Be a Woman," 46.

48. Brophy, "Silence Gives Content," 7; Shanahan, "Single Girl," 23; Dubay, "Virginal Motherhood," 744.

49. Grace, "Woman Today," 40.

50. Mary of Peace, "Woman: Her Meaning," 11; For a discussion of erotic imagery in devotional literature, see Orsi, *Thank you, St. Jude*, 81–82.

51. Lohkamp, "Stronger Heart," 593.

52. Miller, "Rebellious Wife," 49–50.

53. Kersbergen, "Woman's Role," 249.

54. Boberek, "God's Image," 43.

55. Hertz, "Tomorrow's Wife," 719.

56. Van Noenen, "Key," 289; Dubay, "Virginal Motherhood," 749.

57. Parrain, "Personality," 58.

58. Dyer "Eternal Feminine," 27–28.

59. Van Noenen, "Key," 285.

60. Leighton, "Why Brides Cry," 313.

61. Greeley, "Dimension," 18–19.

62. These comments about feminism may support the conclusions of Leila J. Rupp and Verta Taylor who chronicle the existence of a women's rights movement between 1945 and the early 1960s. On the other hand, the articles may also indicate paranoia on the part of some Catholics about women stepping out of their place. See Rupp and Taylor, *Survival in the Doldrums*.

63. "Christ and Women," 52–53.

64. Schmiedler, "Our Tainted Nature," 173–74.

65. Arnold, *Woman and Man*, 24.

66. Ibid., 45.

67. "Woman and the Common Good," 466; "Women Are People," 810; "Husband or Wall," 404.

68. Byrne, "Happy Little," 474–75.

69. Armstrong, "Stop Telling," 28–29.

CHAPTER TWO

1. Lauer, "Women and the Church," 365; emphasis in original.

2. Daly, letter to the editor, *Commonweal*, 603.

3. A small number of Catholic men also wrote supportive articles on the subject of women's liberation in this period. For the purpose of this study, however, I have chosen to focus on the female authors. See for example Meyer, "Deaconess," 79–83; Fichter, "Holy Father Church," 216–19. All of the articles in the large sample were located using the *Catholic Periodicals Index*. The sixty-one periodicals ranged from liberal (*National Catholic Reporter, Commonweal,* and the *Critic*) to moderate (*Sign, Sister Formation Bulletin,* and the *Lamp*) to conservative/devotional (*Ave Maria, Friar,* and *Our Lady's Digest*). A similar range of Catholic scholarly journals also is represented. Twelve of the total feminist articles appeared in *Commonweal*. The frequency of feminist articles in *Commonweal* can be explained by its standing as one of the foremost liberal Catholic periodicals in America. It may also be due, in part, to the fact that the magazine's associate editor at the time was Daniel Callahan, Sidney Callahan's husband. These totals do not include those women whose responses to Sally Cunneen's *Cross Currents* survey on women and the church constituted the bulk of *Sex: Female, Religion: Catholic*.

4. Daly, *Outercourse*, 27.

5. Ibid., 48.

6. Tardiff, *At Home in the World*.

7. Here, Ruether is responding to a general perception of the history of feminist theology that suggests that white feminist theologians were slow to introduce a race critique in their work, privileging gender over race, until forced into a multicultural perspective. Ruether asserts that she and her early colleagues in the sixties began with questions of race and soon produced an integrated race/class/gender critique. She cites Mary Daly as the major exception to this. See Hinton, "Legacy of Inclusion."

8. For a discussion of the differences between reformist and revolutionary feminist theologians in the seventies and eighties, see Gross, *Feminism and Religion*, 48–49.

9. "Woman's Place Is . . .?" *Sign*, July 1965, 23.

10. Sidney Callahan, interview by the author, 13 May 2006.

11. Callahan, e-mail communication with the author, 22 May 2006.

12. While the larger collection of feminist articles has not been addressed by historians, these three monographs have elicited some comment, particularly Daly's *The Church and the Second Sex*. These rare mentions of the three books reveal a perception of Catholic feminists in the earliest period as overly optimistic and unsophisticated. *The Church and the Second Sex* is usually discussed only in the context

of Daly's later, "post-Christian" scholarship, especially because Daly herself repudiated the book five years after its initial publication. Daly's first book has yet to receive scholarly attention in its own right. Only Mary Jo Weaver, a Catholic feminist scholar, addresses Callahan's and Cunneen's books, yet she views them as preludes to later, more sophisticated writing. See Castro, *American Feminism*, 52–53; Weaver, *New Catholic Women*, 65–67.

13. Daly, *Second Sex*, 122. See also Beaton, "Does the Church Discriminate?" 24.

14. Daly, letter to the editor, *Commonweal*, 603.

15. Cunneen, *Sex: Female*, 34.

16. Graef, "As Others See Us," 230.

17. Cunneen, *Sex: Female*, 64.

18. Daly, *Second Sex*, 107; emphasis in original.

19. Ruether, "Becoming of Women," 420.

20. Cunneen, *Sex: Female*, 34.

21. Callahan, *Illusion of Eve*, 32.

22. Heinzelmann, "Priesthood," 505, 507. Although denunciation of a unique feminine nature prevailed in most writings, a handful of feminists chose a strategy emphasizing female difference to stress the positive role women should take in the world. These two approaches echoed the social feminism–rights feminism split of the previous century. See, for example, Burton, "Women Deserve," 27; Van Eyden, "Women Ministers," 213.

23. Callahan, *Illusion of Eve*, 96.

24. "Buried Talents," 15.

25. Jung, "Women at the Council," 279.

26. Maron, "Mary Daly," 23.

27. McEnroy, *Guests in Their Own House*, 125–31.

28. "Buried Talents," 19.

29. Burton, "Lament," 43–44.

30. Callahan, interview by the author.

31. Elizabeth R. Carroll, "The Proper Place for Women in the Church," in Gardiner, *Women and Catholic Priesthood*, 14.

32. "Buried Talents," 19.

33. Carbonneau, "Katherine Kurz Burton's Quest."

34. "Buried Talents," 19.

35. Daly, "Divine Plan for Women?" 4.

36. "Buried Talents," 18.

37. Cunneen, *Sex: Female*, 68.

38. Durkin, "Hats Off," 4.

39. Ruether, "Becoming of Women," 425.

40. Swidler, "Male Church," 387–91.

41. When Catholic feminists spoke about women's sexuality in this period they

meant married women's sexuality. Writers did object to attempts by eternal woman advocates to pigeonhole single women into the role of "spiritual mothers" and called for self-determination for singles, but they did not speak about sex outside of marriage. They were far more likely to talk about the value of sex in marriage than the rights of women to have sex outside of it. In this, Catholic moral teaching still trumped sexual liberation.

42. The 1960 introduction of "the Pill" by John Rock, a Catholic physician, spurred considerable discussion among Catholics; by the midsixties what had largely been a living room dialogue among Catholic couples emerged as a topic of concern in the Catholic media. This discussion rarely addressed the issue of single women's sexuality. The debate centered on married couples' desire to plan their families without violating church teaching. Many hoped the issue would be resolved at the council, but Paul VI announced the formation of a special commission to explore and report on the issue, after which he would render a decision.

43. Ruether, "A Catholic Mother Tells 'Why I Believe in Birth Control,' " 12.

44. "Woman Intellectual," 448.

45. Daly, *Second Sex*, 120.

46. Callahan, *Illusion of Eve*, 70.

47. Ibid., 66.

48. Durkin, "Hats Off," 4.

49. It is unclear how many Catholic women belonged to feminist organizations in the sixties, though Catholic women held several prominent positions in the movement. For example, Sister Joel Reed, president of Alverno College, was one of the founders of NOW, and Elizabeth Farians was NOW's first chair of the Task Force on Women and Religion. Special thanks to Ann Braude for bringing Joel Reed to my attention.

50. Holzhauer, "Doing Daddy In," 102.

51. See Larosa, review of *The Feminine Mystique*.

52. Callahan, *Illusion of Eve*, 150.

53. Ibid., 115.

54. Ibid., 30.

55. Ibid., 31, 112.

56. de Leon, "Liberated Woman?" 5–10; quote at 10.

57. Segers, "New Civil Rights," 204, 207.

58. Cunneen, *Sex: Female*, 8.

59. Beaton, "Does the Church Discriminate?" 24.

60. Callahan, *Illusion of Eve*, 86–87. For a discussion about how Catholic women's attentions to such "worldly adventurous saints" could even help women in the process of leaving the church, see Campbell, *Graceful Exits*, xxv.

61. "Woman Intellectual," 453.

62. Lauer, "Women and the Church," 366.

63. Daly, *Second Sex*, 40.

64. Callahan, *Illusion of Eve*, 36–37.

65. Daly, *Second Sex*, 38.

66. Beaton, "Does the Church Discriminate?" 23.

67. "Liturgical ministry" refers to various functions performed during the Mass, such as lector, sacristan (the person who prepares the sanctuary for Mass), musician, eucharistic minister, and commentator.

68. See, for example, Tobin, "Aggiornamento, Now!" 97.

69. Callahan, *Illusion of Eve*, 116.

70. Cunneen, *Sex: Female*, 147; emphasis in original.

71. Only a few authors in the first phase suggested that women were leaving, or would leave, the church as a result of discrimination. See, for example, Wallace, "Male-Centered Church?" 163; Daly, "Divine Plan," 4.

72. Daly, *Second Sex*, 92.

73. Ibid., 177.

74. Ibid., 11.

75. Ibid., 114; emphasis in original.

76. Ibid., 180.

77. Ibid., 181.

78. Van Eyden, "Women Ministers," 226.

79. Ruether, "Becoming of Women," 423.

CHAPTER THREE

1. Farians, "Pink and Ash," 19 April 1970, in "NOW Papers on Women and Religion."

2. SJIA-US will figure in this narrative, particularly when discussing the relationship between laywomen and women religious, but a full investigation is impossible due to a lack of sufficient archival material. Scattered documents from SJIA-US can be found in the Mary B. Lynch papers, the Women's Ordination Conference Records, and the private papers of Rosalie Muschal-Reinhardt. Newsletters for SJIA-US from 1976 onward are housed in the Sophia Smith Collection at Smith College.

3. A number of factors encouraged an organizational movement at this time. Renewal was on the wane as an issue to inspire organized activism, and the larger women's liberation movement was in its ascendancy. Mary Daly's *The Church and the Second Sex* was being widely read and discussed, and the new nuns were galvanized after several high-profile confrontations with the hierarchy in the late sixties over issues of self-determination.

4. Medina, "Las Hermanas," 4.

5. Kalven, *Women Breaking Boundaries*, 220, 226–67.

6. Elisabeth Schüssler Fiorenza, talk at Grailville, 30 December 1990; quoted in Kalven, *Women Breaking Boundaries*, 210.

7. Ibid., 213.

8. Ibid., 209.

9. Plaskow, "Presidential Address."

10. Patricia Brewster, interview by the author, 21 May 2002. Ann Ida Gannon, long-time president of Mundelein College, became a feminist through her leadership experience serving on numerous national boards and President Richard Nixon's Task Force on Women's Rights and Responsibilities.

11. Barbara Fischer, letter to Jeanne Barnes, 29 August 1970, MBL 2/38, UNDA; emphasis in original.

12. Daly, *Outercourse*, 60.

13. Ibid., 85.

14. Ibid., 102.

15. Elizabeth Farians was among those who participated in the exodus.

16. Daly, *Outercourse*, 138–39; emphasis in original.

17. Daly, *Second Sex*, 2nd ed., 48.

18. Ibid., 15.

19. Farians, Tully-Crenshaw interview, 105.

20. Ibid., 25.

21. "Dance Lightly with the Living Earth."

22. Forty years after this event, in 2006, Farians's act of defiance was honored at a CTS banquet. Farians was once again escorted into the luncheon by Charles Curran and awarded a plaque.

23. Farians, Tully-Crenshaw interview, 65.

24. Ibid., 71.

25. Farians was not the only Catholic feminist to file suit against a Catholic institution for sex discrimination in this period. Annette Walters, a psychologist, NCAN member, and close friend of Margaret Ellen Traxler, sued St. Ambrose College for sex discrimination also in the midseventies.

26. Daly, *Outercourse*, 53, 103.

27. Ibid., 104.

28. Farians, "How NOW Got Religion," in "NOW Papers on Women and Religion." For more on how Farians viewed secular feminists' relationship to religion see Farians, "Justice: The Hard Line," 195.

29. Elizabeth Farians, report of Task Force on Women and Religion, March 1970, MC 480, 1/10 SLRIHU.

30. I thank my mother, Nikki Henold, for her memories on this subject.

31. Farians, "Women in Religion," 4; "Women Strike Church," 26 August 1970, both in "NOW Papers on Women and Religion."

32. Elizabeth Farians, letter to Aileen Hernandez, 7 November 1970, MC 480 1/10, SLRIHU.

33. Elizabeth Farians, letter to Aileen Hernandez, 23 February 1971, MC 480 1/14, SLRIHU.

34. Elizabeth Farians, letter to "The People of God of the Archdiocese of Atlanta," 30 March 1968, MC 480 1/8, SLRIHU.

35. Joint Committee of Organizations concerned with the Status of Women in the Church, "Proposal regarding the status of women in the Roman Catholic Church to be presented to the National Conference of Catholic Bishops," 20 August 1970, in "NOW Papers on Women and Religion."

36. Jeanne Barnes, letter to Elizabeth Farians, 7 November 1970, MC 480 2/4, SLRIHU.

37. Elizabeth Farians, "Opening statement for press conference at the NCCB," 28 April 1971, "NOW Papers on Women and Religion."

38. Bernice McNeela, letter to Elizabeth Farians, 17 March 1971, NCAN-R 3/1, MUA.

39. Elizabeth Farians, e-mail communication with the author, 19 August 2003.

40. Elizabeth Farians, letter to Bernice McNeela, 15 January 1972, MC 480 2/7, SLRIHU.

41. Farians, "Opening statement."

42. Farians, "Justice: The Hard Line," 194–95.

43. Bernice McNeela and Patricia Brunner, letter to Archbishop Leo Byrne, 1 June 1972, MBL 3/26, UNDA.

44. "The National Organization for Women to Challenge Christian Churches on 'The Unfinished Reformation,'" press release, 20 October 1973, MC 496, 84/9, SLRIHU.

45. Farians remains a nonactive member of SJIA-US to this day, if only to support the "wonderful women" in the group who continue their fight for justice in the Catholic Church. Elizabeth Farians, e-mail communication with the author.

CHAPTER FOUR

1. "St. Joan's (Joan of Arc) International Alliance (United States Section)" flyer, ca. 1971, MBL 4/46, UNDA.

2. National Coalition of American Nuns, press release regarding NCAN's "Declaration of Independence for Women," ca. 1972, NCAN-R 2/2, MUA.

3. NAWR, resolutions from the 1974 National Assembly, ARW 30/08, UNDA.

4. Riley, *Transforming Feminism*, 5.

5. Suenens, *Nun in the World*, 23.

6. "Get Rid of the Rabbit Ears, Sister," 16.

7. Linden-Ward and Green, *American Women*, 192. In 1966, 291 American

priests resigned; that number jumped to 1,526 in 1969. National Opinion Research Center, *Catholic Priest*, 279.

8. McNamara, *Sisters*, 632.

9. Riley, *Transforming Feminism*, 2.

10. Lefevere, "Margaret Ellen Traxler."

11. Traxler, "After Selma," 16–17.

12. Margaret Ellen Traxler, memo to NCAN executive board, 2 February 1972, NCAN-R 1/1, MUA.

13. Margaret Ellen Traxler, testimony before the Illinois legislature, 4 February 1975, NCAN-R 1/1, MUA.

14. Jacinta Mann, letter to Sisters of Charity Community newsletter, ca. 1977. NCAN-R 3/2, MUA.

15. NCAN, *If Anyone Can NCAN*, ii.

16. Traxler was not alone in using the feminist Christ image. The NOW Task Force used to sell "Jesus Was a Feminist" buttons. Margaret Ellen Traxler, IWT press release, 9 July 1978, IWT-P 2/2, MUA.

17. Margaret Ellen Traxler, letter to Bishop Raymond Vonesh, July 1972, NCAN-R 1/1, MUA; Margaret Ellen Traxler, letter to Bishop Louis Gelineau, 5 May 1978, MET 7/3, MUA.

18. Ann Gillen, "Study Document on Bishops' 'Theological Reflections on the Ordination of Women,'" April 1973, in NCAN, *If Anyone Can NCAN*, 18.

19. Kelley, "Sr. Helen Kelley Calls Nuns' Coalition Encouraging."

20. Ann Gillen, letter to the editor, *National Catholic Reporter*, ca. 1973, NCAN-R 3/1, MUA.

21. NCAN, *If Anyone Can NCAN*, i.

22. Margaret Ellen Traxler, rough draft of letter to Ildebrando Cardinal Antoniutti, ca. 1971, NCAN-R 1/1, MUA; Margaret Ellen Traxler, letter to Bridget Mary Fitzgerald, 4 November 1971, NCAN-R 3/1, MUA.

23. Margaret Ellen Traxler, letter to Theodore Hesburgh, 1 August 1976, NCAN-R 3/2, MUA.

24. Glenna Raybell, response to Antoniutti letter, ca. 1972, NCAN-R 2/1, MUA. Cardinal Antoniutti was then head of the Sacred Congregation for Religious.

25. Margaret Ellen Traxler, letter to Bishop Raymond Vonesh, July 1972, NCAN-R 1/1, MUA.

26. NCAN, "Declaration of Independence for Women."

27. NCAN, "Statement on Catholic Education," July 1973, in *If Anyone Can NCAN*, 20.

28. Margaret Ellen Traxler, statement before the Illinois House, 22 March 1973, NCAN-R 2/2, MUA.

29. IWT flyer, ca. 1975, IWT-P 2/1, MUA.

30. An extensive collection of material from the Institute for Women Today is housed at the Marquette University Archives.

31. Ethne Kennedy, letter to Cardinal John Dearden, 28 October 1969, ARW 1/5, UNDA; emphasis added.

32. Margaret Ellen Traxler, memo to NCAN executive board, ca. June 1970, NCAN-R 1/1, MUA.

33. Margaret Ellen Traxler, letter to Mary Dennis, 6 July 1970, NCAN-R 3/1, MUA.

34. "Women and Church Ministry," 3; emphasis in original.

35. "Action Plan from Women in the Church" strategy sessions, NAWR convention, August 1973, ARW 3/2, UNDA.

36. Ibid.

37. Elizabeth Thoman, "Liberation and Religious Life," pamphlet from Tele-KETICS, ca. 1974, ARW 30/3, UNDA.

38. Eby, " 'Little Squabble among Nuns'?" 179.

39. LCWR, "History," LCWR home page, <http://www.lcwr.org/lcwr2/history.htm> (28 August 2001). By 1973, membership numbered 648 from 370 religious communities, representing over 150,000 American women religious. To be a member of the LCWR a sister needed to be in the leadership of her own congregation; in this way LCWR members represented the women of their congregations.

40. Traxler, memo to NCAN executive committee.

41. See Daly, "Response to Father Orsy."

42. Henning, "One Sisterhood," 23, 20.

43. For a more comprehensive discussion of this tension within the movement see Trebbi, "Daughters of the Church."

44. The LCWR retained a relationship with Henning and seemed to value her advice; more than once, meeting minutes refer to Henning's warnings about the rift between laywomen and women religious and to LCWR's overtures to laywomen.

45. Karen Whitney, letter to Mary B. Lynch, 12/71, MBL 2/38, UNDA; emphasis in original.

46. WOC, "History: The WOC Story," WOC website, <http://www.womensordination.org> (8 November 2005).

47. The Catholic diaconate is an ordained ministry sharing some functions with the priesthood (i.e., the power to baptize, to officiate at weddings, and to take a limited role assisting the presider at Mass). Deacons cannot consecrate the Eucharist or give absolution. Before Vatican II, the diaconate was usually an interim step for seminarians on the way to priesthood. After the council, the church opened the diaconate to married men.

48. Jeanne Barnes, letter to Elizabeth Farians, 7 October 1969, MC 480 2/3, SLRIHU; Jeanne Barnes, *Journey*, May 1970, 2, Women's History Library, Herstory Collection, reel 6.

49. Ibid., 1.

50. Mary B. Lynch, conference talk MS, 1972, MBL 1/16, UNDA.

51. Ibid.

52. Margaret G. Smith and Marian Kelley, "Speaking about Mary Lynch . . . ," *NewWomen, NewChurch*, November 1979, WOC-R 2/3, MUA.

53. Mary B. Lynch, letter to Josephine Ford, 14 March 1973, MBL 1/06, UNDA.

54. Mary B. Lynch, letter to Deaconess Movement membership, June 1972, MBL 2/22, UNDA.

55. Mary Van Ackere, letter to Mary B. Lynch, 22 August 1974, MBL 2/04, UNDA; Lorraine M. Storck, letter to Mary B. Lynch, 19 January 1972, MBL 2/39, UNDA.

56. Celia Sells, letter to Ethne Kennedy, 23 May 1974, MBL 2/04, UNDA.

57. Celia Sells, letter to Monsignor Ernest Fiedler, 15 August 1973, MBL 2/04, UNDA.

58. Strong evidence suggests that the author is Marilyn Sieg, a member of the DM and the ordination conference task force. "Testimony #20," *AWAPM Bulletin*, 27 April 1975, MBL 3/02, UNDA.

59. Marilyn L. Sieg, "Women in the Ministry and the Unique Life of the Sisters for Christian Community: An Address," 21 August 1973, MBL 4/10, UNDA, 10.

60. Greeley, *Catholic Myth*, 4.

61. Ackere, letter to Mary B. Lynch.

62. C. Virginia Finn, letter to Reverend Paul M. Esser, 14 November 1973, MBL 2/35, UNDA.

63. The charismatic movement, a Catholic form of Pentecostalism, emerged in the late sixties and was noted for its conservatism.

64. Sells, letter to Kennedy; letter to Fiedler.

65. Barbara Fischer, letter to Jeanne Barnes, 29 August 1970, MBL 2/38, UNDA; Colleen H. Flaherty, Deaconess Movement survey response, n.d., MBL 2/40, UNDA.

66. Mary B. Lynch, letter to "Sandy," 21 May 1971, MBL 1/3, UNDA.

67. Rose Horman Arthur, letter to Mary B. Lynch, 31 October 1971, MBL 2/38, UNDA.

68. Mary B. Lynch, letter to bishops MS, 1 January 1975, MBL 1/16, UNDA.

69. Ignatian spirituality is derived from the teachings of Ignatius of Loyola, founder of the Jesuit order of priests. See Regina Griffin, letter to Mary B. Lynch, 14 February 1975, MBL 2/16, UNDA.

70. Trebbi, "Daughters of the Church," 36.

71. Smith and Kelley, "Speaking about Mary Lynch," 15. "Nadine" refers to Nadine Foley, who acted as head of the WOC task force in its first year.

72. Mary Daly, survey response, n.d., MBL 2/40, UNDA; emphasis in original.

73. Elizabeth Farians, "NOW Task Force Cautions Women about Diaconate," 5 March 1971, "NOW Papers on Women and Religion."

74. Arlene Swidler, letter to the editor, *Journey*, Summer 1970, 2, Women's History Library, Herstory Collection, reel 6.

CHAPTER FIVE

1. Maureen Hickey Reiff, interview by the author, 12 June 2006.

2. Ada María Isasi-Díaz, interview by the author, 10 June 2006.

3. Rosalie Muschal-Reinhardt, interview by the author, 10 June 2006.

4. Patricia Hughes, "Who Are These Women?: The Answer Takes Shape," in Gardiner, *Women and Catholic Priesthood*, 174–75.

5. Isasi-Díaz, interview by the author.

6. Mary Daniel Turner, "Synthesis of Ordination Conference," in Gardiner, *Women and Catholic Priesthood*, 136.

7. Arlene Swidler, MS, talk at Graymoor Ecumenical Institute, 10 March 1976, RMR.

8. Elisabeth Schüssler Fiorenza, "Women Apostles: The Testament of Scripture," in Gardiner, *Women and Catholic Priesthood*, 94–99.

9. Rosemary Radford Ruether, "Ordination: What Is the Problem?" in Gardiner, *Women and Catholic Priesthood*, 30–32.

10. Margaret Farley, "Moral Imperatives for the Ordination of Women," in Gardiner, *Women and Catholic Priesthood*, 49.

11. Carroll, "Proper Place," 16.

12. Farley, "Moral Imperatives for the Ordination of Women," 49; Muschal-Reinhardt, interview by the author.

13. Donovan, *Feminist Theory*, 88.

14. Carroll, "Proper Place," 15.

15. Reiff, interview by the author.

16. Anne Elizabeth Carr, "Church in Process: Engendering the Future," in Gardiner, *Women and Catholic Priesthood*, 78.

17. Rosalie Muschal-Reinhardt and women called to ordination, "Women Called to Ordination," in Gardiner, *Women and Catholic Priesthood*, 187.

18. Carr, "Church in Process," 83.

19. Farley, "Moral Imperatives for the Ordination of Women," 48.

20. Muschal-Reinhardt, interview by the author.

21. Frances McGillicuddy, personal note to Rosalie Muschal-Reinhardt, ca. March 1976, RMR; Rosalie Muschal-Reinhardt, letter to Frances McGillicuddy, 16 March 1976, RMR.

22. Bernice McNeela, "Progress of Women in the Catholic Church," *Probe*, January 1975, ARW 32/51, UNDA, 2.

23. Eleanor Kahle, "Practical Problems Facing the Future Priesthood," in Gardiner, *Women and Catholic Priesthood*, 121–128.

24. Arlene Swidler, letter to Rosalie Muschal-Reinhardt, 22 March 1976, RMR.

25. Leonard Swidler, "Sisterhood: Model of Future Priesthood," in Gardiner, *Women and Catholic Priesthood*, 134; emphasis in original.

26. Teresita Basso, a member of the "Women in Solidarity" panel, published an essay, "The Emerging Chicana," focusing particularly on women religious, in 1970. The essay was designed to encourage feminism among Chicana women, advocating involvement in social justice issues for Mexican Americans. The essay also included the rationale of the newly formed Las Hermanas. See Basso, "Emerging 'Chicana,'" 58–65.

27. Mario Barron and Shawn Copcland, respectively, "Women in Solidarity" panel, NAWR National Convention, August 1975, 24, 29.

28. Ibid., 24–27.

29. Ibid., 27–29.

30. Maria Iglesias, "Las Hermanas Statement," in Gardiner, *Women and Catholic Priesthood*, 188.

31. Shawn Copeland, "Black Sister's Response," in Gardiner, *Women and Catholic Priesthood*, 189.

32. Ordination conference task force, "Women in Future Priesthood Now: A Call to Action—A Statement of the Taskforce Planning the Conference," 22 March 1975, MBL 4/36, UNDA.

33. Nadine Foley, "Who Are These Women?" in Gardiner, *Women and Catholic Priesthood*, 6; emphasis in original.

34. Ibid., 4–5; emphasis in original.

35. Carroll, "Proper Place," 24.

36. Carr, "Church in Process," 78.

37. Ruether, "Ordination: What Is the Problem?" 30–34. Ruether was not the only one to question the exclusive focus on ordination. Dorothy Donnelly, executive director of NCAN, asked "is it possible our pursuit of ordination might be a form of idol-worship?" Dorothy Donnelly, "Diversity of Gifts in the Future Priesthood," in Gardiner, *Women and Catholic Priesthood*, 117–19.

CHAPTER SIX

1. Helen M. Wright, "Women's Role in the Church: A Call to Radical Discipleship," talk delivered at 1978 NAWR national assembly, ARW 30/43, UNDA.

2. One liturgy, "St. Michaels—Freedom for Women," was actually celebrated but was taken from Swidler, *Sistercelebrations*.

3. Homilies differ from sermons in that they derive from set readings for the day and not a freely chosen text from scripture. Only men are allowed to preach homilies (and proclaim the Gospel), so if a woman was chosen to give the homily it was called

a "reflection" instead. It was not unusual, however, for Catholic feminists to label their preaching as homilies, a deliberate act of defiance.

4. Henold, "Breaking the Boundaries of Renewal," 97–118.

5. Evidence indicates that some Catholic feminists participated in home masses in this period, even if they did not consider themselves part of the "underground church" movement. Marsie Sylvestro, a woman active in the Catholic feminist movement in the late seventies through the eighties remembers participating in home masses with Bill Callahan, a prominent male supporter of the movement, in the late sixties. Sylvestro, interview by the author. Rosemary Radford Ruether also participated in home masses in this period. Rosemary Radford Ruether, interview by the author, 24 June 2006.

6. Procter-Smith, *In Her Own Rite*, 19.

7. "Underground Catholics Told: Fight, Don't Split," *National Catholic Reporter*, 1 May 1968, 1.

8. Echols, *Daring to Be Bad*.

9. Schneiders, *Beyond Patching*, 74–76.

10. Eller, *Living in the Lap*, 7.

11. Schneiders, *Beyond Patching*, 80.

12. Procter-Smith, *In Her Own Rite*, 18–19.

13. Eller, *Living in the Lap*, 187–88.

14. "The Love of the Church Leaves Us No Choice: A Liturgy of Blessing," in Gardiner, *Women and Catholic Priesthood*, 153.

15. "Our Foremothers—The Witches," October 1980, AMID 1/1/8, BLAUTS.

16. In the ritual of the Mass, the Mass itself is referred to as the "celebration of the Eucharist"; therefore, liturgies were usually called "celebrations."

17. Isasi-Díaz, interview by the author.

18. Reiff, interview by the author.

19. Ada María Isasi-Díaz, memo to Rosalie Muschal-Reinhardt, 16 June 1976, AMID 1/2/WOC Corr. 1/76–6/76, BLAUTS.

20. Each Catholic Mass is divided into two main sections: the Liturgy of the Word and the Liturgy of the Eucharist. Each part is preceded by introductory rites and ends with concluding rites. The Liturgy of the Word consists of the penitential rite, readings (in a Sunday Mass there are three readings: one from the Old Testament, one from an epistle or the Acts of the Apostles, and one from the Gospels), homily, recitation of the Nicene Creed, and offering of the prayers of the faithful, or petitions. The Liturgy of the Eucharist consists of the offering of the gifts of bread and wine, the Consecration, and Communion, when the faithful receive the Eucharist. The words of Consecration include the eucharistic prayer (also referred to as the canon) and the preface to the eucharistic prayer. See Deedy, *Catholic Fact Book*, 107. The Magnificat, or Canticle of Mary, is Mary's prayer, offered when she visited her cousin

Elizabeth (Luke 1:46–55). A litany consists of prayers to individual saints asking for intercession with God.

21. Procter-Smith, *In Her Own Rite*, 13.

22. Workmaster, interview by the author.

23. "St. Michaels—Freedom for Women," liturgy handout, 26 August 1973, MBL 4/04, UNDA; emphasis added. The Sanctus is a prayer recited by the congregation during the Consecration: "Holy, Holy, Holy Lord, God of power and might. Heaven and earth are full of your glory, hosanna in the highest. Blessed is He who comes in the name of the Lord, hosanna in the highest."

24. Collins, "Contemplative Participation," 28–33.

25. Patricia Hughes, "Strategies for Transformation: Healing a Church," in WOC, *New Woman, New Church, New Priestly Ministry*, 133.

26. "After the Death of God the Father" was a precursor to Mary Daly's *Beyond God the Father*.

27. "A Liturgy of Liberation," liturgy handout, 13 January 1974, University Catholic Center, Madison, Wis., MBL 4/04, UNDA.

28. "St. Michaels—Freedom for Women."

29. "Feminist Agape Service," service handout, 6 February 1979, Puebla, N.M., WOC-R 1/3, MUA.

30. For a thorough discussion of Christian feminist thought on Mariology, see Hamington, *Hail Mary*. Major feminist theological works on this subject did not appear until the eighties.

31. Ann Plogsterth, "The Seven Sorrows of Our Lady Queen of Feminists," SJIA-US newsletter, March 1978, 11, SCA.

32. "St. Michael's—Freedom for Women," poem by Joan Krofta, "St. Michaels—Freedom for Women" liturgy handout, 3.

33. "Biblical Foundation for Religious Commitment to Justice," liturgy handout, 30 August 1978, LCWR-R 13/12, UNDA.

34. Judy Dorney, "Mary Magdalene," in *People*, March 1976, ARW 12/30, UNDA. This liturgy was planned and celebrated by the Women's Taskforce of the Paulist Center Community in Boston.

35. Fran Ferder, "National Women's Ordination Study Initiated," press release, ca. 1976, RMR; Ruth MacDonough Fitzpatrick, WOC press release, 6 June 1977, WOC-R 1/2, MUA.

36. Collins, "Lord, Teach Us to Pray," 143.

37. "Love of Christ Leaves Us No Choice," 151.

38. Collins, "Lord, Teach Us to Pray," 145.

39. Priests for Equality, "A Prayer Service for Equality," ca. 1977, WOC-R 1/4, MUA.

40. *Rising Up*, September 1979, WOC Organizations/17, MUA.

41. Baltimore WOC, "I Have a Baptism to Receive," liturgy handout, 28 January 1979, WOC-R 1/2, MUA.

42. Handwritten notes on "Dreams," written for a CCW meeting, ca. 1977, CCW-R 14/18, WLA.

43. Mary Jo Smith, form letter, 21 November 1971, MC 480 2/6, SLRIHU.

44. *Trends*, newsletter of the NAWR Delegate Assembly, 14 August 1976, ARW 30/33, UNDA; NAWR Press Release, NAWR National Assembly, 1976, ARW 30/33, UNDA; "Liturgy of the Word," liturgy handout, 13 August 1976, ARW 30/33, UNDA.

45. International Association of Women Aspiring to the Presbyteral Ministry, bulletin, ca. November 1979, WOC-R 1/4, MUA. Pope John Paul II insisted that only priests be allowed to distribute Communion during papal masses, thus excluding all female eucharistic ministers.

46. Justice for Women Center, "Walk for Justice and Prayer Vigil," 1 October 1979, WOC papal visit 1979, MUA.

47. Boston WOC liturgy, "In Celebration of Women," 30 September 1979, WOC papal visit 1979, MUA.

48. Rosemary Radford Ruether, "Memorandum on an Action to Demonstrate against Discrimination of Women in the Church," ca. 1968, MC 480 1/7, SLRIHU; Elizabeth Farians, letter to Rosemary Radford Ruether, 14 June 1968, MC 480 1/7, SLRIHU (emphasis in original); Arlene Swidler, letter to Elizabeth Farians, ca. May 1968, MC 480 1/7, SLRIHU.

49. International Association of Women Aspiring to the Presbyteral Ministry, bulletin.

50. Donna Quinn, interview by the author, 10 January 2001.

CHAPTER SEVEN

1. Patricia Hughes, "Healing a Wounded Church" (homily), 27 February 1977, ARW 5/24, UNDA.

2. "Dialogue" was used as both a noun and a verb by reformers and was often adapted into the verb "dialoguing." After reading the first draft of my dissertation, my advisor scratched out every use of "dialoguing" with a horrified red gash, but I continue to use this verb form because it is true to my subjects' usage.

3. Bernice McNeela, memo to SJIA membership, 4 August 1975, RMR; "Where the Spirit Is There Is Freedom," SJIA-US promotional material, ca. 1975–76, RMR; Catharine Stewart-Roache, letter to "Joan," 4 December 1975, WOC Conferences/7, MUA. "Joan" most likely refers to Joan Campbell.

4. Study Commission on Woman in Society and in the Church, "Report Presented to the Synod of Bishops," October 1974, MBL 4/1, UNDA, 4.

5. Pope Paul VI, "Women: Balancing Rights and Duties," *Origins* 5, no. 35 (1976).

6. "One Part of the Dialogue," in Gardiner, *Women and Catholic Priesthood*, 11.

7. Ada María Isasi-Díaz, letter to "friends," 8 March 1981, AMID 1/3/WOC Corr. 10/80–12/81, BLAUTS.

8. Ada María Isasi-Díaz, handwritten notes, ca. 1975, AMID 1/4/WOC meeting notes 11/75–10/81, BLAUTS.

9. Ada María Isasi-Díaz, unsent memo to Rev. Charles Mulligand, ca. 1976, AMID 1/1/RRTF Corr. 75–78, BLAUTS; RRTF meeting minutes, 14 December 1975, AMID 1/1/RRTF Minutes 1975–77, BLAUTS.

10. Ada María Isasi-Díaz, letter to "Judi," ca. 1976, AMID 1/1/RRTF Corr. 75–78, BLAUTS.

11. Ada María Isasi-Díaz, confidential memo to RRTF steering committee, 12 September 1978, AMID 1/1/RRTF Corr. 75–78, BLAUTS.

12. Isasi-Díaz, interview by the author.

13. Muschal-Reinhardt, "Love, Power and Justice," 58.

14. Rosalie Muschal-Reinhardt, memo to Bernice McNeela, 25 September 1975, RMR.

15. Rosalie Muschal-Reinhardt, interview by the author, 2 June 2005.

16. Quinn, interview by the author.

17. Ibid.

18. Ibid.

19. Ibid.

20. CCW Annual Report, 1976, CCW-R 13/2, WLA.

21. Quinn, interview by the author.

22. Muschal-Reinhardt, interview by the author, 2 June 2005; Reiff, interview by the author.

23. Each diocese's vicar of religious was responsible for all matters concerning diocesan priests and women religious.

24. The directory was an example of systematic discrimination. It included names of hospital chaplains, usually priests, but not heads of hospitals, who were sisters. Likewise, it included parish pastors but not school principals.

25. "Highlights in the History of Chicago Catholic Women 1974–1985," ca. 1985, CCW-R 13/2, WLA.

26. O'Brien, "New Way," 4–5; Finn, "Train," 10.

27. Rosalie Muschal-Reinhardt, letter to WOC Core Commission, 26 October 1976, CCW-R 21/24, WLA.

28. Deedy, *Catholic Fact Book*, 53.

29. Sacred Congregation for the Doctrine of the Faith, "Declaration."

30. Ann Patrick Ware, "Perplexed Thoughts upon Leaving the Church after Mass," 25 May 1977, NCAN-R 3/2, MUA. For an additional example of feminists expressing anger through sarcasm, see Popson, letter to the editor. Popson, a laywoman, created a list of fifteen new requirements for priesthood, including "must

be an only child," "must be born of a Virgin," and "must have a messianic complex." She wondered, "with the exception of the last requirement, how many present 'priests' might be subject to having their ordinations revoked as invalid?"

31. WOC, "WOC Welcomes Declaration," press release, 28 January 1977, CCW-R 16/20, WLA. This document was misdated in the original. The incorrect date reads 28 January 1976.

32. NCAN, *If Anyone Can NCAN*, 30.

33. WOC, "WOC Welcomes Declaration"; Joan Chittister, LCWR press release, 28 January 1977, LCWR-R 8/5, UNDA.

34. Rochester Regional Task Force on Women in the Church, "A Response to the Vatican Declaration about the Ordination of Women," 1 February 1977, WOC-R 1/2, MUA. See also Quixote Center, press release, 3 February 1977, WOC-R 1/5, MUA; and Chicago WOC, press release, 22 February 1977, WOC-R 1/2, MUA.

35. The most publicized of these was held by WOC's Washington chapter, as mentioned above. See Washington D.C. WOC, "Publick Notice," ca. 27 February 1977, WOC-R 1/2, MUA.

36. Chicago WOC press release, 22 February 1977.

37. Washington D.C. WOC, press release, 27 February 1977, WOC-R 1/2, MUA.

38. Chicago WOC press release, 22 February 1977; emphasis in original.

39. Christian Feminists, newsletter, ca. 1977, WOC Organizations/17, MUA; Kathleen Keating and Jane Marie Luecke, letter to select NAWR members, 1 April 1977, ARW 5/24, UNDA.

40. CCW and WOC Lenten calendar, 1977, WOC-R 1/2, MUA.

41. *WOC Newsletter*, April 1977, WOC-R 3/3, MUA, 1. Only a few bishops, most of whom were old friends of the movement, came to dialogue, and the NCCB released a discouraging statement affirming the "Declaration." The NCCB did, however, call for the authentication and expansion of women's ministries; they also conceded that "efforts to open up new and greater opportunities for leadership by women are imperative" and promised to "vigorously pursue this matter." "Excerpt from the Statement of the United States National Conference of Catholic Bishops," 5 May 1977, WOC-R 1/2, MUA.

42. Rosalie Muschal-Reinhardt, memo to "sisters," ca. 1977, WOC-R 2/2, MUA; emphasis in original.

43. Ibid., 1.

CHAPTER EIGHT

1. Catharine Stewart-Roache, "Public Declaration by Deacon Candidates in New Mexico," *WOC Newsletter*, April 1977, WOC-R 3/3, MUA, 4–5.

2. Catharine Stewart-Roache, "Body of Christ," in "Break-Fast," liturgy handout, May 1977, WOC-R 1/4, MUA.

3. Catharine Stewart-Roache, letter to Archbishop Roberto Sanchez, 15 February 1978, WOC-R 3/2, MUA.

4. Mary Hunt, interview by the author, 23 June 2005; Muschal-Reinhardt, Reiff, Quinn, interviews by the author.

5. Bednarowski, *Religious Imagination*, 19–20.

6. Albert, "Revolutionary Loyalists." In explaining why Catholic feminists remained in the church, psychologist Sheila Pew Albert argued that they "are mature adults who hold the tension between these opposing forces because of factors unique to the spirituality of Catholicism." These factors included "the uniquely Catholic 'sacramental imagination' " and "the holding power of the Catholic community"; Winter, Lummis, and Stokes, *Defecting in Place*; Weaver, *New Catholic Women*, 71.

7. Song sheet, "Songs for the Wounded," ca. November 1979, WOC papal visit 1979, MUA; Ritamary Bradley, "Kiss Boy Babies Only," September 1979, DQP 5/Pope's Visit 1979 3 of 3, WLA.

8. Baltimore WOC and Baltimore Catholic Women's Seminary Fund, liturgy handout, "I Have a Baptism to Receive," 28 January 1979, WOC-R 1/2, MUA.

9. Diann Neu, Martha R. Colburn, and Michael Donahue, letter to the Jesuit School of Theology at Berkeley Community, 7 November 1979, WOC-R 3/1, MUA.

10. Mary Luke Tobin, SL, "Opening Remarks," in WOC, *New Woman, New Church, New Priestly Ministry*, 15. Several months prior to Baltimore, WOC invited Pope John Paul I to attend the Baltimore conference and explore new ideas for priestly ministry. John Paul I was elected pope 26 August 1978 and died suddenly on 28 September 1978. Shortly thereafter he was succeeded by John Paul II.

11. Fran Ferder, "An Experience of Priesthood," in WOC, *New Women, New Church, New Priestly Ministry*, 101–9.

12. WOC Core Commission, minutes, 1/5–7/79, WOC-R 2/4, MUA.

13. Eileen Stenzel, "The Ordination of Women: A Statement of Strategy," in WOC, *New Women, New Church, New Priestly Ministry*, 141–45.

14. For comments about the "anti-ordination conference," see Rosemary Radford Ruether, letter to Dolly, Rosalie, and WOC task force, 7 December 1978, WOC-R 2/4, MUA; press coverage of the Baltimore conference was generally negative, far more so than the coverage in Detroit. This can be explained, in part, by an incident that occurred at the major press conference for the event. Mary Hunt, one of the prominent speakers, was perceived as being rude and condescending to the journalists. When asked a question she responded with frustration and said that the answer could be found in "theology 101." See McCarthy, "Sanity and 'Sister Says.' "

15. Papa, "Women Mix Social Change, Ordination Aims," 18.

16. *CCW Update*, 12/78, CCW-R 14/5, WLA.

17. Billie Poon, letter to Rosalie Muschal-Reinhardt, 17 February 1979, WOC Corr./20, MUA.

18. Mary E. Hunt, letter to Abigail McCarthy, 9 January 1979, WOC Corr./20, MUA; Papa, "Women Mix Social Change, Ordination Aims," 18.

19. "Recommendations from the Assembly," in WOC, *New Woman, New Church, New Priestly Ministry*.

20. Strong feelings on this issue emerged in a series of individual and group interviews I conducted with Maureen Hickey Reiff, Rosalie Muschal-Reinhardt, Ada María Isasi-Díaz, and Marsie Sylvestro. Hunt and Schüssler Fiorenza themselves were cited as a cause of much of this tension as they came to be more dominant in the movement's leadership over time; they were viewed, at times, as being insensitive and hierarchical. When invited to comment on tensions among the leadership in this period, neither Hunt nor Schüssler Fiorenza raised the issue.

21. Hunt, interview by the author; "Finest hour" comment made by Ada María Isasi-Díaz and Rosalie Muschal-Reinhardt, interviews by the author, 10 June 2006.

22. Questions for discussion focused on women's relationships to the institutional church, the priesthood, and ministry. Taken as a whole, the responses are notable for marked pessimism about the institutional church, affirmation of women already ministering, and conviction that Catholicism needed a new vision of church that feminists could model. Participants believed that ordaining women into present structures would not renew a church desperately in need of systemic change. It also was becoming clear that many women seemed ready to consider a break with the church. Yet 71.8 percent of participants still attended weekly Mass. See Jean Gehret, Ada María Isasi-Díaz, and Virginia Power, "Pre-Conference Process" in WOC, *New Women New Church New Priestly Ministry*, 159.

23. Fiorenza refers here to the declaration's "second argument," that is, the claim that women cannot be priests because they cannot image Christ.

24. Elisabeth Schüssler Fiorenza, "To Comfort or to Challenge: Feminist Theological Reflections on the Pre-Conference Process," in WOC, *New Women, New Church, New Priestly Ministry*, 43–60.

25. Elisabeth Schüssler Fiorenza, interview by the author, 6 March 2006.

26. Schüssler Fiorenza, "To Comfort or to Challenge," 129–30.

27. Carroll, "Prayer as Life's Alchemy," 5.

28. Quinn, interview by the author. Callahan, who worked extensively with Maureen Fiedler and Dolly Pommerleau at the Quixote Center, was censured by the Jesuits in 1979 for his work on this issue.

29. "Alternative Liturgy," in WOC, *New Women, New Church, New Priestly Ministry*, 154–55.

30. Isasi-Díaz and Muschal-Reinhardt, interviews by the author, 10 June 2006.

31. Quinn, interview by the author.

32. Judging from photographs, the Saturday evening Mass was very well attended, but the alternative liturgy certainly indicates a shift in the movement.

33. Schüssler Fiorenza, *Discipleship of Equals*, 130; Schüssler Fiorenza, interview by the author.

34. Ruether, letter to Dolly, Rosalie, and WOC task force; emphasis in original.

35. Ada María Isasi-Díaz, memo to WOC Core Commission, ca. summer 1979, WOC-R 2/4, MUA.

36. The general consensus was that local groups were still at the level of consciousness-raising; many were hardly ready for political action, let alone leaving the church or celebrating sacraments on their own.

37. WOC Core Commission minutes, 1/5–7/79, MUA

38. Sylvestro, interview by the author.

39. Fuller, "Tale of Journeying." See also Farians, "Justice: The Hard Line," 195, for a similar opinion.

40. See Rosen, *World Split Open*, part 3.

41. References to lesbianism are rare in Catholic feminist documents of the period. Scattered references from the first half of the decade indicate the desire to separate lesbian rights from the ERA, as Catholic feminists believed the debate would scare Catholics away from supporting the amendment. Several documents suggest that some Catholic feminists wanted to keep lesbian rights separate from feminism (similar to the abortion issue) because they could not support the cause on moral grounds. The issue arose at the 1978 WOC convention when a speaker, theologian Mary Hunt, spoke in support of homosexuals. Several WOC members wrote to complain after the conference and probably voiced objections at the conference itself. See, for example, South Central Region WOC, letter to WOC Core Commission, 26 December 1978, WOC-R 3/1, MUA. In addition, WOC's 1978 convention in Baltimore failed to pass a recommendation supporting "the inclusion of lesbians and gay men in the public ministry of the Church," indicating internal division on the issue. See "Recommendations from the Assembly," in WOC, *New Woman, New Church, New Priestly Ministry*, 176–78. On the other hand, as early as 1975, CCW showed support for homosexuals and called for ministry to them; Lois McGovern, a founding member of CCW, served as a chaplain for Dignity Chicago in the late seventies. In the early eighties, Marsie Sylvestro, Mary Hunt, and Diann Neu helped found the Conference for Catholic Lesbians, an alternative to Dignity. Also in the late seventies, Jeanine Grammick, a member of NCAN, cofounded New Ways Ministry, an advocacy organization that also ministered to gay and lesbian Catholics. Many Catholic feminists rallied in support of Grammick and New Ways Ministry from its inception, although as of 1979 WOC's board was still unable to reach a consensus for support. See WOC Coordinating Committee, minutes, 5/18–20/79, WOC-R 2/4, MUA.

42. Margaret Ellen Traxler, letter to Louellen Lorenti, 22 November 1977, MET 7/3, MUA.

43. Mary Ann Ihm, letter to Rosalie Muschal-Reinhardt, 7 September 1979, WOC Corr./20, MUA.

44. Zelle Andrews, letter to Rosalie Muschal-Reinhardt, 27 June 1978, WOC-R 2/4, MUA.

45. Margaret Ellen Traxler, letter to Ellie Smeal, 6 April 1978, MET 7/3, MUA.

46. Anne E. Carr, "Questions for the Future," in *New Woman, New Church, New Priestly Ministry*, 85.

47. Many historians claim universal agreement among feminists on abortion rights. A representative view is Chafe, *Road to Equality*, 73: "all feminist activists, whatever their organizational affiliation, could easily support abortion reform." See also Berkeley, *Women's Liberation*, 53. Ruth Rosen recounts, in her only mention of Catholic feminists, the experiences of two former women religious who with "other activist nuns waged a war with the Vatican" over abortion rights after which they decided to leave the church. This characterization of Catholic feminism as centered on abortion rights is misleading. See Rosen, *World Split Open*, 264–65. In contrast, Sara Evans says that Hispanic women, because they were Catholic and antiabortion, stayed away from the movement. This also is misleading because many Catholic Hispanic women, particularly women religious, participated in the movement through Las Hermanas as well as through WOC, NAWR, NCAN, and the LCWR. See Evans, *Personal Politics*, 298.

48. Jacinta Mann, letter to Sisters of Charity Community newsletter, ca. 1977. NCAN-R 3/2, MUA.

49. For an example of how a pro-life woman religious explained this dilemma, see Kathleen Keating, letter to Mary Sarah, 9 September 1977, ARW 30/17, UNDA.

50. Margaret Ellen Traxler, letter to the editor, *Houston Chronicle*, 29 November 1977, MET 7/3, MUA.

51. Margaret Ellen Traxler, letter to Annette Walters and Jacinta Mann, ca. 1977, MET 7/3, MUA.

52. For a further example of this dilemma in action, see Baltimore Task Force on Women in the Church, September 1979, WOC-R 3/1, MUA. In this document, a local Catholic feminist group refused to take a stand on the issue but thoroughly castigated the NCCB for not thinking through the consequences for poor women of an antiabortion constitutional amendment.

53. Margaret Ellen Traxler, letter to Betty Ford, 16 August 1975, MET 7/1, MUA.

54. Margaret Ellen Traxler, letter to Mary Eunice, 4 October 1975, MET 7/1, MUA.

55. *NCAN Newsletter*, June 1982, 2; quoted in Trebbi, "Daughters of the Church Becoming Mothers of the Church," 48. Because NCAN could not issue policy statements without approval of the entire membership, NCAN's failure to pass a resolution in favor of abortion rights suggests the organization was split on the issue throughout the seventies.

56. For a retrospective discussion of Catholic feminists' ambivalence about abortion in the seventies and eighties, see Riley, *Transforming Feminism*, 7.

57. Frances Kissling, interview by the author, 23 June 2006.

58. Catholic feminists achieved some modest success within the church on this issue. An extensive 1978 letter-writing campaign to the NCCB Committee on Women in the Church resulted in that Committee recommending that the NCCB support the ERA publicly. The NCCB elected to remain neutral, but the feminists still considered their influence on the hierarchy to be a gain. The National Council of Catholic Women might have voiced its opposition, but every major group of sisters, except the conservative Consortium Perfectae Caritatis, came out strongly in favor and urged participation in the ratification campaign. Women religious in particular threw themselves into ERA work. By 1977, NCAN members alone had testified twice before the U.S. Congress and in twenty state legislatures. Ann Ida Gannon, longtime president of Mundelein College and former member of President Richard Nixon's Task Force on Women's Rights and Responsibilities, served as cochair of ERA Illinois, a coalition of pro-ERA organizations in that crucial state. For an enlightening discussion of the clash between the activist styles of ERA Illinois and NOW (after Gannon's tenure in the organization), see Mansbridge, *Why We Lost*, chap. 12.

59. Segers, "Sister Maureen Fiedler," 175–85.

60. Section 29 of the Pastoral Constitution on the Church in the Modern World (*Gaudium et Spes*) reads, "Any kind of social or cultural discrimination in basic personal rights on the grounds of sex, race, color, social conditions, language or religion, must be curbed and eradicated as incompatible with God's design." Flannery, *Pastoral Constitution*, 163–282. References to this passage were ubiquitous among Catholic ERA advocates. Another favorite tactic of Fiedler's was to proclaim that both John F. Kennedy and Theodore Hesburgh (president of the University of Notre Dame), two icons of American Catholicism, supported the ERA.

61. A prime example of the desire to separate abortion and ERA was Ann Ida Gannon, who said explicitly that she was co-chair of ERA Illinois because she wanted to disavow the idea that abortion, lesbianism, and ERA were connected. See Kleiman, "Sister Ann Ida Pushing Spirit of ERA in '76."

62. See Eleanor Smeal, form letter, October 1977, ARW 40/15, UNDA, and attached "Mary O'C" to "Maggie," handwritten note, 20 October 1977, ARW 40/15, UNDA.

63. Kissling, interview by the author.

64. See for example Ruether, *Liberation Theology*.

65. Shawn Copeland, interview by the author, March 2001; Jamie Phelps, interview by the author, 8 January 2001.

66. Phelps, interview by the author.

67. Isasi-Díaz, interview by the author.

68. Boston WOC was probably the most left-leaning of all the WOC chapters; Barbara Zanotti's influence was very much in evidence here.

69. A "provincial" is the leader of a regional group of Sisters of Mercy. All communities within that region fall under the provincial's authority.

70. Theresa Kane, interview by the author, 28 August 2001.

71. Theresa Kane, "Welcome to Pope John Paul II," 7 October 1979, DQP 5/ Pope's US Visit–1979, 1 of 3, WLA.

72. Later, during the whole of the pope's address, the women religious wearing blue armbands, led by the Quixote Center's Maureen Fiedler, stood in silent protest against continued sexism in the church. In a flyer distributed at the shrine, the women stated that their protest was a moral imperative. They stood in solidarity with all women, they said, and called the church to repentance for the sin of oppression. While they claimed they believed the church could change, they also warned that the church's "refusal to address sexism within itself makes continued church membership a difficult question for many women." "On the Occasion of Pope John Paul II's Address to Women Religious," 7 October 1979, DQP 5/Pope's US Visit–1979, 1 of 3, WLA. Kane was aware of what the sisters in blue armbands were planning but was not involved in their protest. In her words, the two protests were "separate but not unrelated." Kane, interview by the author.

73. "Blessed are you among women" is a phrase from the "Hail Mary" prayer. Catherine Doyle, letter to Theresa Kane, 16 December 1979, LCWR-R 36/2, UNDA.

74. Marjorie Lynch, letter to Theresa Kane, 10 October 1979, LCWR-R 36, UNDA.

75. Muschal-Reinhardt, interview by the author, 6 June 2005.

EPILOGUE

1. Priscilla Ballou, "The Gospel of Priscilla," ca. early to mid-1980s, WOC-R 1/3, MUA.

2. Kerry Maloney, liturgy handout ca. early to mid-1980s, WOC-R 1/3, MUA.

3. Priscilla Ballou, e-mail communication with the author, 18 June 2002.

4. Schüssler Fiorenza, *In Memory of Her*, 349.

5. Thibodeau, "Veiled Dissent," 105. For more on Women-Church, see Livesay, "Women at the Doors."

6. Diann L. Neu, "Women-Church on the Road to Change," in Winter, Lummis, and Stokes, *Defecting in Place*, 241.

7. Ruether, *Women-Church*, 5.

8. Ibid.

9. For the latter position, see Ferraro and Hussey, *No Turning Back*.

10. Hunt and Kissling, "*New York Times* Ad," 124–26.

bibliography

ORAL HISTORY INTERVIEWS CONDUCTED BY THE AUTHOR

Priscilla Ballou
Patricia Brewster
Sidney Callahan
Shawn Copeland
Elizabeth Farians
Mary Hunt
Ann Ida Gannon
Ada María Isasi-Díaz
Theresa Kane
Frances Kissling
Gratia L'Esperance
Deni Mack
Agnes Mary Mansour
Rosalie Muschal-Reinhardt
Jamie Phelps
Donna Quinn
Maureen Hickey Reiff
Rosemary Radford Ruether
Elisabeth Schüssler Fiorenza
Marie Sheehan
Joan Sobala
Marsie Sylvestro
Joan Workmaster

ARCHIVAL COLLECTIONS

Cambridge, Mass.
 Schlesinger Library, Radcliffe Institute, Harvard University
  Elizabeth Farians, Papers of NOW Officers, 1965–73
  National Organization for Women Records
Chicago, Ill.
 Women and Leadership Archives, Loyola University Chicago
  Ann Ida Gannon, BVM, Papers
  Chicago Catholic Women Records
  Donna Quinn Papers
  Madonna Kolbenschlag Papers
Milwaukee, Wis.
 Marquette University Archives
  Annette Walters Papers
  Institute for Women Today Records
  Margaret Ellen Traxler Papers
  Marjorie Tuite Papers
  National Association of Laymen Records
  National Coalition of American Nuns Records
  Women's Ordination Conference Records
New York, N.Y.
 Burke Library Archives at Union Theological Seminary
  Ada María Isasi-Díaz Papers
Northampton, Mass.
 Sophia Smith Collection, Smith College Archives
  Saint Joan's International Alliance—United States Section Newsletters
Rochester, N.Y.
 Rosalie Muschal-Reinhardt Private Collection (now archived at the Women and
  Leadership Archives, Loyola University Chicago)
Silver Spring, Md.
 Sisters of Mercy of the Union National Archives
South Bend, Ind.
 University of Notre Dame Archives
  Leadership Conference of Women Religious of the United States Records
  Mary B. Lynch Papers
  National Assembly of Religious Women (U.S.) Records

PRIMARY SOURCES

A. M., Sr. "Minors in Their Father's House." *Ave Maria*, October 1966, 5.

Alberse, James D. "Is There a Man in Your House?" *Friar*, March 1957, 6–9.

Armstrong, April Oursler. "Stop Telling Women They're Unhappy!" *Family Digest*, January 1962, 4–7.

Arnold, F. X. *Women and Man: Their Nature and Mission*. New York: Herder and Herder, 1963.

Aubuchon, Andre. "The Role of Woman in Salvation." *Priestly Studies* 29 (1963): 2–12.

——. "To Be a Woman Is to Be a Cradle." *Our Lady's Digest*, May–June 1965, 46.

Beaton, Catherine. "Does the Church Discriminate against Women on the Basis of Their Sex?" *Critic*, June–July 1966, 20–27.

Boberek, Aurelius. "God's Image in Woman." *Marriage*, March 1962, 41–45.

Bowen, James V. "Woman Power." *Marriage*, September 1969, 20–22.

Brennan, Margaret. "Standing in Experience: A Reflection on the Status of Women in the Church." *Catholic Mind* 74 (1976): 19–32.

——. "Women in the Family of God." *Catholic Mind* 72 (1974): 38–46.

Brophy, Liam. "Silence Gives Content." *Catholic Home Journal*, October 1956, 6–7.

"The Buried Talents" symposium. *Sign*, October 1966, 15–19.

Burke, Mary. "The Church and the Equal Rights Amendment." *America* 132 (1975): 374–81.

Burton, Katherine. "The New Breed of Women." *Sign*, September 1965, 48.

——. "The Sisters' Quiet Revolution." *Sign*, February 1966, 51.

——. "Why Not Give Us Women a Break?" *Sign*, April 1963, 62.

——. "Women Deserve an Even Break." *Sign*, May 1966, 27.

Byrne, Katharine M. "Happy Little Wives and Mothers." *America* 94 (1956): 474–75.

——. "Who Wants an Intellectual Wife?" *Today*, June 1960, 10–12.

Callahan, Sidney. "The Future of the Sexually Liberated Woman." *Critic*, March–April 1972, 78–80.

——. *The Illusion of Eve: Modern Woman's Quest for Identity*. New York: Sheed and Ward, 1965.

——. "Toward Liberating Families." *Living Light* 8 (1971): 54–60.

——. *The Working Mother*. New York: Macmillan Publishing Co., 1971.

Carroll, Elizabeth. "Prayer as Life's Alchemy." In *The Wind Is Rising*, 4–5. Baltimore, Md.: Quixote Center, 1978.

Celestine. M. "The Image of the Sister." *Sisters Today* 37 (1966): 223–46.

Chisholm, Patricia. Letter to the Editor. *National Catholic Reporter*, 28 June 1968, 4.

"Christ and Women." *Homiletic and Pastoral Review* 56 (1955): 51–53.

Chrysantha, M.,OSF. "A Blueprint for Christian Women." *Catholic Educational Review* 56 (1958): 221–29.

Clark, Cynthia. "Church Women and Christian Unity." *Catholic World* 202 (1966): 278–82.

Cunneen, Sally. *Sex: Female, Religion: Catholic.* New York: Holt, Rinehart, and Winston, 1968.

Daly, Mary. *Beyond God the Father: Toward a Philosophy of Women's Liberation.* Boston: Beacon Press, 1973.

———. "A Built-In Bias." *Commonweal* 81 (1965): 508–11.

———. *The Church and the Second Sex.* 1968. 2nd ed., New York: Harper Colophon Books, 1975.

———. "The Courage to See: Religious Implications of the New Sisterhood." *Christian Century* 88 (1971): 1108–11.

———. "A Divine Plan for Women?" (letter to the editor). *National Catholic Reporter,* 15 June 1966, 4.

———. Letter to the Editor. *Commonweal* 79 (1964): 603.

———. "Response to Father Orsy." In *Proceedings of the Conference of Major Superiors of Women National Assembly—1968.* Washington D.C.: Merkle Press, 1969.

———. "The Spiritual Revolution: Women's Liberation as Theological Re-education." *Andover Newton Quarterly* 12, no. 4 (1972): 163–200.

De Leon, Shirley. "What Is a Liberated Woman?" *Sign,* August 1970, 5–10.

Deferrari, Teresa Mary, CSC. "Women Theologians in the Church." *Sisters Today* 37 (1966): 392–99.

Donnelly, Doris. "The Advancement of Women . . . A Call of the Spirit." *Catholic Charismatic,* March–April 1976, 12–15.

Dozier, Carroll T. "Woman: Intrepid and Loving." *Catholic Mind* 73 (1975): 58–64.

Dubay, Thomas, SM. "Virginal Motherhood." *Review for Religious* 24 (1965): 744–59.

———. "Wonder and Woman." *Sisters Today* 41 (1970): 362–70.

Durkin, Martha. "Hats Off! It's a Revolution" (letter to the editor). *National Catholic Reporter,* 20 July 1966, 4.

Dyer, Ralph J. "The Eternal Feminine." *Marianist,* January 1956, 22–27.

Farians, Elizabeth. "Justice: The Hard Line." *Andover Newton Quarterly* 12, no. 4 (1972): 191–200.

———. "NOW Papers on Women and Religion." Self-published pamphlet, ca. 1971–72.

Fichter, Joseph H., SJ. "Holy Father Church." *Commonweal* 92 (1970): 216–19.

Flannery, Austin, ed., *Vatican Council II: Constitutions, Decrees, Declarations; The Basic Sixteen Documents.* Northport, N.Y.: Costello Publishing Co., 1996.

Ford, J. Masingberd. "The Ordination of Women?" *Continuum* 5 (1968): 738–43.

Friedan, Betty. *The Feminine Mystique.* New York: W.W. Norton and Co., 1963.

Gardiner, Anne Marie, ed. *Women and Catholic Priesthood: An Expanded Vision; Proceedings of the Detroit Ordination Conference.* New York: Paulist Press, 1975.

"Get Rid of the Rabbit Ears, Sister." *Ave Maria,* 16 January 1965, 16.

Gorman, Ralph. "Women—The Silent Half." *Sign,* June 1965, 8.

Gorres, Ida. "Women in Holy Orders?" *Month* 34 (1965): 84–93.

Grace, William J. "Woman Today." *Grail*, April 1957, 39–43+.

Graef, Hilda. "As Others See Us: This Masculine Church." *Priest* 25 (1969): 227–30.

———. "Women in the Church of Today." *Catholic World* 207 (1968): 206–10.

Greeley, Andrew M. "That Extra Dimension." *Ave Maria*, 23 November 1963, 17–19+.

Grumbach, Doris. "Father Church and the Motherhood of God." *Commonweal* 93 (1970): 268–69.

Gutierrez, Gustavo. *A Theology of Liberation: History, Politics, and Salvation.* Translated by Sister Caridad Inda and John Eagleson. Maryknoll, N.Y.: Orbis Books, 1973.

Harper, Lucille S. "Woman's Place Is Not Where You Think It Is." *Catholic Layman*, June 1965, 40–44.

Harrington, Madeleine. "What Every Single Girl Knows." *America* 107 (1962): 624+.

Haughey, John C. "Women's Lib—Catholic Style." *America* 123 (1970): 454.

Heinzelmann, Gertrud. "The Priesthood and Women." *Commonweal* 81 (1965): 504–7.

Henning, Clara Maria. "Are Women Theologians Being Taken Seriously?" *Momentum*, December 1972, 14–19.

———. "The One Sisterhood." *Catholic Mind* 71 (1973): 20–23.

———. "Women in the Priesthood." *Commonweal* 99 (1974): 360–63.

Hertz, Solange. "Tomorrow's Wife and Mother." *America* 116 (1967): 718–22.

Herzfeld, Norma Krause. Letter to the Editor. *Commonweal* 64 (1956): 373.

Hitchcock, James. "Women's Liberation: Tending toward Idolatry." *Christian Century* 88 (1971): 1104–7.

Holzhauer, Jean. "Doing Daddy In." *Commonweal* 79 (1963): 100–102.

Holzschlag, Phyllis. "Is Catch-22 Male Chauvinist?" *Commonweal* 93 (1970): 69–70.

"Husband or Wall." *America* 109 (1963): 404.

Jarrott, Catherine A.L. "Applause and Advice" (letter to the editor). *National Catholic Reporter*, 15 December 1965, 4.

Kelley, Helen. "Sr. Helen Kelley Calls Nuns' Coalition Encouraging." *Trans-Sister*, September 1969, 1–2.

Kersbergen, Lydwine van. "The Search for Woman's Role." *Catholic World* 181 (1955): 431–36.

———. "Toward a Christian Concept of Woman." *Catholic World* 182 (1955): 6–11.

———. "Woman's Role in the Vocation of Virginity." *Worship* 29 (1955): 242–53.

Lacey, Mother M. Gregory. " 'Soul Size' Challenge." *America* 102 (1959): 157–59.

Larosa, Barbara. Review of *The Feminine Mystique* by Betty Friedan. *Sign*, May 1963, 54.

Lauer, Rosemary. "Women and the Church." *Commonweal* 79 (1963): 365–68.

Le Fort, Gertrud von. *The Eternal Woman*. Translated by Marie Cecelia Buehrle. Milwaukee, Wis.: Bruce Publishing Co, 1954.

Leighton, Sally. Letter to the Editor. *America* 101 (1959): 654.

———. "Why Brides Cry." *America* 98 (1957): 312–13.

Lohkamp, Nicholas, OFM. "Woman: 'The Stronger Heart.'" *Homiletic and Pastoral Review* 63 (1963): 586–94.

Mahowald, Mary B. "Feminism, Socialism, and Christianity: Individualistic or Communalistic Ideologies?" *Cross Currents* 25 (1975): 33–50.

Maron, Edward. "Mary Daly and the Second Sex." Interview. *U.S. Catholic*, September 1968, 21–24.

Martin, Rita. "Answer, Anyone?" Letter to the Editor. *National Catholic Reporter*, 15 December, 1965, 4.

Mary Eileen. "Some Aspects of the Art of Teaching Women." *Catholic Educational Review* 55 (1959): 533–39.

Mary of Peace. "Woman: Her Meaning in Surrender." *Cord*, January 1966, 7–15.

Mary Theresita. "The Nun in the World Talks Back!" *Extension* 59 (1964): 20–23.

McCarthy, Abigail. "The Long and Subtle Servitude." *Commonweal* 101 (1975): 415+.

———. "Sanity and 'Sister Says,'" *National Catholic Reporter*, 8 December 1978, 775.

McClesk, Donna. "The 'New Woman.'" *Marriage*, March 1968, 38–46.

McIntyre, Bonaventure. "The Nobility of Christian Womanhood." *Friar*, August 1963, 96–97.

"McIntyre to Oust 200 Updating Nuns." *National Catholic Reporter*, 15 November 1967, 1.

McNeela, Bernice. "Progress of Women in the Catholic Church." *Probe*, January 1975, 2.

McWilliams, Nancy. "Feminism and Femininity." *Commonweal* 92 (1970): 219–21.

"Men's Lib." *Triumph*, October 1970, 42.

Meyer, Charles R. "Deaconess, Priestess, and Bishopess." *Catholic Digest*, April 1966, 79–83.

Miller, Donald F., CSSR. "How to Treat a Rebellious Wife." *Ligourian*, April 1959, 49–50.

Mueller, Therese. Review of *The Eternal Woman*, by Gertrud von Le Fort. *Worship* 29 (1955): 304.

Murray, Michele. Letter to the Editor. *Commonweal* 74 (1961):207–8.

National Coalition of American Nuns. *If Anyone Can NCAN: Twenty-Years of Speaking Out*. Chicago: NCAN, 1989.

Papa, Mary. "Women Mix Social Change, Ordination Aims," *National Catholic Reporter*, 24 November 1978, 1+.

Parrain, P. "The Personality of Woman." *Family Digest*, May 1958, 53–59.

Raymond, Janice G. "Nuns and Women's Liberation." *Andover Newton Quarterly* 12, no. 4 (1972): 201–12.

Rogers, Katherine. Letter to the Editor. *America* 101 (1959): 654.

Ruether, Rosemary Radford. "The Becoming of Women in Church and Society." *Cross Currents* 17 (1967): 418–26.

———. "A Catholic Mother Tells 'Why I Believe in Birth Control.'" *Saturday Evening Post*, 4 April 1964, 12+.

———. "The Cult of True Womanhood." *Commonweal* 99 (1973): 32.

———. "Is Roman Catholicism Reformable?" *Christian Century* 82 (1965): 1152–54.

———. *Liberation Theology: Human Hope Confronts History and American Power.* New York: Paulist Press, 1972.

———. *New Woman, New Earth: Sexist Ideologies and Human Liberation.* New York: Seabury Press, 1975.

———. "Theology by Sex." *New Republic*, 10 November 1973, 24–26.

———. *Women-Church: Theology and Practice of Feminist Liturgical Communities.* San Francisco: Harper and Row, 1985.

———. "Women's Liberation in Historical and Theological Perspective." *Soundings* 53 (1970): 363–73.

Sacred Congregation for the Doctrine of the Faith. "Declaration on the Question of the Admission of Women to the Ministerial Priesthood." Encyclical read 15 October 1976. Rome: The Vatican.

Sattler, Henry V. "Why Female? Why did God Create Both Man and Woman?" *Marriage*, May 1965, 8–9.

Schiavone, Margaret D. Letter to the Editor. *America* 101 (1959): 654.

Schmiedler, Edgar. "Our Tainted Nature's Solitary Boast." *American Ecclesiastical Review* 137 (1957): 168–75.

Segers, Mary C. "The New Civil Rights: Fem Lib!" *Catholic World* 211 (1970): 203–7.

"Seven Women Write of Woman's Role." *America* 105 (1961): 218–19.

Shanahan, Louise. "Love and the Single Girl." *Extension*, November 1967, 22–25.

Stone, Naomi Burton. "How to Live with and Laugh at Male Chauvinism." *Momentum*, December 1972, 20–23.

Suenens, Leon Joseph Cardinal. *The Nun in the World: Religious and the Apostolate.* Westminster, Md.: Newman Press, 1963.

Swidler, Arlene. Letter to the Editor. *National Catholic Reporter*, 28 June 1968, 4.

———. "The Male Church: A History to Live Down." *Commonweal* 84 (1965): 387–91.

———. ed. *Sistercelebrations: Nine Worship Experiences.* Philadelphia: Fortress Press, 1974.

Tansey, Anne. "Why Must Men Run the Show?" *Catholic Layman*, June 1966, 51–58.

Tardiff, Mary, ed. *At Home in the World: The Letters of Thomas Merton and Rosemary Radford Ruether.* Maryknoll, N.Y.: Orbis Books, 1995.

Tobin, Mary Luke. "Aggiornamento, Now!" *Hospital Progress*, September 1965, 6+.

Traxler, Mary Peter. "After Selma, Sister, You Can't Stay Home Again!" *Extension* 60 (1965): 16–18.

Van Eyden, Rene. "Women Ministers in the Catholic Church?" *Sisters Today* 40 (1968): 211–26.

Van Noenen, Athanasius. "The Key and the Sword." *Cross and Crown* 7 (1955): 276–89.

Wallace, Cecilia. "Male-Centered Church?" (letter to the editor). *Commonweal* 86 (1967): 163.

"Woman and the Common Good." *America* 101 (1959): 466.

"The Woman Intellectual and the Church: A Commonweal Symposium." *Commonweal* 85 (1967): 446–56.

"Women Are People." *America* 104 (1961): 810.

"Women in Church Ministry." *Probe*, March 1971, 1–4.

Women's History Library. *Herstory: Microfilm Collection*. Berkeley, Calif.: Women's History Library, 1972.

Women's Ordination Conference. *New Woman, New Church, New Priestly Ministry: Proceedings of the Second Conference on the Ordination of Roman Catholic Women, November 10-12, 1978, Baltimore, Maryland*. Edited by Maureen Dwyer. New York: Kirkwood Press, 1980.

Yzermans, Vincent A. "The Hand That Rocks the Cradle." *Magnificat*, September 1956, 42–45.

SECONDARY SOURCES

Alpert, Sheila Pew. "Revolutionary Loyalists: A Psychological Study of American Catholic Feminists." Ph.D. diss., California Institute of Integral Studies, 1996.

Banks, Olive. *Faces of Feminism: A Study of Feminism as a Social Movement*. Oxford: Robertson and Co., 1981.

Becker, Penny Edgell. " 'Rational Amusement and Sound Instruction': Constructing the True Catholic Woman in the *Ave Maria*, 1865–1889." *Religion and American Culture* 8 (1998): 55–90.

Bednarowski, Mary Farrell. *The Religious Imagination of American Women*. Bloomington: Indiana University Press, 1999.

Berkeley, Kathleen. *The Women's Liberation Movement in America*. Westport, Conn.: Greenwood, 1999.

Berryman, Phillip. *Liberation Theology*. New York: Pantheon Books, 1987.

Bingemer, Maria Clara Luchetti. "Woman: Time and Eternity; The Eternal Woman and the Feminine Face of God." In *Special Nature of Women*, edited by Anne Carr and Elizabeth Schüssler Fiorenza, 98–107. Philadelphia: Trinity, 1991.

Braude, Ann, ed. *Transforming the Faiths of Our Fathers: Women Who Changed American Religion*. New York: Palgrave Macmillan, 2004.

Brown, Alden V. *The Grail Movement and American Catholicism, 1940–1975*. Notre Dame, Ind.: University of Notre Dame Press, 1989.

Brownmiller, Susan. *In Our Time: Memoir of a Revolution*. New York: Dial, 1999.

Burns, Jeffrey M. *Disturbing the Peace: A History of the Christian Family Movement, 1949–1974*. Notre Dame, Ind.: University of Notre Dame Press, 1999, 2.

Cadorette, Curt. "Liberation Theology: Context and Method, Introduction." In *Liberation Theology: An Introductory Reader*, edited by Curt Cadorette, 1–12. Maryknoll, N.Y.: Orbis Books, 1994.

Campbell, Debra. *Graceful Exits: Catholic Women and the Art of Departure*. Bloomington: Indiana University Press, 2003.

Carabillo, Toni, Judith Meuli, and June Bundy Csida, eds. *The Feminist Chronicles, 1953–1993*. Los Angeles: Women's Graphics, 1993.

Carbonneau, Robert. "Katherine Kurz Burton's Quest for Catholic Feminine Identity in a Male-Dominated Church: 'Woman to Woman' in *Sign Magazine* (1933–69)." Unpublished paper, 1987.

Castro, Ginette. *American Feminism: A Contemporary History*. Translated by Elizabeth Loverde-Bagwell. New York: New York University Press, 1990.

Chafe, William H. *The Road to Equality: American Women since 1962*. New York: Oxford University Press, 1994.

Cochran, Pamela D.H. *Evangelical Feminism: A History*. New York: New York University Press, 2005.

Cohen, Martha. *The Sisterhood: The True Story of the Women Who Changed the World*. New York: Simon and Schuster, 1988.

Collins, Mary, OSB. *Contemplative Participation: Sacrosanctum Concilium Twenty-Five Years Later*. Collegeville, Minn.: Liturgical Press, 1990.

——. "Principles of Feminist Liturgy." In *Women at Worship: Interpretations of North American Diversity*, edited by Marjorie Procter-Smith and Janet R. Walton, 9–28. Louisville, Ky.: Westminster John Knox Press, 1993.

Cott, Nancy F. *The Grounding of Modern Feminism*. New Haven, Conn.: Yale University Press, 1987.

Cunneen, Sally. "Spirit of Equality Often Permeates Sacred Texts." Review of *What Men Owe to Women: Men's Voices from World Religions*, edited by John C. Raines and Daniel C. Maguire, *National Catholic Reporter*, 27 April 2001, <http://www.sacredchoices.org/bookreview.htm>. 2 December 2002.

Daly, Mary. *Outercourse: The Be-Dazzling Voyage*. London: Women's Press, 1992.

"Dance Lightly with the Living Earth." <http://www.cincinnati.earthsave.org/elizabeth.htm>. 19 August 2002.

Deedy, John. "Beyond the Convent Wall: Sisters in the Modern World." *Theology Today* 40, no. 4 (1984), <http://theologytoday.ptsem.edu/jan1984/v40-4-article4.htm>. 20 September 2002.

——. *The Catholic Fact Book*. Chicago: Thomas More Press, 1986.

Dolan, Jay. *The American Catholic Experience: A History from Colonial Times to the Present*. Notre Dame, Ind.: University of Notre Dame Press, 1992.

Donovan, Josephine. *Feminist Theory: The Intellectual Traditions of American Feminism*. New York: Continuum, 1994.

Douglas, Susan J. *Where the Girls Are: Growing Up Female with the Mass Media*. New York: Times Books, 1994.

DuPlessis, Rachel Blau, and Ann Snitow, eds. *The Feminist Memoir Project: Voices from Women's Liberation*. New York: Three Rivers, 1998.

Dwyer-McNulty, Sara. "Moving beyond the Home: Women and Catholic Action in Post–World War II America." *U.S. Catholic Historian* 20 (2002): 83–97.

Ebest, Sally Barr, and Ron Ebest, eds. *Reconciling Catholicism and Feminism? Personal Reflections on Tradition and Change*. Notre Dame, Ind.: University of Notre Dame Press, 2003.

Eby, Judith Ann. " 'A Little Squabble among Nuns'?: The Sister Formation Crisis and the Patterns of Authority and Obedience among American Women Religious, 1954–1971." Ph.D. diss., Saint Louis University, 2000.

Echols, Alice. *Daring to Be Bad: Radical Feminism in America, 1967–1975*. Minneapolis: University of Minnesota Press, 1989.

Eller, Cynthia. *Living in the Lap of the Goddess: The Feminist Spirituality Movement in America*. New York: Crossroads Press, 1993.

Elliot, Lawrence. *I Will Be Called John: A Biography of Pope John XXIII*. New York: E.P. Dutton and Co., 1973.

Evans, Sara. *Born for Liberty: A History of Women in America*. New York: Macmillan Publishing Co., 1989.

——. *Personal Politics: The Roots of Women's Liberation in the Civil Rights Movement and the New York*. New York: Knopf, 1979.

Ferraro, Barbara, and Patricia Hussey, with Jane O'Reilly. *No Turning Back: Two Nuns' Battle with the Vatican over Women's Right to Choose*. New York: Poseidon Press, 1990.

Finn, James. "The Train Leapt the Tracks." *Commonweal* (special supplement), 26 December 1986, 10.

Fisher, James Terrence. *The Catholic Counter-Culture in America, 1933–1962*. Chapel Hill: University of North Carolina Press, 1989.

Franck, Irene, and David Brownstone. *Women's World: A Timeline of Women in History*. New York: HarperCollins, 1995.

Garcia, Alma M., ed. *Chicana Feminist Thought: The Basic Historical Writings*. New York: Routledge, 1997.

Garry, Laurie Wright. "The Women's Ordination Conference (1975–1994): An Introduction to a Movement." Ph.D. diss., Marquette University, 2000.

Gatlin, Rochelle. *American Women since 1945*. Jackson: University Press of Mississippi, 1987.

Greeley, Andrew M. *The Catholic Myth: The Behavior and Beliefs of American Catholics*. New York: Touchstone, 1990.

Gross, Rita M. *Feminism and Religion: An Introduction.* Boston: Beacon Press, 1996.

Hamington, Michael. *Hail Mary? The Struggle for Ultimate Womanhood in Catholicism.* New York: Routledge, 1995.

Hanson, Margaret M. "Role of Grievance, Efficacy, and Cost in the Women's Movement in the Catholic Church." Ph.D. diss., Iowa State University, 1993.

Harlan, Judith. *Feminism: A Reference Handbook.* Santa Barbara, Calif.: ABC-CLIO, 1998.

Haskins, Susan. *Mary Magdalen: Myth and Metaphor.* New York: Riverhead Books, 1993.

Henold, Mary J. "Breaking the Boundaries of Renewal: The American Catholic Underground, 1966–1970." *U.S. Catholic Historian* 19, no. 3 (2001): 97–118.

Hennesey, James, SJ. *American Catholics: A History of the Roman Catholic Community in the United States.* New York: Oxford University Press, 1981.

Hinton, Rosalind. "A Legacy of Inclusion: An Interview with Rosemary Radford Ruether." *Cross Currents,* Spring 2002, <http:www/crosscurrents.org/Ruetherspring2002.htm>. 3 December 2002.

Hunt, Mary E., and Frances Kissling, "The *New York Times* Ad: A Case Study in Religious Feminism." *Journal of Feminist Studies in Religion* 3, no. 1 (1987): 115–27.

Hyman, Paula E. "Jewish Feminism Faces the American Women's Movement: Convergence and Divergence." In *American Jewish Women's History: A Reader,* edited by Pamela S. Nadell, 297–312. New York: New York University Press, 2003.

Kalven, Janet. *Women Breaking Boundaries: A Grail Journey, 1940–1995.* Albany: State University of New York Press, 1999.

Kane, Paula, James Kenneally, and Karen Kennelly, eds. *Gender Identities in American Catholicism.* Maryknoll, N.Y.: Orbis Books, 2001.

Katzenstein, Mary Fainsod. *Faithful and Fearless: Moving Feminist Protest inside the Church and Military.* Princeton, N.J.: Princeton University Press, 1998.

Kenneally, James. "A Question of Equality." In *American Catholic Women: A Historical Exploration,* edited by Karen Kennelly, CSJ, 125–51. New York: Macmillan Publishing Co., 1989.

Kennelly, Karen, ed. *American Catholic Women: A Historical Exploration.* New York: Macmillan Publishing Co., 1989.

Kleiman, Carol. "Sister Ann Ida Pushing Spirit of ERA in '76," *Chicago Tribune,* 24 June 1976, 22.

Klein, Ethel. *Gender Politics.* Cambridge, Mass.: Harvard University Press, 1984.

Langley, Winston E., and Vivian C. Fox, eds. *Women's Rights in the United States: A Documentary History.* Westport, Conn.: Greenwood, 1994.

Lefevere, Patricia. "Margaret Ellen Traxler Lived Her Passion for Justice." *National*

Catholic Reporter, 1 March 2002, <http://www.natcath.com/NCR_
Online/archives/030102/0301021.htm>. 18 August 2002.

Lerner, Gerda. *The Creation of Feminist Consciousness*. New York: Oxford University
Press, 1993.

Linden-Ward, Blanche, and Carol Hurd Green. *American Women in the 1960s:
Changing the Future*. New York: Twayne Publishers, 1992.

Little, Joyce A. *The Church and the Culture War: Secular Anarchy or Sacred Order*. San
Francisco: Ignatius Press, 1995.

Livesay, Jennifer. "Women at the Doors: Gender, Protest, and Belief in a
Midwestern Women-Church Group." Ph.D. diss., Indiana University, 1998.

Mankiller, Wilma, Gwendolyn Mink, Marysa Navarro, Barbara Smith, and Gloria
Steinem, eds. *The Reader's Companion to United States Women's History*. Boston:
Houghton Mifflin, 1998.

Mansbridge, Jane J. *Why We Lost the ERA*. Chicago: University of Chicago Press,
1986.

Massa, Mark S. *Catholics and American Culture: Fulton Sheen, Dorothy Day, and the
Notre Dame Football Team*. New York: Crossroads, 1999.

McEnroy, Carmel. *Guests in Their Own House: The Women of Vatican II*. New York:
Crossroad Publishing Co., 1996.

McNamara, Jo Ann Kay. *Sisters in Arms: Catholic Nuns through Two Millennia*.
Cambridge, Mass.: Harvard University Press, 1996.

Medina, Lara. "Las Hermanas: Chicana/Latina Religious-Political Activism, 1971–
1997." Ph.D. diss., Claremont Graduate University, 1998.

Meyerowitz, Joanne, ed. *Not June Cleaver: Women and Gender in Postwar America,
1945–1960*. Philadelphia: Temple University Press, 1994.

Milhaven, Annie Lally, ed. *The Inside Stories: Thirteen Valiant Women Challenging the
Church*. Mystic, Conn.: Twenty-Third Publications, 1987.

Morris, Charles R. *American Catholic: The Saints and Sinners who Built America's
Most Powerful Church*. New York: Vintage Books, 1997.

Muschal-Reinhardt, Rosalie. "Love, Power and Justice." M.Div. thesis, Jesuit School
of Theology in Chicago, 1977.

National Opinion Research Center. *The Catholic Priest in the United States:
Sociological Investigations*. Washington D.C.: United States Catholic Conference,
1972.

O'Brien, David. "A New Way of Doing the Work of the Church." *Commonweal*
(special supplement), 26 December 1986, 4–5.

Orsi, Robert A. *Thank You, St. Jude: Women's Devotion to the Patron Saint of Hopeless
Causes*. New Haven, Conn.: Yale University Press, 1996.

Plaskow, Judith. "1998 Presidential Address: The Academy as Real Life; New
Participants and Paradigms in the Study of Religion." *Journal of the American
Academy of Religion* 67 (1999): 521–38.

Pogrebin, Letty Cottin. "Anti-Semitism in the Women's Movement." *Ms. Magazine*, June 1982, 46.

Popson, Martha. Letter to the Editor, *Catholic Messenger*, 10 February 1977.

Procter-Smith, Marjorie. *In Her Own Rite: Constructing Feminist Liturgical Tradition.* Nashville, Tenn.: Abingdon, 1990.

Rader, Rosemary. "Catholic Feminism: Its Impact on United States Catholic Women." In *American Catholic Women: A Historical Exploration*, edited by Karen Kennelly, CSJ, 182–219. New York: Macmillan Publishing Co., 1989.

Redmont, Jane. *Generous Lives: American Catholic Women Today.* New York: William Morrow and Co., 1992.

Riley, Maria. *Transforming Feminism.* Washington, D.C.: Sheed and Ward, 1989.

Rosen, Ruth. *The World Split Open: How the Modern Women's Movement Changed America.* New York: Viking, 2000.

Rowbotham, Sheila. *A Century of Women.* New York: Penguin, 1997.

Ruether, Rosemary Radford, and Rosemary Skinner Keller, eds. *In Our Own Voices: Four Centuries of American Women's Religious Writing.* San Francisco: HarperCollins, 1995.

Rupp, Leila, and Verta Taylor. *Survival in the Doldrums: the American Women's Rights Movement, 1945 to the 1960s.* New York: Oxford University Press, 1987.

Ryan, Barbara. *Feminism and the Women's Movement: Dynamics of Change in Social Movement Ideology and Activism.* New York: Routledge, 1992.

Schneiders, Sandra Marie. *Beyond Patching: Faith and Feminism in the Catholic Church.* New York: Paulist Press, 1991.

———. *With Oil in Their Lamps: Faith, Feminism, and the Future.* New York: Paulist Press, 2000.

Schüssler Fiorenza, Elisabeth. *Discipleship of Equals: A Critical Feminist Ekklesia-logy of Liberation.* New York: Crossroad, 1993.

———. *In Memory of Her: A Feminist Theological Reconstruction of Christian Origins.* Boston: Crossroad, 1983.

Segers, Mary. "Sister Maureen Fiedler: A Nun for Gender Equality in Church and Society." In *Religious Leaders and Faith-Based Politics: Ten Profiles*, edited by Jo Renee Formicola and Hubert Morken, 175–85. Lanham, Md.: Rowman and Littlefield, 2001.

Shreve, Anita. *Women Together, Women Alone: The Legacy of the Consciousness Raising Movement.* New York: Viking Penguin, 1989.

Stanton, Helen. *Christian Feminism: An Introduction.* London: Darton, Longman and Todd, Ltd., 1998.

Steichen, Donna. *Ungodly Rage: The Hidden Face of Catholic Feminism.* San Francisco: Ignatius Press, 1991.

Thibodeau, Tracy Memoree. "Veiled Dissent: The Mobilization of White Feminists in the RCC." Ph.D. diss., Southern Illinois University, 1998.

Thomas, Samuel L. "Catholic Journalists and the Ideal Woman in Late Victorian America." *International Journal of Women's Studies* 4 (1981): 89–100.

Trebbi, Diana. "Daughters of the Church Becoming Mothers of the Church: A Study of the Roman Catholic Women's Movement." Ph.D. diss., City University of New York, 1985.

Walton, Janet R. *Feminist Liturgy: A Matter of Justice*. Collegeville, Minn.: Liturgical Press, 2000.

Weaver, Mary Jo. *New Catholic Women: A Contemporary Challenge to Traditional Religious Authority*. San Francisco: Harper and Row, 1985.

Winter, Miriam Therese, Adair T. Lummis, and Allison Stokes, eds. *Defecting in Place: Women Claiming Responsibility for Their Own Spiritual Lives*. New York: Crossroad, 1994.

Woloch, Nancy. *Women and the American Experience*, 2nd ed. New York: McGraw Hill, 1994.

index

Chicago Catholic Women (CCW), 9,
    141, 159, 180, 182–87, 193
Chittester, Joan, 103
Christian Family Movement (CFM), 18–
    20
Christian Feminists, 194
Church and the Second Sex, The (Daly),
    37, 60–62, 70, 251 (n. 12)
Church Women United, 66, 122, 169
Clericalism, feminist critiques of, 47–
    49
Cody, John, 185
Conference for Catholic Lesbians, 218,
    269 (n. 41)
Consciousness-raising, 66, 84, 96, 98–
    101, 104–5, 131, 143, 152, 160–61,
    269 (n. 36). *See also* Feminist
    consciousness
Conference of Major Superiors of
    Women (CMSW). *See* Leadership
    Conference of Women Religious
Congregation for the Doctrine of the
    Faith (CDF), 24, 189
Copeland, Shawn, 133–34, 225–28
Crowley, Patty, 184
Cultural feminism, 138–39, 143
Cunneen, Sally, 37, 248 (n. 3), 252
    (n. 12)
Curran, Charles, 74

Daly, Mary, 23, 36, 38–39, 45, 52, 56–57,
    60–62, 64, 69–72, 92, 103, 106, 114,
    142, 151, 248 (n. 3)
Deaconess Movement (DM), 8, 64–65,
    104–15
Dearden, John, 78, 97
Declaration on the Question of the
    Admission of Women to the Minis-
    terial Priesthood, 167–69, 189–95,
    200–201
Dialogue, 78, 107, 115, 119, 168–73,

175–77, 180–82, 193–95, 204, 211,
    222–23, 228, 266 (n. 41)
Dingman, Maurice, 107–8, 182
Donnelly, Dorothy, 261 (n. 37)
Dozier, Carroll T., 182
Durbeck, Patricia, 197

Eighth Day Center for Justice, 183
Equal Rights Amendment (ERA), 95,
    100, 103, 157, 159, 223–24, 271
    (nn. 58, 60–61)
Eternal Woman, 23–33; and American
    Catholic writers, 28–33; and Catholic
    feminists, 43–44, 62, 152
Eucharist, 110, 146–47, 149–50, 155,
    162–65, 211–12

Farians, Elizabeth, 1, 16–17, 63–64, 72–
    81, 106, 114, 142, 164, 255 (n. 22), 256
    (n. 45)
Farley, Margaret, 123–26, 128–29
Feminine Mystique, The (Friedan), 3, 14,
    16, 53–54
Feminist consciousness, 55, 168; adop-
    tion of, 4, 66, 84, 104, 108, 139–40,
    154, 195, 202, 228, 247 (n. 5). *See also*
    Consciousness-raising
Feminist movement: history of, 246–
    47 (n. 2), 247 (n. 3); holiness of, 138,
    140, 151; and religion, 6, 18, 74, 76,
    80, 81
Feminist spirituality movement, 143–45
Feminist theologians, 10, 67, 208, 242,
    268 (n. 20)
Feminist theology, 56–57, 119, 123–25,
    208–10, 228, 242, 251 (n. 7)
Ferder, Fran, 155, 205
Ferraro, Barbara, 239–40
Fiedler, Maureen, 223, 238, 271 (n. 60),
    272 (n. 72)
Finn, Virginia, 114

Foley, Nadine, 130, 135, 187
Ford, Betty, 2, 221
Ford, Josephine, 107
Friedan, Betty, 3, 14, 16, 74
Fuller, Georgia, 17, 192, 218–19

Gannon, Ann-Ida, 255 (n. 10), 271
  (nn. 58, 61)
Gillen, Ann, 92
Glenmary Sisters of Appalachia, 87
Gospels, as motivation for Catholic fem-
  inism, 6, 85
Grail, the, 18–20, 66–67, 142, 146, 208
Grammick, Jeanine, 269 (n. 41)
Gumbleton, Tom, 182

Hallinan, Paul J., 78
Harvard Memorial Exodus, 71, 80
Henning, Clara Maria, 103, 258 (n. 44)
Hogan, Joseph, 176–77
Hughes, Patricia, 137, 167, 187, 193
Hunt, Mary, 199, 207–10, 224, 236,
  238–40, 267–68 (nn. 14, 20–21),
  269 (n. 41)
Hussey, Patricia, 239–40
Hyde, Henry, 2, 221–22

Iglesias, María, 134, 225
Ihm, Mary Ann, 220
Illusion of Eve, The (Callahan), 37
Immaculate Heart of Mary (IHM) sis-
  ters, 87
Impastato, Fara, 99
Institute for Women Today (IWT), 96,
  169
International Association of Women
  Aspiring to Presbyteral Ministry
  (IAWAPM), 113
Isasi-Díaz, Ada-María, 1, 122, 147–48,
  172–78, 187, 201, 214, 226, 236, 268
  (n. 20)

Jadot, Jean, 156
John Paul II, 103, 202, 205, 228–32,
  237–38
Joint Committee on the Status of
  Women in the Church, 9, 65, 78–80

Kahle, Eleanor, 131
Kalven, Janet, 66
Kane, Theresa, 2, 103, 229–32, 235
Keating, Kathleen, 221
Kennedy, Ethne, 97, 114
Kissling, Frances, 223–25, 238–40
Kopp, Audrey, 89

Las Hermanas, 66, 132, 134, 226–27,
  261 (n. 26), 279 (n. 47)
Lauer, Rosemary, 35–36
Laywomen, 8, 129–32, 184–85
Leadership Conference of Women
  Religious (LCWR), 8, 97, 101–3, 146,
  154, 241, 258 (n. 39)
Le Fort, Gertrud von, 26–28, 43
Lesbianism, 217–19, 224, 269 (n. 41)
Liberation theology, 92, 127–28, 151,
  214
Liturgical movement, 141–42; and
  women, 58, 99
Liturgy, 6, 126–27, 137–65, 211–13;
  with female presiders, 147–48, 213,
  233–36; as protest, 63, 100, 138, 145,
  157–65, 192–93
Loyal opposition, 6–7, 59, 94, 120, 198
Lynch, Mary B., 1, 106–15 passim, 119–
  20, 130

Maloney, Kerry, 233
Mann, Jacinta, 91, 221
Mansour, Agnes Mary, 238
Marriage Encounter retreat, 67
Mary (Mother of God), 51–52, 152–55,
  157, 231–32

McGillicuddy, Frances, 64, 114, 129–31
McGovern, Lois, 269 (n. 41)
McNeela, Bernice, 79, 131
Ms. (magazine), 15
Muschal-Reinhardt, Rosalie, 117, 121, 130, 148, 172, 175, 178–82, 184–85, 187–88, 194–95, 199, 201, 208, 218, 220, 232, 236, 268 (n. 20)
Mujerista theology, 2
Murphy, Eileen, 107
Murphy, Frank, 182

National Assembly of Religious Women (NARW), 247 (n. 7). *See also* National Assembly of Women Religious
National Assembly of Women Religious (NAWR), 8, 66, 85, 97–101, 133, 141, 146, 160
National Association of Laymen, Women's Rights Committee, 65, 78, 160
National Black Sisters Conference (NBSC), 66, 132, 215, 228
National Coalition of American Nuns (NCAN), 1, 6, 65, 78, 85, 89–96, 191, 241, 271 (n. 58)
National Conference of Catholic Bishops (NCCB), 63, 78–80, 97, 105, 107, 109, 119, 186, 201, 266 (n. 41)
National Council of Catholic Women (NCCW), 95, 271 (n. 58)
National Organization for Women (NOW), 17, 71, 74, 78, 80, 247 (n. 6). *See also* Task Force on Women and Religion
Neal, Marie Augusta, 127–28
Neu, Diann L., 236, 269 (n. 41)
New nuns, 18, 21, 85–87, 110, 142, 174, 217
New York Times advertisement, 238–39
Nuns. *See* New nuns; Women religious

Onk, Mary Beth, 192

Patriarchy, 123–24, 144
Phelps, Jamie, 214–15, 225–26
Pommerleau, Dolly, 216–17
Poon, Billie, 207
Praxis, 126, 151
Priesthood: renewal of, 123–28
Priests for Equality, 188, 192, 212
Protest, 64, 71, 76–77, 157–65, 191–93, 201
Proulx, Amedee, 182

Quinn, Donna, 117, 173, 182–87, 199, 212–13, 220–21, 224, 238
Quixote Center, 169, 192

Radical feminism, 18; among Catholic feminists, 65, 68–81, 85
Raybell, Glenna, 94
Raymond, Jan, 75, 77
Reiff, Maureen Hickey, 117, 147, 184, 192, 199, 268 (n. 20)
Riley, Maria, 17, 85, 88
Rochester Regional Task Force on Women and the Church (RRTF), 176–77, 191
Roman Catholic Womenpriests, 241–42
Ruether, Rosemary Radford, 17, 39–40, 49, 56, 61, 92, 123–25, 135–36, 142, 164, 184, 208, 213–14, 221, 224, 237, 238, 248 (n. 3)

Saint Joan's International Alliance– United States Section (SJIA-US), 8, 64–65, 71, 74, 83, 85, 120, 130–31, 146, 180, 254 (n. 2)
Saint Mary's College (South Bend), 38, 74
Saints, 55
Sanchez, Roberto, 171, 182, 197

Schüssler Fiorenza, Elisabeth, 66, 92, 123–25, 210–11, 213–14, 221, 224, 236, 268 (n. 20)
Second Vatican Council, 3, 16, 21–23, 39, 45, 70, 86, 179, 223
Self-immolation, 31
Sexuality: Catholic Church's view of, 49–50; and feminists, 55, 252–54 (n. 41). *See also* Birth control
Sheehan, Lawrence, 78
Sieg, Marilyn, 110
Sister Formation Conference (SFC), 20, 86, 102
Sisters of Mercy, 238
Smeal, Eleanor, 224
Social justice, 6, 85, 89, 95, 100–101, 154
Spirituality, 111–12, 138–39, 145, 149; as act of protest, 137
Stenzel, Eileen, 205
Stewart-Roache, Catharine, 170–71, 197–98
Stuhlmueller, Carroll, 215
Surrender, 13, 27, 29
Sustained ambivalence, 6, 197–232. *See also* Ambivalence
Swidler, Arlene, 64, 114, 123, 131, 146, 164
Swidler, Leonard, 132
Sylvestro, Marsie, 117, 216–18, 268 (n. 20), 269 (n. 41)

Tarango, Yolanda, 226
Task Force on Women and Religion, 1, 71, 74–77, 169, 192, 218–20, 257 (n. 16). *See also* National Organization for Women
Theology. *See* Feminist theology
Tobin, Mary Luke, 46, 93, 101, 204–5
Traxler, Margaret Ellen, 2, 17, 64, 89–99 passim, 103, 182, 219, 220–22, 238

Tuite, Marjorie, 122, 158, 175, 184, 211, 225, 237–38
Turner, Mary Daniel, 122

Underground church, 142, 262 (n. 5)

Vatican II. *See* Second Vatican Council

Walters, Annette, 219, 255 (n. 25)
Ware, Ann Patrick, 190
Whitney, Karen, 104
Williamson, Cris, 145, 162
Wolff, Madeleva, 74
Women-Church, 139, 236–37, 241
Women Exploring Theology workshop, 66
Women of the Church Coalition (WCC), 9, 173, 183, 194, 236
Women religious, 88; and feminist movement, 91, 98–99; as feminists, 87, 120; and laywomen, 88, 103, 129–31, 184–85; and racism, 132; and sisterhood, 87
Women's Alliance for Theology, Ethics, and Ritual (WATER), 236, 241
Women seminarians, 67, 107, 119, 155, 179, 243
Women's ordination, 11, 84, 110, 121, 123, 188, 189–95, 205–7, 241–42; and Episcopal Church, 119–20. *See also* Aspiring priests
Women's Ordination Conference (WOC), 9, 141, 188, 191, 201–2, 213–15, 226, 229, 241; in Baltimore (1978), 163–64, 173, 203–14, 227–28, 267 (n. 14); in Detroit (1975), 114, 117–36, 155–56, 169
Workmaster, Joan, 15, 149–50
Wright, Helen, 140

Zanotti, Barbara, 212, 215